The Lewis and Clark Expedition

The Lewis and Clark Expedition
Then and Now

Edited by David Kvernes
Southern Illinois University-Carbondale

The Center for Western Studies
Augustana College
2004

Published by The Center for Western Studies
Mailing address: Box 727, Augustana College, Sioux Falls, SD 57197
Street address: Augustana College, 2201 S. Summit Ave., Sioux Falls, SD 57197
E-mail address: cws@augie.edu
Copies of our book catalog may be obtained by calling 605-274-4007 or by visiting our web page at www.augie.edu/CWS.

The Center for Western Studies in an archives, library, museum, publishing house, and educational agency concerned principally with collecting, preserving, and interpreting prehistoric, historic, and contemproary materials that document native and immigrant cultures on the northern prairie-plains. The Center promotes understanding of the region through exhibits, publications, art shows, conferences, and academic programs. It is committed, ultimately, to defining the contribution of the region to American civilization.

Library of Congress Cataloging-in-Publication Data

The Lewis and Clark Expedition : then and now / edited by David Kvernes.
p. cm. -- (Prairie plains series ; no. 11)
Includes bibliographical references and index.
ISBN 0-931170-82-6 (alk. paper)
1. Lewis and Clark Expedition (1804-1806) 2. West (U.S.)--Discovery and exploration. 3. West (U.S.)--Description and travel. 4. Lewis, Meriwether, 1774-1809. 5. Clark, William, 1770-1838. I. Kvernes, David. II. Augustana College (Sioux Falls, S.D.). Center for Western Studies. III. Title. IV. Series.

F592.7.L6925 2004
917.804'2--dc22 2004054560

Cover image: *Lewis and Clark's Spirit Mound* by Ron Backer. Courtesy Ron Backer, Palm Desert, CA

Publication made possible by grants from First Dakota National Bank and Augustana College's Mellon Fund Committee

Number 11 in the Prairie Plains Series

Printed in the United States of America
by Pine Hill Press, 4000 W. 57th Street, Sioux Falls, SD 57106

Contents

Contributors

Joseph Basile, Ph.D., is associate professor of English at the University of South Dakota.

Tim S. Beck, M.A., teaches history at Roncalli High School, Aberdeen, South Dakota.

Ralph J. Coffman, Ph.D., is professor of history and archaeology at Fitchburg State College in Massachusetts.

Joan K. Warner Dolence, M.A., works with thesis and dissertation writers at the University of Tennessee.

John D. W. Guice, Ph.D., is professor emeritus of history at the University of Southern Mississippi.

Tom Kilian, Ph.D., is director of the Rural Initiative Center and founder of Kilian Community College, Sioux Falls, South Dakota.

David Kvernes, Ph.D., is professor emeritus of English at Southern Illinois University-Carbondale.

Ronald Laycock is president of the Lewis and Clark Trail Heritage Foundation and a member of the National Lewis and Clark Bicentennial Council.

Rex C. Myers, Ph.D., is lecturer in history and freshman studies at Lawrence University in Wisconsin.

Rev. Elmer S. Odland served parishes in Lignite, Washburn, and Minot, North Dakota, and Rushford, Minnesota.

Rita Easterby Olson, M.A., is a doctoral student in English at the University of South Dakota.

Laurinda W. Porter, Ph.D., is professor of communication studies at St. Cloud State University in Minnesota.

Kent Scribner, M.P.A., is a development officer with the University of South Dakota Foundation.

Jerry L. Simmons, M.D., is a pathologist with the Laboratory of Clinical Medicine, Sioux Falls, and is a professor at the University of South Dakota Medical School.

Robert C. Steensma, Ph.D., is professor emeritus of English at the University of Utah, Salt Lake City.

Brad Tennant, M.A., is a history instructor at Presentation College in South Dakota.

Harry F. Thompson, Ph.D., is director of research collections and publications at the Center for Western Studies, Augustana College, South Dakota.

Norma Clark Wilson, Ph.D., is professor of English at the University of South Dakota.

Introduction

David Kvernes

Driving north on Interstate 29 in western Iowa, travelers are frequently reminded by road signs that they are following the Lewis and Clark Trail. But natural signs provide reminders as well. There to the left, across a broad expanse of river bottomland and hidden behind a low line of trees, lies the Missouri River. Beyond it, on the Nebraska side, bluffs form a dark undulating line on the western horizon, and beyond those bluffs stretch the beginnings of the northern plains, a vast grassland at the time of the Voyage of Discovery. Then suddenly on the right appear the explorers themselves—on a large billboard, with Sacagawea standing in front, arm outstretched, pointing the way.

If on the one hand travelers have the reality of the river bottoms and bluffs that the expedition members also saw as they struggled northward against the Missouri current, on the other they have one of the myths that have grown up around this journey—Sacagawea as chief guide to the expedition. Both reality and myth are amply treated in this collection of essays, which were first presented at sessions of the Dakota Conference on Northern Plains History, Literature, Art, and Archaeology in Sioux Falls, South Dakota, from 1998 to 2002. Several more, dealing with the food eaten by expedition members, would almost certainly been included had they not already appeared in a book published by the Center for Western Studies, the sponsor of the conference. That book, *The Lewis and Clark Expedition: Food, Nutrition, and Health* (2003) by Elaine Nelson McIntosh, provides insights into the diet and health of the explorers that can be found nowhere else.

A majority of these essays deal with Lewis and Clark on the northern plains, which is understandable given the site of the conference where they were first presented. Yet it is also appropriate in light of the amount of time the explorers spent in this area. It was eleven months from the time they passed the mouth of the Platte River in Nebraska until they reached the Great Falls of the Missouri at the edge of the Rockies in Montana. Precisely half that time was spent wintering at the Mandan villages in North Dakota. Their time in this area was much briefer on the return journey, but that segment still added more than a month to the total spent on the northern plains. The focus in this collection on local sites and events on the northern plains, particularly in the Dakotas, and the fact that many of the authors are residents or former residents of the areas they describe gives these essays a flavor that is missing from other collections of this sort. The essays by Odland on the replica of

Fort Mandan and by Wilson and Scribner on Spirit Mound are good examples. Yet other places and events important in the Lewis and Clark story, from Jefferson's Monticello to The Dalles on the Columbia River, also appear in these essays, and no effort was made to limit the subjects covered.

The phrase "Then and Now" in the title of this collection points to an obvious truth: since the period when the Lewis and Clark story unfolded, from 1804 to 1806 and for several decades before and after those dates, new controversies have arisen, new books have been written, and even new artifacts have appeared, especially in the twentieth century. Recent controversies are examined in essays by Thompson and Guice, and mid-twentieth-century books and articles by Bernard DeVoto are at the center of Steensma's treatment of that historian of the American West.

The "Then" section begins with Rex Myers' investigation of a piece of fiction, but it is fiction with a decidedly historical base, set in the period just before the two captains set out. To introduce us to that historical context, Myers covers actual pre-Lewis and Clark explorations of the West before launching into an account of what the pseudonymous Don Alonso Decalves tells us in his *New Travels to the Westward.* Myers also makes some shrewd guesses about the real author behind Decalves' tale, based on a careful examination of the evidence. Whereas Myers covers vast areas of the West in his treatment of these fictional travels, Tom Kilian pinpoints one episode in the travels of the Frenchman Perrin du Lac up the Missouri in 1802. Kilian gives us a fine narrative account of his attempt to discover remnants of a cedar monument placed on the highest of the Bijou Hills in central South Dakota by the Frenchman. Although Kilian and his partner find no remains, they come away satisfied that they have done all that could be done.

Central to our perceptions of the Lewis and Clark Expedition are the journals kept by expedition members, and one of the things that make this expedition unique is the quantity and quality of those journals. As the historian Donald Jackson points out, they were the "writingest explorers" in our history, and for their gift we must thank President Jefferson, in addition to the journal keepers themselves. He insisted on their making a written record not only of the events and places visited along the way but also of the plants, animals, and Indian tribes they observed and the geography of the lands through which they passed. When the fame of Lewis and Clark fell into eclipse in the mid and late nineteenth century, it happened in part because their journals were less available than those of other explorers such as John C. Frémont and John Wesley Powell. The next two essays in this collection deal directly with the expedition journals. In "The Literary Struggles of Lewis and Clark," Joseph Basile tells us that in addition to supplying President Jefferson with the facts about their trip, the captains sometimes "felt compelled or inspired...to elevate their narrative styles, in effect to poeticize the wilderness." Basile makes the case that they were successful in this attempt and provides us with a new appreciation of their skill as writers. Joan Warner Dolence takes a quite different approach to the journals in "The Rhetoric of Imperialism in the Lewis and Clark Journals: Camp Dubois to the Mandan Villages." She shows how the explorers' attitudes toward the lands they crossed, as reflected in their journals, encouraged the appropriation of those lands by white settlers. Using several recent studies of the "rhetoric of empire" as a starting point, she demonstrates how the explorers' language reflects "their tendency to survey the area with a view toward establishing commercial and military" domination.

Traveling through uncharted wilderness can be hazardous to the physical well being of the travelers, as the expedition members discovered. In his essay Dr. Jerry Simmons examines some of the many illnesses and injuries suffered by Lewis and Clark's crew. He makes good use of his experience as a flight surgeon in Vietnam to compare that kind of medical practice with the efforts of the captains to keep their men healthy. Brief quotations from the journals describing medical problems are annotated by Dr. Simmons, again using his own wilderness medicine experience. Even the physical hazards of sexual encounters with Indian women are noted, along with the treatments applied to contain the infections. Those sexual encounters become the main focus of Brad Tennant's essay, in which he describes the ways these experiences differed as the expedition moved from the Mandan to the Shoshone to the Chinook in the far West. By providing background on the attitudes of the expedition members as well as on Indian customs and beliefs, he shows how we can best interpret these encounters without the bias that might so easily come into play.

Indian customs of a quite different sort are the subject of Laurinda Porter's essay on honoring and gift giving among the Lakota. By carefully describing those customs as practiced in the early nineteenth century, she is able to point out how Lewis and Clark's dealings with the Indians were successful when they were in accord with Lakota practice and how they failed when not. Interviews with three contemporary Indians are used to provide descriptions of both early nineteenth-century and current customs related to honoring and gift giving.

Trade networks and mechanisms used by Indians across the West, from South Dakota to The Dalles on the Columbia River, are examined by Ralph Coffman, who focuses on two trade institutions: the trade center and the rendezvous. He is able to draw new connections between artifacts used by the Shoshone, as reported by Lewis and Clark, and those used much earlier by Hopewellian cultures as far east as Ohio. As Coffman makes clear, Lewis and Clark's accounts of the Indian groups they met determined the course of relations between Indians and Americans for decades to come.

The "Then" section closes with an account of how well the explorers succeeded in fulfilling President Jefferson's expectations, as set forth in his instructions to Lewis and in other documents. Brad Tennant and Tim Beck conclude that the captains did indeed fulfill those expectations despite the reservations of some recent historians on the important issue of the discovery of a commercially useful water route to the Pacific by way of the Missouri and the Columbia Rivers. Tennant and Beck place particular emphasis on the captains' contributions to our knowledge of the plants, animals, geographic features, and Indian cultures which they encountered.

The "Now" section opens with essays addressing two modern controversies related to Meriwether Lewis: the validity of evidence that he fathered a son by a Yankton Sioux woman and the questions surrounding his death—was it murder or suicide? On the first, Harry Thompson begins by telling of the occurrence, in the baptismal records of an Episcopal mission in south-central South Dakota, of a listing of a sixty-eight-year-old man who claims Lewis as his father. Thompson goes on to investigate the question of "how we write history" and specifically the nature and validity of "documentary, or source based, history." On the second issue—suicide or murder—John Guice presents the arguments on both sides in great detail but maintains that a strong case can be made for murder, this in spite of the majority opinion among respected historians in favor of suicide. Guice does not claim to prove murder, but he asks that the evidence for it be given more serious consideration than it has received in the past. These two essays are joined not simply by having Lewis as subject. Both suggest that exhuming his remains and conducting DNA tests on them offer the possibility of settling the controversies.

Stories of heroic endeavors shade into myth at some point, especially if they become part of a whole nation's identity, so it should come as no surprise that a number of myths have sprung up around the Lewis and Clark Expedition. Ronald Laycock and David Kvernes touch upon some of them while treating Sacagawea, the Indian interpreter and only woman to make the journey, and also in dealing with other members of the expedition. Laycock focuses on Sacagawea as she appears in Eva Emery Dye's 1902 historical novel, *The Conquest: The True Story of Lewis and Clark*. He shows how Dye's commitment to the women's suffrage movement motivated her to embroider lavishly the story of the Indian woman in order to create a heroine for the suffrage movement. Other writers in the first half of the twentieth century used Dye's work as a resource, and thus the myths have persisted. The entire expedition crew, excluding only the two captains, are the subject of Kvernes's essay. He sets out to show how increasing attention has been paid to these "outsiders" over the course of the past century in contrast to their neglect in the nineteenth. Again, Sacagawea figures prominently, as does Clark's black slave York, but the other crew members are also shown to benefit from a variety of changes in public attitudes and the availability of new evidence in the twentieth century.

One of the historians who have paid attention to the ordinary expedition members was Bernard DeVoto, whose career as a chronicler and champion of the West, and particularly of Lewis and Clark, is traced by Robert Steensma. Among other things, he shows how DeVoto's fiction writing, some of it published under a pseudonym and none of it well received by the critics, helped to shape his fine narrative style when he came to write history. Steensma captures for us the sense of combative enthusiasm that makes DeVoto so engaging as a historian.

Among revisionist historians of the late twentieth century the term colonialism figures prominently. Rita Easterby Olson adopts it as the theme of her essay, which describes the ways the journal accounts encouraged colonization of the West and the subsequent dispossession of the Native populations. Postcolonial theory, beginning with Edward Said's *Orientalism*, provides a starting point for her argument, which is developed by a close reading of the journals.

Artifacts related to the Lewis and Clark Expedition have a way of turning up in unexpected places, even in our own day. The necklace of grizzly bear claws that was recently discovered among uncatalogued South Pacific relics at the Peabody Museum of Archeology at Harvard University is a case in point. Not a case in point is perhaps the largest artifact of all, a full-sized replica of Fort Mandan that appeared close to the original site of the fort in central North Dakota, exactly where one would expect it. It was constructed by a dedicated band of Lewis and Clark enthusiasts. The Reverend Elmer Odland was one of the leaders of that band, and his essay recounts the steps that led to its appearance: hatching the idea, choosing a site, raising the money, and finally building the fort and dedicating it. He tells a heartening story of community action to preserve local history.

One of the better known geographic features on the northern plains linked to the Lewis and Clark Expedition is Spirit Mound in extreme southeastern South Dakota. It was visited by Lewis, Clark, eleven other members of the expedition, and Lewis's dog on a sweltering day in late August 1804. Norma Wilson, a professor at the nearby University of South Dakota, describes the Native American traditions associated with the mound and then brings us forward to the present, telling of visits to this site with several Native American writers and hearing accounts of Native traditions about it from others. We get a strong sense that the mound is still a living presence in the hearts of Native Americans. The recent efforts that have restored Spirit Mound to something like its natural state when Lewis and Clark visited provide hope that these traditions will be preserved for a long time to come. How that restoration to a natural state came about is one of the subjects of Kent Scribner's essay,

"Spirit Mound after Lewis and Clark." He takes us through the two-hundred years since the historic visit, summarizing the history of the area around the mound, telling us who owned the property and how it was treated as the decades passed, and concluding with details of the campaign to restore it.

Covering as it does a great variety of subjects and an equally great span of time, from the decades before the explorers set out to the present, this collection will, we trust, provide readers with both delight and instruction.

The Lewis and Clark Expedition
Then: The Journey Begins

Before the Corps: Don Alonso Decalves' 1786-1787 "Exploration" of the West

Rex C. Myers

Thomas Jefferson and Connecticut Yankee John Ledyard spent the summer of 1785 in Paris concocting a fantastical plan to explore the American West. Years later, Jefferson remembered the details and excitement of their plotting: "I then proposed to him to go by land to Kamchatka [Russia], cross in some of the Russian vessels to Nootka Sound, fall down into the latitude of the Missouri, and penetrate to, and through that to the United States." In fact, Jefferson proposed Ledyard walk across North America from west to east: "He eagerly seized the idea."[1]

In fiction, Don Alonso Decalves spent that same summer in New Orleans, smitten with "the unknown parts of America" and "a desire to explore them." At summer's end, Decalves "came to a positive determination to make an attempt the ensuing year."[2] Ledyard's effort failed when Russian authorities arrested and returned him to Europe, but Decalves' apocryphal exploration took place in 1786-1787 and found its way into print by May 1788 as *New Travels to the Westward or, Unknown Parts of America*. Don Alonso Decalves joined a long list of writers who did not let fact stand in the way of a good story about the West.

Fiction played an important role in developing the West, not only as genre for more recent shoot-'em-up novels and grade "B" movies, but much earlier in the process of European exploration. Two dominant dreams fed personal and national fantasies: anticipation that the region contained wealth comparable to the riches Spain exploited in Central and South America; and the presumption that one could easily traverse the area through a Northwest Passage at best, or a series of interlinked waterways at least. Lewis and Clark drew the last maps to belie dreams of an easy crossing, but prospects of hidden treasure fired imaginations well into the present era.

Fantasies fed fabrications like tributaries to real and imagined western rivers, or hopes of precious nuggets in so much geographic gravel. Native oral traditions wove legends into understandable and memorable pasts. Retelling and translation for Europeans garbled or confused stories as facts, sometimes inadvertently, sometimes not. European chroniclers, often eager to over-extend their knowledge or enhance perceptions of their own importance, left out "I was told" caveats to descriptions of far-off places. Imprecise inter-montane lakes, west-flowing rivers, crystal peaks, and fecund prairies and mountain ranges too often converted into specific map points. That is the magnanimous explanation for falsehoods. Others lied. They did not accurately report what they saw or they created entire river systems and native tribes out of whole cloth. It made no difference. Stories of wealth and geography lingered on maps and in public consciousness like verses committed to memory.

To Alvar Nunez Cabeza de Vaca belongs the honor of being the first European to cross North America. Accounts of his eight-year traverse (1527-1535) from Florida to the Pacific coast fueled rich dreams of copper, emeralds, and pearls as they circulated through Mexico and Spain.[3] Estevanico, an African slave who accompanied de Vaca, became a principal in Father Marcos de Niza's 1539 penetration north of Mexico into pueblo villages along the upper Rio Grande. Estevanico forged ahead of Niza's main party, antagonized natives with arrogant behavior, and died at their hands. But as couriers shuttled between the African and Niza, they brought back details the priest could hardly wait to share. Niza reported seven towns in a region called "Cibola," including "the biggest, most populous, and richest" city in the world, comprising stone buildings two, three and four stories high. Turquoise ornamented buildings and people were found; a unicorn—"half as big again as...a large cow"—roamed prairies; and such gold abounded "that the natives of it deal in vessels and jewels for the ears and little plates with which they scrape themselves to relieve themselves of sweat."[4] Niza mixed unsubstantiated reports with observed reality, but the two melded into a fantasy of "somewhat white" Indians in Cibola enjoying silver and gold in "greater use and more abundance than in Peru."[5] Little wonder Francisco Vazquez de Coronado and a thousand men spent 1540-1542 looking for wealth and unicorns from the Rio Grande to Kansas.[6]

French explorers farther north and a century later had no firmer grasp on reality. Jean Nicolet's purported 1634 landing on the shore of what is now Green Bay, dressed in a "grand robe of China damask, all strewn with flowers and birds of many colors" to greet the Winnebago as "people of the sea," presents a striking case in point.[7] When Louis Jolliet and Father Jacques Marquette descended the Mississippi in 1673 and passed the mouth of the Missouri, they assumed it provided access to "the Vermillion Sea or California."[8] Priest Louis Hennepin and Sieur de La Salle retraced this route between 1678 and 1680, the good father returning to France and publishing his *Description of Louisiana* in 1683 with an edited reissue in 1697. Hennepin reported "civilized tractable" tribes along the Mississippi, with laws, and "a king who commands as a sovereign." He waxed on. "It is as warm as Italy. The corn ripens there in fifty days. The soil bears two crops a year. There are found there palm trees, canes, laurels, forests of mulberry trees" and more. In Hennepin's 1697 retelling, he turned his eyes westward along the Missouri recounting Indian stories that it took only ten or twelve days to reach the headwaters—a single mountain from which rivers flowed east and west. “Beyond this mountain the sea is seen and great vessels, [and] that these rivers are peopled by a great number of villages”[9]

As Hennepin used his imagination and pen to extend the scope of his explorations, another Frenchman made a similar expedition farther north. Louis Armand de Lom d'Arche, Baron de Lahontan, had been on the western frontier for some time when, in the late summer of 1688, he returned to Fort Michilimackinac and physically settled in for winter. His creative mind traveled more widely. In a well-structured deceit, the Baron wrote to a friend on September 18 that he intended “to travel through the southern Countries that I have so often heard of.”[10] Quill in hand, ink bottle at the ready, Lahontan pressed on, fictitiously leaving the fort by canoe on September 24 with twenty men and five Indians. They went through Green Bay, up the Fox River, portaged to the Wisconsin, floated down to the Mississippi, then turned upstream until on November 3 he and his party discovered Long River.

The next four months Lahontan explored—all fictitiously, visiting Essanapes and Gnacsitares tribes in villages with 500 to 600 armed men. Cacick, king of the Gnacsitares, offcred Lahontan “a great many Girls…pressing me and my Retinue to serve ourselves,” but the French explorer demurred—how could they be enjoyed without good bread and wine?[11] Also at the Gnacsitares village, Lahontan met four Mozeemleks from a tribe to the south and west. They looked Spanish with bushy beards, swarthy complexions, and long hair, and told the explorer their tribe could field 20,000 warriors. These four ersatz natives described their village beside a river that sprang from the same ridge of mountains as the Long River. This mountain range was only six leagues wide, but very high and rugged. Three hundred leagues downstream from the Mozeemlek village the river emptied into a salt lake 300 leagues in circumference around which where six “noble Cities” of flat-roofed stone houses and hundreds of smaller towns. Residents called themselves Tabuglauk and were artisans in copper.[12]

Lahontan said he left a lead plate with the French coat of arms at the headwaters of Long River in January and began his return, supposedly arriving back at Fort Michilimackinac May 28, 1689: “Thank God, I am now return'd from my Voyage upon the Long River.”[13] He drew a detailed map of the west-to-east flowing Long and showed its headwaters interlinked with the Mozeemlek's westward flowing river. Ever helpful, the French explorer concluded his account with suggestions for future expeditions: “Men ought to be between 30 and 40 years of Age; of dry constitution, of peaceable Temper, of an active and bold Sprit, and inur'd to the fatigues of Voyages.” Their number should include “some Trumpeters and Fidlers, both for animating his Retinue, and raising the admiration of the Savages.”[14]

"R. Longue" appeared on H. Moll's "A New Map of North America" in 1713, drawn to suggest that from its headwaters to the Pacific was a distance of not more than a few miles.[15] Three years later, a young French voyageur named Jacques de Noyon, who had, in fact, explored the region north of where Lahontan imagined the Long River, reported Indians told him a river entering Lake of the Woods also emptied into the Western Sea and that Indians in the area had metal axes and coins bearing Chinese characters which they had traded from ships along the sea coast.[16] Bobe, a Quebec priest, gathered information from travelers passing through the city and in 1720 presented the governor of New France with a manuscript entitled *Memoir for the Discovery of the Western Sea*. Bobe stated that the Pacific lay no more than 200 leagues west of the source of the Missouri (and/or the Long.) He proposed six possible routes to the western sea. Two paths speculated avenues west from the lower Mississippi and Missouri. The remaining four used headwaters of both rivers as jumping off points, including a course west from Lake of the Woods to a river called "Cerf," which entered Lake Takamamiouen and led, in turn, to another river that emptied into the Pacific. One route simply directed exploration overland through the "vast and beautiful plains" of Assiniboine country.[17]

Etienne Venyard, Sieur du Bourgmont, provided details of the lower portion of what became known as Louisiana. Between 1714 and 1725, the French adventurer explored, mapped, and wrote about the Missouri basin—"the most beautiful lands in the world"—as far up as the Niobrara River. The Missouri, Bourgmont reported confidently in his 1714 *Exact Description of Louisiana*, provided easy access to Spanish territory with its many silver mines. He also found copper, lead, mulberry trees for silk, and the "most handsome tribe of all these continents," the Omahas, who were "white and blond, like Europeans...[and] live without warring on their neighbors."[18] To the north, Pierre La Verendrye and his sons Louis and Francois, between 1739 and 1742, wandered the vast and beautiful plains. They saw shining or snowy mountains others reported seeing, heard of silver riches and tribes of dwarves, as well as met an Indian who spoke Spanish and said that Spain's outposts were only weeks away by horseback.[19]

Concurrently, a Dutch-born Frenchman named Antoine Simon La Page du Pratz spent sixteen years among native groups along the lower Mississippi. In September 1751, he began a series of articles in the *Journal Oeconomique*, which became a three-volume history of Louisiana published in French in 1758. An English translation appeared in 1763 entitled *The History of Louisiana, or of the Western Parts of Virginia and Carolina*. In his first *Journal* article, du Pratz stated his belief that "the principal qualities of an historian are truth and accuracy," but he had never traveled north of Natchez and relied on the writings of others, such as Bourgmont, for details that lacked both truth and accuracy.[20]

For information about the West beyond French exploration, du Pratz recorded his conversation with a "wise old man" named Machacht-ape, who recounted a five-year trip to the "nation of the West, or the Canzas." He ascended the Missouri to its headwaters then crossed to the "Fine River" which flowed past villages of the Otters and into a "great Water on the west." The Otters feared bearded men who came from the setting sun, kidnapped children for slaves, dressed in knee-length coats, had firearms, and wore shoes of red or yellow. Du Pratz included "A Map of Louisiana, with the course of the Missisipi" in his 1763 edition. He showed the Missouri flowing almost due west from the Mississippi, unrestricted by mountains.[21] North of the Missouri, du Pratz drew in Lahontan's Long River with a large lake at its headwaters and a tantalizingly short portage to a west-flowing "Beautiful River" in the land of the Northern Otters.[22]

A new breed of dreamers focused their attention west of the Mississippi at mid-century—Colonial Americans. The Loyal Land Company of Virginia in 1753 proposed sending Dr. Thomas Walker up the Missouri to search for its "communication with the Pacific Ocean" but abandoned the idea when the French and Indian War began.[23] Robert Rogers and his Rangers occupied Detroit and other western forts during that war, and Rogers thought Parliament should fund a Pacific expedition. He forwarded his proposal in a 1765 publication, *A Concise Account of North America*, lauding riches in an area he had never seen. The next year, as Agent to the Western Indians and Governor Commandant at Michilimackinac, Rogers wrote instructions for Captain James Tute "commanding a party for the discovery of the North West Passage from the Atlantick into the Passifick Occian, …or for the discovery of the great Reriver Ourigan."[24] Rogers predicted Tute would find "an inhabited country and great riches," including gold which he believed natives carried westward and traded with the "Japancies."[25]

Tute, in turn, delegated expedition responsibility to Jonathan Carver, who left his boss at Prairie de Chien on May 6, 1767, and returned to Michilimackinac on August 29, reporting a trip "upwards of three thousand miles."[26] In a relative straight line, such exploration would have taken Carver nearly to the Pacific coast and back, but he accumulated this distance wandering northern plains. When he returned to Boston that fall, he began to write a journal for publication. A thread of "Natives say" ran through his narrative but not always visibly in the warp and woof of tales he wove, or with geographic points on his maps. Carver proved remarkably accurate, reporting plains tribes and topography, but outside that region he waffled about what he actually witnessed. A "River of the West"—the Oregon—flowed to the South Sea. All great North American rivers—St. Lawrence, Mississippi, Bourbon (north flowing), and the Oregon—"rise within a few leagues of each other." Carver provided more details: bearded men in very large canoes floated the Pacific; Shining Mountains covered with "crystal stones, of an amazing size" sparkled in the sun; white Indians existed; "gold so plenty[ful]...that [Indians] make their most common utensils of it" awaited; and a mountain of red marble used for native pipe making rose from the prairie.[27]

The Great Plains, Carver said, were "a most delightful country, abounding with all the necessities of life, that grow spontaneously..."; with "trees bending under their loads of fruits such as plums, grapes, and apples..."; meadows abundant in hops and vegetables; ground nuts as large "as hens eggs"; and enough maple trees to "produce sugar sufficient for any number of inhabitants." In the western mountains, Carver reported seeing a large cat-like animal of a "reddish or orange cast" with "black spots of different figures" on the skin and black striped ears. "This creature is nearly as fierce as a leopard, but will seldom attack a man." [28]

Carver published his *Travels through the Interior Parts of North America in the Years 1766, 1767 and 1768* in London during 1778. The immensely popular work went through more than two dozen printings/editions in English, French, and German between that date and 1838. The first American edition (1784) appeared in Philadelphia under the imprint of Joseph Crukshank and Robert Bell. Crukshank reissued it in 1789 and again in 1792.[29] For many, Carver's accounts of the West were the most thorough and readily available. He assured readers in a 1781 printing that he had not "as travelers are sometimes supposed to do, amused them with improbable tales, or wished to acquire importance by making his adventures favour the marvellous."[30] But Carver had his skeptics. Peter Pond, himself a western narrator, observed in his 1785 vernacular that Carver "gave a good a count of the small part of the western countrey he saw but when he a Leudes to heresasa he flies from facts in two many instances."[31]

A jumble of information about the West bubbled into the awareness of Americans, Englishmen, and Spaniards by the mid-1780s. Francois Barbe-Marbois, first secretary of the French legation in the U.S., sent all state governors a questionnaire seeking details about their jurisdictions. Only Virginia's governor took him seriously—Thomas Jefferson began to gather information that ultimately saw print in his *Notes on the State of Virginia*, published in 1787.[32] As Jefferson gathered material about Virginia from the Atlantic to the Mississippi, Sir Joseph Banks, president of the Royal Society in London, received a suggestion from Peter Pond and Alexander Henry that the Society fund exploration of "A Proper Rout, by Land, to Cross the Great Cotenant of America."[33]

When the Virginia governor got wind of the proposal in late 1783, he hurriedly wrote to his friend George Rogers Clark, then in the very western part of the state gathering specimens of mammoth bones for Jefferson, and asked if the frontiersman "would like to lead such a party?" Clark declined because of personal finances (Virginia owned him money for earlier services) but thought it was a good idea, something three or four men might accomplish thoroughly over the space of four or five years, and certainly "an Expence worthey the attention of Congress."[34]

That same year, two New England men published accounts of their 1778 explorations of the Pacific Coast as part of Capt. James Cook's 1776-1779 expedition. Both John Ledyard and John Rickman extolled the wealth in sea otter fur to be harvested by whoever controlled the Pacific coast of North America.[35] Individually and together, Ledyard and now Ambassador Thomas Jefferson hatched several schemes to explore the region, the most far-fetched of which was Ledyard's abortive effort to reach the Pacific coast of North America via Russia and then walk east to the United States.[36]

Spain took official possession of Louisiana following the 1763 end of the French and Indian War. In 1785, Governor Estaban Rodrigues Miro, at the request of his superiors, wrote a description of the region. His report admitted to no exploration after the French abandoned the area in 1758 but contained accurate details about the Missouri as far up as the Niobrara and Sioux rivers. The Spanish Governor speculated on Missouri headwaters not too far from those of the Rio Grande or the Colorado, and a large waterfall two hundred leagues upriver from the Aricaras which gave surrounding mountains their name: "La Montana que Canta" (the mountain which sings.)[37]

Connecticut-born Peter Pond worked both sides of the United States' northern border in 1785. On one hand he presented Congress with a map of the western Great Lakes used later in boundary negotiations; on the other, he encouraged Parliament to aid fur traders by establishing posts all the way to the Pacific. For both interests he felt sure that "only a narrow stretch of unknown territory remained to be crossed to make the long desired northwest passage a reality."[38] Pond, although critical of Carver's western hearsay stories, did not hesitate to report "what the savages told me." All western tribes were united, peaceful, used canoes but not firearms, and had "Negroes" living among them. These Indians possessed horses, mules, and asses, but also animals from Central America, notably the "lama with its beautiful wool." Perhaps most noteworthy, Pond said all the western rivers flowed to the South Sea, suggesting one in particular and recommending Alexander Mackenzie explore it two years later. [39] Mackenzie did, but the river that ultimately bore his name flowed to the Arctic, not the Pacific.

Thomas Jefferson's *Notes on the State of Virginia*, researched and revised between 1780 and 1782, saw print (in England) during 1787. Thorough, and eager to provide insights about Virginia and regions bordering it to the west, Jefferson shared interesting information on Louisiana. He, too, believed in a "westwardly" flowing river on the other side of the mountains, expressed fascination with mammoth bones, and wanted to believe "traditional testimony of Indians" that the wooly beast "still exists in the northern and western part of America."[40] He wondered aloud, albeit skeptically, about the possibility of a volcano in the region as a source of pumice found floating down the Missouri. He suspected the Missouri had its origins in high, snowy mountains, yet remained uncertain about the proximity of the river's headwaters to those of the Rio Grande or the River of the North, [41] hoping, like the English and the Spanish, that the distance from those mountains to the Pacific might be as little as 100 miles.[42]

Hope, fantasy, and just plain bad information translated themselves onto maps. As Estaban Miro admitted in 1785 to having no information about Louisiana newer than 1758, map makers used even older data. The result was a "playground for cartographical imagination."[43] Frenchman Robert de Vaugondy issued nearly identical maps in 1750 and 1772, notable for capturing the region as Baron Lahontan imagined it in 1688: the Long River watershed, an enormous body of salt water—"Lake Salso"—around which lived Moozemlek Indians to the north and the coppersmith Tahuglauks to the south, a rendition of du Pratz's "Beautiful River" resembling an east-west Missouri flowing unobstructed from the Mississippi to the Pacific, and another stream draining the salt lake—a "River of the West"—and reaching the Pacific at about fifty degrees north latitude.[44] His Majesty's Geographer, Thomas Kitchin, drew English maps in 1765 and 1787; prolific Italian cartographer Antonio Zatta included two maps of the region in his multi-volume, 218-map *Atante Novissimo* (1776-1785); and a dozen others tried their hands at drawing maps without contributing more than incidental notations of "Extensive Meadows full of Buffaloes," or "Mountain of bright Stones," or "civilized people," or a Chinese colony along the Pacific, perhaps the source of Jacques de Noyon's 1716 coins.[45] Lahontan's 1688 misinformation prevailed for a century like Gresham's Law for cartography—no better information replaced it.

Into this geography and international milieu walked Don Alonso Decalves. Two editions of *New Travels to the Westward* appeared in 1788. John Trumbull of Norwich, Connecticut, published one; John W. Folsom of Boston, the other. Folsom's advertisement in *The Boston Gazette* and the *Country Journal*, Monday, May 19, 1788, announced the thin volume, priced at one shilling:

New Travels to the Westward

Or unknown Parts of America

Being a tour of almost fourteen months

This work

(being worthy of the perusal of every enterprising American)

> contains an account of the country upwards of two
> thousand miles west of the Christian parts of
> North America; with an account of
> White Indians, their manners, habits
> And many curious particulars,
> Never before published.
> Attested by three other persons.

Between 1788 and 1805, this little publication went through at least nineteen printings, some as *New Travels to the Westward*, others as *Travels*, in states from Maine to Kentucky, including a German language edition out of Philadelphia in 1796.[46] Length depended on type setting: Trumbull's 1788 edition ran thirty-four pages; Folsom's, set in a larger font and with more space between lines, came out at forty-four.

Trumbull printed a notice of his second edition in *The Norwich Packet and Country Journal*, a newspaper he edited, on Friday, March 6, 1789. He added a portion of the author's preface in which Decalves apologized for the work's "humble style":

> [T]he Author
> never had the advantage of a liberal edu-
> cation, consequently has nothing to recom-
> mend it, but a simple statement of facts,
> without exaggeration.[47]

The preface itself continued:

> I make no doubt, if my observations were dressed out by an accomplished historian, or had I the talents of a poet, (for which I had sufficient subject) they would have been received with much greater avidity; but such as they are, in the simple unaffected language of truth, I submit to the Public....[48]

Alas, would that Decalves really had "facts without exaggeration" in the "simple unaffected language of truth." The Don proved an accomplished storyteller.

By his own account, Alonso Decalves left his native Spain at the age of twenty-one in 1780 and moved with his family to New Orleans. When he finally set out on June 1, 1786, to explore "the unknown parts of America," his small party included himself and three others: brother John, Dutchman Peter Vanshuts, and an Indian named Tomhegan.[49] They used a large canoe and paddled up the Mississippi at the rate of thirty miles per day for thirty-one days, an effort that would have brought them near the mouth of the Missouri, a river which Decalves never acknowledged.

Caching their canoe and dividing gear evenly, they set out afoot westward through "large tracts of land, where not a tree could be seen for miles" the beauty of which "exceeds even a romantick description." When they encountered trees, they were picturesque groves of walnut and beech. They also found ample game: buffalo, deer, bear, and wild turkeys and streams full of fish. It was a prairie that Hennepin, Bourgmont, and Carver would have recognized. On August 25, after nearly two months of walking, they began ascending "into a higher country." In time, "Sublime Mountains," whose "height[s] were truly astonishing," came into view—mountains most previous explorers said were there and all cartographers had scattered variously across their maps. Decalves' party reached the range's crest on September 4 and the next day scaled a very high peak, but retreated quickly when everyone but John Decalves got altitude sickness.

Descending into "a fine, level country," they encountered and followed a "considerable river," flowing generally west—probably the one du Pratz's informant Machacht-ape observed. On September 26, John Decalves and Tomhegan killed a large animal (eight feet, seven inches long) "in the form of a cat" with "rows of spots in bright vermilion" on its sides, black spots on its belly, and a tufted tail. Jonathan Carver would have been proud. The group then built a raft and continued their journey downriver.

On October 5, they encountered their first natives, fortuitously friendly and dramatically impressed with European firearms when the group killed a large white [grizzly] bear as a demonstration. Two days later, natives led them to their village of huts around Lake Brumbock, certainly large enough to be Lake Salso, although Decalves fails to mention salinity. He did describe tribe members as over six feet tall, well-proportioned, robust, with "bright and sparkling" eyes, "free from that spiteful look common among Indians in the east," and with speech "more like the language of civilized nations, than that of Savages"—Indians like Hennepin reported a century earlier. Active and swift of foot, many natives lived 100 years and more. Attired in tanned hides, Decalves' hosts fed him a variety of meats, "samp made of Indian corn," and "delicious" goat's milk.

Eager to show off their visitors, natives took the party across Lake Brumbock on October 10 and down the River Astungo, "as large as the Missisippi [sic] above the mouth of the Ohio." Six days later, after passing through rich lands, they arrived at the capital, Astungo, on an island in its namesake river, with several thousand inhabitants, all "as white as a swan, or the whitest sheep."

King Knipperdoling[50] greeted them warmly, showed them through beautiful, multi-story, flat-roofed stone buildings, with isin-glass windows and exterior murals—remarkably like buildings Lahontan described. Gold (from mines in the southern part of the region), pearls, furs, and feathers decorated rooms and inhabitants alike, including the king's seven wives and thirty children. Decalves demonstrated the power of his rifles to the king's covetous delight. But these people lived in peace—Knipperdoling could muster an intimidating 4000 warriors if necessary—worshipping the sun and moon, with the king himself as a trinity. Outside the city, Decalves and his party enjoyed a "beautiful and temperate climate," saw "large and handsome settlements, compassed by fine fields...[of]...every kind of produce that grows in America, except wheat." He observed mulberry trees and silk worms, but no silk garments; saw cattle, mules, goats, and sheep; tasted "ordinary" wine from local grapes; walked through Indian corn over ten feet tall; then heard locals tell of medicinal and vegetable roots that grew spontaneously.

Extraordinarily, they met another European—John Van Delure, another Dutchman. Decalves created a life for Delure that included fur trading along the Pacific Coast in the fall of 1784. When Delure and a companion went ashore and got lost overnight, they returned to the coast only to discover that ship and crew had hastily abandoned them to escape a mob of Indians angry at the rape of their women. Delure avoided the tribe's wrath but found himself alone (his companion soon died) in a strange land. He contemplated walking eastward across North America and headed up the Astungo River, a clear River of the West look-alike. After about 350 miles, Delure abandoned his idea of a transcontinental hike and settled in a small village 150 miles north of Astungo city. There he took a wife (the nineteen-year old daughter of a "rich sachem"), fathered a son, and settled into a comfortable existence. Decalves and his compatriots wintered in Delure's village, a community of dwarf-like residents the explorer described in terms far inferior to those of Astungo: "Short, thick, and ill shaped...they resembled Negroes..." with complexions and hair "milk white."

Decalves and his party decided to leave in the spring of 1787 and invited Delure to join them. He declined, preferring to remain with his wife and son. The explorers departed Delure's village on April 27 and Astungo on May 7, after selling Knipperdoling two of their rifles as well as half their lead and powder for 400 pounds of gold and fur. As they crossed the Sublime Mountains in mid-June, they found the source of pumice Jefferson reported on the Missouri, witnessing a volcanic eruption to the south: "Ten thousand vollies of lived flames." On the other side of the mountains they struggled through thick vegetations and set a prairie fire to ease their passage. Reaching the Mississippi July 9th, they located their cached canoe three days later. On July 27, 1787, they arrived back in New Orleans, bearded, attired in furs, and unrecognizable, even to Decalves's father. The Don looked back on the country he had seen with unequivocal optimism: "I believe...that the extent of the country west of any Christian inhabitants [and] north of New Mexico...to be greater than is at present possessed by any Potentate in Europe." In the immediate future he foresaw a profitable trade in furs and gold.

Prescient coincidences between Decalves' 1788 narrative and Lewis and Clark's journals (1803-1806) catch the reader's eye, the phrase "we proceeded on" among them.[51] Decalves, like Lewis, reached the crest of the mountains and "to our astonishment, we beheld a chain of mountains directly before us."[52] They met their first western Indians in nearly identical scenes—"The women ran off as fast as their legs would carry them";[53] encountered and killed a grizzly bear; returned to cached canoes, each with one small hole;[54] came home in unrecognizable frontier form.

Concomitant with *New Travels'* publication notice in the *Norwich Packet*, appeared a prospectus for the "new City of Athens," projected at the junction of the Mississippi and Missouri, "the most desirable spot in the known world." Surrounding land enjoyed a "soil where almost every thing grows spontaneous[ly]," replete with "corn, wine and oil…on its hills, and milk and honey in its valleys." More specifically, spring water, salt, stone, coal, lead, iron, copper, and marble quarries all existed within an hour of the proposed city. Beyond that, fur riches of the upper Missouri "will one day bring more wealth into the cofers [sic] of the merchant, than the mines of Peru or Mexico to the Spanish monarch." Freedom of religion, unlimited economic opportunity, and a nurturing climate for the arts will emerge:

> Again shall Athens bid her columns rise,
> Again her lofty turrets reach the skies,
> Science again shall find a safe retreat,
> And commerce here as in a centre meet.[55]

Don Herico Ignatius Ferinando Cuspes, Secretary for the Athens Company, supposedly translated the document. Side-by-side front-page publication of the book notice and Athens prospectus suggest deliberate action and close association.

Don Alonso Decalves was as apocryphal as Knipperdoling's kingdom. Nothing in any edition of *New Travels to the Westward*, or newspapers advertising it, identified Decalves beyond his own preface. Not lost on the careful reader, however, is Decalves' broad knowledge of extant 1780s information about Louisiana. Fruitful prairies, fanciful vegetation (mulberry trees included), high mountain ranges with a large salt lake set therein, great westward flowing rivers, animals real and imagined, furs, gold, white Indians, African-like Indians, a king to rule over them, volcanoes—the impressive list belies coincidence. Whoever wrote *New Travels* read widely.

Likewise, the publication's timing appears opportune. Antoine du Pratz's 1763 English language edition of *The History of Louisiana* fed public interest in the West following the French and Indian War. Robert Roger's *Concise History* found wide readership two years later, and Pacific fur trade information from John Ledyard and John Rickman expanded awareness of the region's amazing riches. Thomas Jefferson's own *Notes on the State of Virginia* added grist to the mill. Most notably, Jonathan Carver's 1784

American edition of *Travels through the Interior Parts of North America*, coupled with its frequent republication, indicated a broad market for such literature. Decalves initial title *New Travels* positioned the work before Carver's readers as a sequential account of the region. Thomas Jefferson himself had all these pre-Decalves books in his library; and there can be little doubt that the author of *New Travels to the Westward* read a similar collection.[56]

Fabricating names had a frontier tradition parallel to creating fictions. Lahontan set the standard. Decalves used two names that went beyond coincidence. Tomhegan, the native traveling companion, was a name from the American Revolution—a "rascally" Abenaki Indian who sided with the British and raided what is now Bethel, Maine.[57] King Knipperdoling shared his name with a German Anabaptist leader whose brief rise to prominence in 1535-1536 was less benevolent but did include multiple wives. Those names reaffirm Decalves' highly literate background.

Candidates for the false Don do not readily suggest themselves. For sheer knowledge, Louisiana Governor Estaban Rodrigues Miro and John Ledyard are tantalizing candidates. Miro gathered much published material as well as oral reports from Missouri River trappers before he wrote his 1785 report. Ledyard had both interest and inclination, spending most of the mid-1780s trying to promote fur trade in the region or figure out how to walk across it (like Delure); he demonstrated ability, witnessed by his 208-page publication of Captain Cook's voyages in 1783 and narratives of his Russian travels composed from June 1787 forward. He possessed the knowledge since he had access to Thomas Jefferson's library while both were in France in 1785 and 1786. It may also be worth noting that Ledyard lived pleasantly among the Iroquois Indians for three and one half months while a student at Dartmouth in 1772 and 1773. A Connecticut native who published his 1783 account of Captain Cook's voyage with Nathaniel Patten in Hartford, Ledyard might logically choose a home-state venue for other writing. Unfortunately, for the sake of an easy answer, neither Miro's nor Ledyard's papers contain anything suggesting authorship of *New Travels to the Westward*.[58]

Publication data suggest an alternate hypothesis. With nascent copyright laws, the only person guaranteed financial gain on a book title was the publisher/printer. Anyone with a printing press could and did pirate titles. The shortness of *New Travels* made it an easy target. Two hundred years have clouded precise printing details surrounding the many editions of *New Travels*, but it appears most publishers did only one press run. Samuel Bragg, Jr. (Dover, New Hampshire) in 1796 and 1797, as well as A. Stoddard (Hudson, New York), 1799 and 1801, did two. *Norwich Packet* editor John Trumbull issued at least three.[59]

The thirty-three year old Trumbull, therefore, deserves a more deliberate look. A Norwich community historian described the editor as "remarkable for his genial humor, and [he] always had a merry turn or witty remark at hand."[60] An imprint of *New Travels* bearing John Trumbull's name as publisher and printer appeared with a 1788 date. An advertisement for another edition of the same works appeared in his newspaper on March 6, 1789, and when he printed the work yet again in 1790, the title page bore a note, "The Third Edition." There is also the possibility Trumbull issued *New Travels* a fourth time in 1796.[61] The quick succession of Trumbull editions—1788, 1789, 1790—suggests he had the greatest interest in the publication and was not copying anybody else's work, although he reset type for each edition. Coupled with his newspaper's 1789 front-page advertisement and side-by-side publication of the Athens pseudo-prospectus, Trumbull obviously had a unique relationship with *New Travels to the Westward*.[62]

We do not know Trumbull's reading habits, but undoubtedly he admired Carver's popularity. In conjunction with his newspaper, he printed and sold maps, almanacs, books, pamphlets, novels without attribution, and other items "in frequent editions."[63] In June 1787, he printed a large map of the world which included Captain Cook's discoveries and was "approved, by several Gentlemen." Two months later he began selling a map of the western United States by the country's Surveyor General, Thomas Hutchins, and in April 1788 he reprinted Col. Isaac Sherman's assessment of the Western Reserve, which reported an ideal city site where the Cuyahoga River entered Lake Erie with "iron ore, stone, coal, and...valuable salt Springs" close by.[64] Accounts of westward land speculation or settlement opportunities appeared almost weekly in the *Packet* during 1788. Trumbull's humor and wit may have found satirical expression in the writings of Alonso Decalves and Herico Cuspes.[65] If editor John Trumbull was not the author of *New Travels* or the new Athens prospectus, he knew who was and understood their motivations well. For modern historians their identities are lost.

While authors of these writings undoubtedly separated fact and fiction in their own minds, there is no way to tell if the general public did so. Decalves' profession of "a simple statement of facts" and the "unaffected language of truth" resembled affirmations of veracity both Carver and Pond used in recommending their own works. In 1788, even the best-read American—Thomas Jefferson—did not have a precise idea of what the region between St. Louis and the Pacific held in the way of rivers, mountains, volcanoes, or woolly mammoths. At least fourteen different publishers/printers of *New Travels* gambled on broad public interest in the area, letting book buyers sort out their own perceptions. That said, it is worth noting that Thomas Jefferson did not have a copy of *New Travels to the Westward* in his library when he sold it to Congress in 1815.[66]

But Decalves did not have the last word on Astungo. In 1801 at Windsor, Connecticut, appeared a related publication:

A
NARRATIVE
Of a voyage taken by
Capt. James VanLeason
From Amsterdam to China,
And from thence to the
Western Continent of North-America;
...
also, an acount of
Mr. Vandelure's
Being left behind on the continent,
By the misconduct of the ship's company,
where he lived almost seven years.

At least eight different editions saw print between 1801 and 1819, but no *New Travels* publisher also issued this narrative. The 1801 number attributed authorship to both James Vanleason and John Vandelure; in subsequent reissues Vandelure took sole authorship.[67]

In format, *Narrative* always resembled a fake letter John Vandelure wrote from Holland to his uncle in Philadelphia, usually dated August 24, 1796. Vandelure told of his partnership with Vanleason in a 1783-84 trading enterprise with the ship "Trumbull." First the two men traded in China, then went to the Pacific coast of North America for furs. From there, Vandelure picked up the story of his abandonment at the mouth of the "great river," apparently with pen, ink, and a journal which he maintained on a daily basis. He repeated accounts of his subsequent residency among natives in the village he named Lottowongo, his marriage (to a native wife he first called Mary and subsequently Polly), and his children—a boy and, later, a girl. Vandelure's yarn meshed with meeting Decalves' party during the winter of 1786-87, then launched into a long morality tale of his success in converting to Christianity first his wife, followed by her sachem father's entire household, and ultimately King Knipperdoling himself. Vandelure also taught his family and in-laws how "to talk Dutch." In 1791, Vanleason returned with the "Trumbull" to the mouth of the Astungo, made contact with Vandelure (who bore him no ill will for the seven-year exile), and shortly thereafter transported to Amsterdam the Dutchman's and the sachem's households, plus furs worth twenty thousand pounds sterling. Vanleason, and ultimately his brother, fell in love with the now Christianized sisters of Vandelure's wife and married them. Everyone prospered under "a gracious God in his good providence." Vandelure prospered to the tune of four ships and a fortune of 80,000 pounds. An 1816 edition may have been the most forthright when it called the story "A Religious Tale."[68]

Characters aside, the style and focus of Vandelure/Vanleason's publication do not necessarily argue for the same authorship as *Travels*. Indeed, by naming his ship the "Trumbull," whoever wrote *Narrative* may have subtly pointed to the author of the *Travels*, who first "carried" the Vandelure and Vanleason stories. Beyond that, the *Narrative* has extensive dialogue, clearly retains a pseudo-letter format, and maintains a pronounced proselytizing flavor; traits not found in Decalves' writing. *Narrative* is also not as tightly written. Title pages used the name "Vandelure," but texts most often exhibited a "Deluer" spelling; the Mary/Polly duality is not clear at several points; and Vandelure is not as precise about the river Astungo's geography as was Decalves. Vandelure's overwhelming interest in converting natives also portends, even coincides with, early nineteenth-century frontier revivalism,[69] while his seven-year residence in Knipperdoling's kingdom may have been tailored to suit a long-standing American interest in "Indian captive" literature.[70] As a sequel to Alonso Decalves' original *Travels*, the new *Narrative* may have enjoyed success and public interest because of its predecessor. Perhaps sales improved or revived after 1803 with the purchase and exploration of Louisiana. One edition of *Travels* and five printings of Vandelure's narrative appeared after that date.[71]

Real exploration of Louisiana began in earnest about the time Alonso Decalves' fabrication first found its way into print. The Spanish deliberately began to expand their knowledge of and exert their control over a region they inherited in 1763 but would only hold until century's end.[72] England, its ubiquitous fur trading personnel insinuated among upper Missouri River tribes, and its flag carried overland by Alexander Mackenzie to the Arctic Ocean (1789) and the Pacific (1793), more accurately understood geography between the northern prairies and those two bodies of water.[73] Thomas Jefferson, chief among Americans interested in what lay west of the new nation,[74] encouraged exploration informally throughout the 1790s and in 1803 finally succeeded in implementing George Rogers Clark's suggestion, making Lewis and Clark "an Expense worthey the attention of Congress."

Those and subsequent efforts sparked new fictions about the American West. Don Alonso Decalves' *New Travels to the Westward* stands apart, however, as a unique published apocrypha, dismissible because Trumbull or someone else created it of whole cloth, admirable for the satirical application of profound knowledge about the region. On one hand it would be generous to say Decalves continued the travel saga traditions of Candide or Gulliver, but without socio-political lessons; on the other, he most certainly preceded late eighteenth- and nineteenth-century European travel-in-America narratives. Most important, *New Travels to the Westward*, although fiction, is the first account of pure travel in the West. There is no pretense of exploration or trade. It is as if Decalves picked a point on a real map (Lake Salso, for instance, or the Essenapes' homeland) and spun his yarn of travel and return. In the account of his wanderings through the region, he captured both the sense of place and the romance of adventure that future writers would explore at greater length. As such a fabrication, it is truly a work "dressed out by an accomplished historian...[with]...the talents of a poet" about a region that "exceeds even a romantick description."

Before Lewis and Clark: The Monument of Perrin du Lac

Tom Kilian

The recent revival of interest in Lewis and Clark among scholars and the general public has focused wide attention on the Northern Plains in our nation's history. With due respect to the stunning accomplishments of Lewis and Clark, too little has been made of the succession of explorers and traders who preceded them up the Missouri and whose knowledge, journals, and maps made the famous expedition more possible and better prepared.

Bienville, the French Governor of the Territory of Louisiana, writing on April 22, 1734, said that a French voyageur from New Orleans had lived for several years among the Arikara on the Upper Missouri (Robinson 1905, 26). There were at least two other voyageurs with him. It may be possible that this man was the Frenchman to whom the Verendryes referred as living near Ft. Pierre when they arrived from the west in 1743. If not, these men were additional early arrivals.

In 1787, Don Andres LaGariniere of St. Louis sent Joseph Garreau, age 23, to the Upper Missouri. Garreau stayed on, settled down with the Arikara, and was still active when Maximilian of Wied found him among the Mandans 46 years later (*SDHC* vol. 7, 228). Jacques D'Eglise is known to have traveled to the Upper Missouri to trade with the Rees in 1790, 1792, and 1794 (Karolevitz 1975, 20). Jean Baptiste Truteau led his party upriver in 1794 and built the first house in what is now South Dakota, a few miles south of present Pickstown (Kingsbury 1975, 24). James Mackay traveled up to the White River in 1795-96 and explored the country along the Niobrara (*SDHC* vol. 7, 228). Almost certainly there were others who were less well known and who left no journals for modern historians to dissect. Given all of the boatmen, hunters, and other retainers who accompanied these adventurers, there must have been a substantial number of men with knowledge of the Upper Missouri in St. Louis in 1800.

In 1802, a Frenchman from Paris joined the procession of explorers to the Upper Missouri. His name was Perrin du Lac, and he also traveled extensively in the United States east of the Mississippi (Robinson 1925, 582). He wrote a book describing his adventures in America entitled *Travels through the Two Louisianas, and among the Savage Nations of the Missouri; Also in the United States, along the Ohio, and the Adjacent Provinces, in 1801, 1802 and 1803. With a Sketch of the Manners, Customs, Character and the Civil and Religious Ceremonies of the People of these Countries* (*SDHC* vol. 41, 92). It first appeared in Paris in 1805 and was translated from the French by Richard Phillips, in London, in 1807.

In 1802, du Lac came up the Missouri River as far as the White River, which flows into the Missouri a few miles south of the city of Chamberlain (du Lac 53). His brief account of his travels in what is now South Dakota was based on that voyage. He began preparations for his venture in the spring of 1802, in St. Louis. In assembling men and equipment in preparation to ascend the Missouri, du Lac secured a large "perioque," able to accommodate ten men and a cargo of "everything required for the savages," including "Woollen clothing, blue and scarlet clothes, guns, gunpowder, lead, vermillion, copper cauldrons, knives, wines and silver trinkets." His boat would probably have been from forty to fifty feet long, with ends pointed and from three to four feet deep, in order to contain all the men, cargo, tents, and equipment. Such boats later came into common use in the trade on the Missouri. He set out on his expedition on May 18, 1802.

Du Lac produced a map of his travels, the "Carte Du Missouri L'An 1802," which was attached to the French edition of his book and which provides substantial details of the area through which they passed.

Among his companions on the trip was a man he described as an old trader on the Illinois River, who is believed by some scholars to have been either Jean Baptiste Truteau or James Mackay (Schell 1961, 32-36). Mackay was a Scotsman employed by a French-owned company during the Spanish regime in Louisiana. In their employ, he had gone up the Missouri as far as the White and had journeyed overland in that area. The evidence seems to support Mackay as the companion for at least two reasons. First, MacKay's overland travels west of the Missouri in what is now Nebraska, between the Niobrara and the Loup, are noted in great detail on du Lac's map. This would seem to be unlikely if Truteau had been his companion. And, from any thoughtful reading of Truteau's own journal, which reflects his ineptitudes of management and judgment on his travels on the Missouri in 1794, it is difficult to imagine that du Lac would have chosen him as a guide and advisor.

The only notation of a fort or post of any kind on du Lac's map is the showing of Jean Baptiste Truteau's house, built in 1794 and popularly called the Pawnee House. On the map, it is called the Second Poste de la Compagnie. Having attained the mouth of the White River, du Lac turned around and began his return journey downriver on August 28, 1802. All of du Lac's report of his trip within present-day South Dakota is contained in about two pages. He kept very irregular notes of having passed the Niobrara and of some encounters with the Poncas.

Du Lac made one entry of keen interest to us now. Concerning the installation of a monument, an accomplishment for which he is well known, he wrote:

> At a little distance from the mouth of the White River, I perceived a mountain more elevated than any of those on the banks of the Missouri. The weather being extremely fine I took with me two hunters, an interpreter, and a young savage as guide. When we ascended it halfway, the cold became very sensible and we had brought nothing to defend ourselves from it. My companions lighted a large fire, near to which we slept during the night. At daybreak, we continued and before sunrise had gained the summit, the green which surrounded us presented the appearance of a calm sea. Some of my companions having shot a calf and some squirrels, we regaled ourselves on them. I proposed to employ some little time in raising a monument which might attract the attention of travelers in those distant countries. For want of stone, I used wood and having cut some cedars 20 inches in diameter, cleared the trunks and made them square; these we fixed in the ground so that each side was turned to one of the cardinal points. On one side, I engraved my name, with this inscription: "Sitis cognoscendi"; on another, those of my companions; on another, "Deo et Naturae"; and on the fourth, the date of my arrival. (*SDHC* vol. 23, 1-2; Jennewein 1961, 240).

Such an account fires the imagination. Here was a monument of cedar, widely known as a wood of enduring qualities. It was placed in a setting which borders on the arid, as well drained as could be possible. It was placed in a location inaccessible to all but the very determined. By some miracle, might it have escaped disasters of natural and human agency and still be there? Or at least some trace—a burned or battered stump—still in place?

The date of the monument placement was August 26, 1802. In "A Short History of Brule County" in the *South Dakota Historical Collections*, volume 23, John H. Bingham and Nora V. Peters have noted that it is sixteen miles south from the mouth of the White River to the nearest summit of the Bijou Hills, that there is no comparable elevation in the vicinity, and that it is most probably the "mountain" of which du Lac wrote. This is an observation that can be readily confirmed today by any interested traveler in that area.

The Bijou Hills did not receive their name until well after du Lac had come and gone. They were named for a French trader, either Louis or Joseph Bissonette of St. Louis, who built a trading post at the southern foot of these hills in 1812. He was nicknamed "Bijou" by the English-speaking traders and rivermen who had difficulty pronouncing his French name. Bijou's trading post was located in the SE 1/4 of Section 30, Township 100 North, and Range 71 West in the present LaRoche Township of Charles Mix County.

The Bijou Hills are the highest elevations in a large area in every direction and have served as landmarks from the earliest times. The hill nearest the river, readily seen from the river, has an elevation of 2,028 feet, over 600 feet higher than nearby present-day Chamberlain. About a mile to the southeast, in Charles Mix County, there is an elevation of 2,125 feet. The location of the hills nearest the river is in the SE 1/4 of Section 30, Township 101

North, Range 70 West. These hills are well supplied with cedar. Squirrels are found in the trees along the river below the summit of the hills, as they were when du Lac visited.

If the monument was on the summit of the Bijou Hills, where might one expect it to have been? (*SDHC* vol. 24, 510). There are several "summits" of these hills, depending on the vantage point from which they are viewed. I discussed the question with a field associate of long standing, Durand C. Young. We examined the literature of the time and place and discussed the question with Will G. Robinson, then state historian. We resolved to try to find some trace of du Lac's monument.

We assembled our field equipment and set out for the Bijou Hills on June 23, 1961, early in the morning. Arriving in the area of the hills, we stopped briefly to survey and collect relics at the site of Proteau's Post, located south of the Ola community in the Southwest 1/4 of the Northwest 1/4 of Section 22, Township 101, Range 70. Pressing on, we stopped and inquired in the town of Bijou Hills for access roads or trails leading to the edge of the highest hills near the Missouri. By late afternoon we had chosen a site and set up camp at the base of a high butte. It was a beautiful evening with an exceptional sunset, and Young recently recalled the dramatic sight of a large buck with a huge rack of horns, seen as a black silhouette above us on the butte against a scarlet sky.

We awoke to a clear morning and the prospect of a hot day. Following breakfast over a fire, we were off to explore the slopes of the butte. By midmorning the sun was bearing down. Even though it was June, the brushy vegetation on the slope of the butte was dry, harsh, and scratchy. There was a profusion of rattlesnakes and we had to pick our way carefully. It soon became apparent that, from our location below, we would be unable to spot the highest point chosen by du Lac for his monument. We decided that we must resort to a technique that had served us well in locating sites in other settings in the past. We would try to recreate du Lac's situation. He was on the river, moving upstream from the south when he came upon the mountain. From that vantage, it should be possible to see what du Lac saw as the summit of the mountain.

We went down to the river on the southwest side of the butte in order to look back up and see how the summit would appear from that vantage point. The results were dramatic: one summit stood out plainly from the river. It would be the point most clearly defined from the river and a site almost certainly to be chosen to place a monument visible from the river. We studied the contours of the hill so that we could move up to the spot without losing it at close range.

The next morning found us picking our way slowly up along the edge of the scrubby, rocky slope to the top. Arriving at the top, we had an arresting view of the country around in all directions. It was a marvelous sight. Hawks were overhead and the great grassy breaks of the river seemed to run out forever. We found the summit to be different than it appeared from below, a sort of ridge with a north and a south point or drop-off. The south point appeared to be the highest, and we moved toward it, searching as we went for any sign of a monument, rock cairn, or other evidence of human disturbance.

On arrival at the top of the south summit, we came upon a dramatic sight. There has been a very substantial landslide at that point, a large section of the butte having fallen away from the peak in a large section. The slide had left a sharp, nearly vertical, cliff, which we could look over and down and see the huge pile of broken rock and rubble below at the foot of the created cliff. And farther down, at the sides of the rock fall, was a very large stand of cedar trees.

And so our situation rapidly became clear. If we were on the right summit, as we firmly believed, the search for du Lac's monument was over. If the monument or any sign of it had still existed at the time of the slide, it was now buried under countless tons of rock below, for the point at which it must have been placed had been the highest crest! The setting was right and the large and only nearby stand of cedar from which the monument could have been made was directly below us. We looked at the scene for a long time; there was little else to be done.

Going back down the side of the butte and breaking camp and on our way home, we had no real sense of defeat. We felt we had come as close as anyone ever would to finding du Lac's cedar monument. We had done what was possible and we had learned much in the doing. We believed that we were in the right place but simply very much too late.

The Literary Struggle of Lewis and Clark

Joseph Basile

> The very baldness of ordinary American life is in deadly hostility to scenic representation...the passions which belong to human nature must be delineated, in America, subject to the influence of that despot—common sense.
>
> —James Fenimore Cooper, *Notions of the Americans*

> What, after all, does the practicalness of life amount to? The things immediate to be done are very trivial. I could postpone them all to hear this locust sing. The most glorious fact in my experience is not anything that I have done or may hope to do, but a transient thought, or vision, or dream, which I have had. I would give all the wealth of the world, and all the deeds of all the heroes, for one true vision. But how can I communicate with the gods, who am a pencil-maker on the earth, and not be insane?
>
> —Henry David Thoreau, *A Week on the Concord ad Merrimack Rivers*

Of the various struggles that form the journey and journals of Lewis and Clark, perhaps the most neglected has been their literary dilemma.[1] Lewis and Clark, while zealously endeavoring to fulfill their charge to inform President Jefferson of the diverse details of the expedition, felt compelled or inspired, from time to time, to elevate their narrative styles, in effect to poeticize the wilderness. Thus, an examination of their journals reveals their willingness to cross literary as well as geographical boundaries. By expressing the tension between America's practical pursuits and its aesthetic aspirations, Lewis and Clark demonstrate a pattern evident in nineteenth-century American writers as diverse as Thoreau, Whitman, Hawthorne, and Poe.

As James Fenimore Cooper observes in *Notions of the Americans*, "the passions which belong to human nature must be delineated, in America, subject to the influence of that despot—common sense." Cooper's shrewd appraisal reveals a major obstacle to imaginative expression as the young nation's writers seek to advance what Lewis P. Simpson, in *The Federalist Literary Mind*, has called "the Republic of Letters" (12). Most of the major authors of the American Renaissance would, sooner or later, come to decry this apparent mania for pragmatism. Consider, for example, Thoreau's lament in *A Week on the Concord and Merrimack Rivers* that, as "a pencil-maker on earth," he could not "communicate with the gods...and not be insane." Notice the speaker's assertion in Whitman's "When I Heard the Learn'd Astronomer" that, vividly if unaccountably, he must remove himself from the lecture-hall and gaze "in perfect silence at the stars." Recall Hawthorne's wry castigation of the well-fed old-timers in "The Custom-House" chapter of *The Scarlet Letter*, perpetuating an environment such as the one in "The Artist of the Beautiful," unappreciative of—and even detrimental to—the creative process. Or listen to Poe, who called his collected poems "mere trifles," proclaim, in "Israfel":

> If I could dwell
> Where Israfel
> Hath dwelt, and he where I,
> He might not sing so wildly well
> A mortal melody,
> While a bolder note than this might swell
> From my lyre within the sky.

Interestingly enough, prior to the formulations of Thoreau, Whitman, Hawthorne, and Poe, Lewis and Clark emerge on the scene, not primarily as professed members of the literati, but as practical-minded men who, nevertheless, at least occasionally, manifest their own desire to be temporary "artists of the beautiful."

Bernard DeVoto celebrates the journals as "the first report on the West, on the United States over the hill and beyond the sunset, on the prairie of the American future. There has never been another so excellent or influential" (lii). William Least Heat-Moon avers that Lewis and Clark "presented their permanently important historical and anthropological record clearly and poignantly, often writing under trying and dangerous conditions." "In our time," he asks, "who of the many astronauts has written anything to compare in significance or force of language?" (230). And Stephen E. Ambrose offers colorful and insightful appraisals of Lewis and Clark as writers. Of the former, he states,

> Though his sentences remained convoluted and cried out for punctuation, he managed to carry them off by retaining a flow of narrative interspersed with personal observations and reactions, all held together by using the right phrase at the precise moment in an arrangement of words that stands the ultimate test of being read aloud and making perfect sense while catching the sights and sounds and drama and emotion of the moment in a way that can be compared to the stream of consciousness of James Joyce or William Faulkner, or the run-on style of Gertrude Stein—only better, because he was not making anything up, but describing what he saw, heard, said, and did. (67)

Of Clark, Ambrose notes, he "was a great writer about the events in which he participated, and described the country he was passing through with a lovely lyric quality, but he could be disappointingly terse when writing about an event he had not seen with his own eyes" (144).

A modest but representative sampling of the writing of both Lewis and Clark reveals the intriguing ranges of their styles. Note the laconic depiction by Lewis of Mount St. Helens and Mount Hood:

> We had a view of Mt. S. Helens and Mount Hood. The first is the most noble-looking of its kind in nature. Its figure is a regular cone. Both these mountains are perfectly covered with snow—at least the parts of them which are visible. The highlands in this valley are rolling, though by no means to steep for cultivation. They are generally fertile, of a dark rich loam and tolerably free of stone.[2]

Even more drastically understated is Clark's mention of a dangerous situation involving Lewis, only a few days into the expedition: "Captain Lewis near falling from the pinnacles of rocks, 300 feet. He caught at 20 feet" (28). I am inclined to agree with Ambrose's assessment that "surely Lewis told Clark more than Clark recorded about such a life-threatening incident. As soldiers, who either learned lessons or died, they had a need to talk over incidents that threatened the expedition. They had to avoid unnecessary risks. So Lewis must have told Clark in some detail how he came to fall, and how he saved himself—but this didn't make it into Clark's journal entry" (144).

Yet Lewis and Clark did not consistently rely on mere factual succinctness. Both were capable of moving to a more evocative mode of expression, as these examples will demonstrate. Lewis, fascinated by the mating buffalo, reports: "It is now the season at which the buffalo begin to copulate, and the bulls keep a tremendous roaring. We could hear them for many miles, and there are such numbers of them that there is on continual roar. Our horses had not been acquainted with the buffalo. They appeared much alarmed at their appearance and bellowing" (340-41). Clark likewise attempts to convey a powerful force of nature:

> The mosquitoes were so troublesome to the men last night that they slept but little. Indeed, they were excessively troublesome to me. My Mosquito bier has a number of small holes worn through which they pass in. I set out at an early hour intending to proceed to some other situation. I had not proceeded on far before I saw a ram of the bighorn animal near the top of a larboard bluff. I ascended the hill with a view to kill the ram. The mosquitoes were so numerous that I could not keep them off my gun long enough to take sight, and by that means missed. (369)

While such a passage, particularly when compared to Lewis's account of the buffalo, may seem to be merely nit-picking, it reveals Clark's ability, like his partner's, to provide a more intimate and less scientific glimpse of the environment.

Ironically, at those times when Lewis experiences his greatest jubilation, he also expresses his keenest artistic intensity and frustration. Literary romanticism in America truly could not be far off. In a passage from Lewis which, over the past several years, I have used in classes as a "Set Piece" to suggest his artistic struggle—and which, in his brilliant recent work Ambrose has also examined—note Lewis's sense of mounting urgency as he seeks the words to capture the splendor of the Great Falls of Missouri:

> I hurried down the hill, which was about 200 feet high and difficult of access, to gaze on this sublimely grand spectacle....
>
> Immediately at the cascade, the river is about 300 yards wide. About 90 to 100 yards of this, next the larboard bluff, is a smooth even sheet of water falling over a precipice of at least 80 feet; the remaining part, about 200 yards wide, on my right, forms the grandest sight I ever beheld. (177)

Three more paragraphs follow, adding to the sense of Lewis "all but trip[ping] over himself in attempting to describe the falls," as Ambrose so vividly puts it (237). Then Lewis, using primarily the imagery of art and photography rather than the musical imagery of Poe's "Israfel," confesses, as does Poe, his stylistic inadequacy:

> After writing this imperfect description, I again viewed the Falls, and was so much disgusted with the imperfect idea which it conveyed of the scene, that I determined to draw my pen across it and begin again; but then reflected that I could not perhaps succeed better than penning the first impressions of the mind. I wished for the pencil of Salvator Rosa, a Titian, or the pen of [James] Thompson, that I might be enabled to give to the enlightened world some idea of this truly magnificent and sublimely grand object which has, from the commencement of time, been concealed from the view of civilized man. But this was fruitless and vain. I most sincerely regretted that I had not brought a camera obscura with me, by the assistance of which even I could have hoped to have done better, but, alas, this was also out of my reach. (178-79)

With the spirit of a chastened but resolute wordsmith, he continues: "I therefore, with the assistance of my pen only, endeavored to trace some of the stronger features of this scene by the assistance of which, and my recollection aided by some able pencil, I hope still to give the world some faint idea of an object which at this moment fills me with such pleasure and astonishment; and which of its kind, I will venture to assert, is second to but one in the known world" (179).[3]

While Clark may not exhibit such a blatant sense of artistic frustration, he nevertheless reveals a tension similar to Thoreau's: both reveled in the amassing of scientific or naturalistic details while finding it impossible to refrain from interacting on an emotional level with their surroundings. Thus Clark, in the following passage, provides a revealing mixture of factual details and a personal signature:

> On this hill, several artificial mounds were raised; from the top of the highest of those mounds I had an extensive view of the surrounding plains, which afforded me one of the most pleasing prospects I ever beheld; under me a beautiful river of clear water about 80 yards wide, meandering through a level and extensive meadow, as far as I could see.... Went to the rock which jutted over the water and marked my name and the day of the month and year. (34)

One of the most telling indications of Clark's reservations about his literary abilities is amply recorded by Ambrose:

> On learning of Lewis's suicide, the publishers, C. and A. Conrad of Philadelphia, told Jefferson that they had a contract to produce the journals and asked what they should do now. "Govr. Lewis never furnished us with a line of the M.S.," they told Jefferson, "nor indeed could we ever hear any thing from him respecting it tho frequent applications to that effect were made to him"
>
> Jefferson replied that the journals were coming to Monticello, and so was Clark; that they would consult, that Clark would come on to Philadelphia to see what could be done.
>
> When Clark arrived at Monticello, there was apparently some talk about Jefferson's taking over the journals and doing the editing to prepare them for the printer. There was no man alive who had a greater interest in the subject, or one who had better qualifications for the job. But he was sixty-five years old and desired to spend his remaining years at Monticello as a gentleman farmer. In January 1810, Lewis's cousin William Meriwether wrote Clark, "Mr. Jefferson would not undertake the work."
>
> Clark took the journals to Philadelphia, where he called on the men who had helped Lewis prepare for the expedition and those whom Lewis had hired to do drawings and calculations—Charles Willson Peale was one of them. On February 3, 1810, Peale wrote his brother, "I would rather Clark had undertaken to have wrote the whole himself and then have put it in the hands of some person of talents to brush it up, but I found that the General was too diffident of his abilities." (479)

Thus, as Ambrose points out, "After some false starts, Clark persuaded Nicholas Biddle to undertake the work" (470).

While Lewis and Clark strikingly left the editing and publication of their journals to other hands, they nevertheless provided American literature with a vivid and enduring work, rife with literary tensions. Charles Kuralt, an aficionado of the explorers, asserts in *Charles Kuralt's America*, "Lewis and Clark deserve a Homer to tell of the Odyssey, one of the most heroic and successful treks in all of human history. They may have one someday, as their trip through the Rockies, hard reality in the pages of their maps and diaries, fades into legend in the mists of time" (194). Shortly after Kuralt's statement, Ambrose's superb book appeared, and then, a short time later, the highly acclaimed film by Ken Burns and Dayton Duncan, coupled with their well-crafted volume, *Lewis & Clark: An Illustrated History*. Whatever authors may vie for the distinction of being a suitable Homer, I would maintain that, in their own candid and cogent ways, Lewis and Clark themselves should be regarded as America's homespun Homers.

The Rhetoric of Imperialism in the Lewis and Clark Journals: Camp Dubois to the Mandan Villages

Joan K. Warner Dolence

In *Imperial Eyes: Travel Writing and Transculturation*, Mary Louise Pratt, professor of Spanish and Comparative Literature and director of Stanford University's Program in Modern Thought and Literature, defines "contact zone" as "the space in which peoples geographically and historically separated come into contact with each other and establish ongoing relations, usually involving conditions of coercion, radical inequality, and intractable conflict."[1] In many ways, Lewis and Clark's Voyage of Discovery represents a voyage into the contact zone. The expedition entered territory historically held by Native Americans in order to establish trade relations and notify Western tribes of their "new father in Washington." In addition, Lewis and Clark led a military and scientific expedition into an area only recently purchased from the French and still largely administered by the Spanish. French, British, and Spanish trappers, traders, and explorers had preceded Lewis and Clark up the Missouri River at least as far west as the Mandan villages in present-day North Dakota. As they pushed up the Missouri in the summer and fall of 1804, Lewis and Clark and their crew encountered remnants of these earlier influences in the form of rafts headed down the Missouri stacked with furs, dilapidated trading houses by the side of the river, and sketchy maps locating landmarks and native settlements.

One could consider interactions among the crew themselves an example of relations in the contact zone. In addition to the land-owning captains, Lewis and Clark, the expeditionary crew consisted of sergeants and privates of humbler means and less authority; hired boatmen and translators, many of them of mixed French and Native American ancestry; Clark's slave, York; and, later, translator Toussaint Charbonneau and his Shoshone wife Sacagawea. Although relations within the group proved largely harmonious, the expedition was structured as a military undertaking, complete with the hierarchy inherent in such a grouping. The captains employed court martial hearings and lashings in the early months of the expedition to establish and maintain the discipline of the group. The social, geographical, and ethnic disparities as well as the differences in rank among the expeditionary members establish this group as one typical of the contact zone.

The social, geographical, and ethnic differences between expeditionary members and the Native Americans they encountered on this first leg of the journey also illustrate relations in the contact zone. One incident, which took place on September 25, 1804, near present-day Pierre, South Dakota, demonstrates the often unstable nature of interactions in areas where "peoples geographically and historically separated come into contact with each other."[2] After holding a council with several Teton Sioux chiefs, Lewis and Clark invited the chiefs aboard their keelboat, where the captains offered them whiskey. According to Clark, the captains soon had trouble convincing the chiefs to disembark. Clark wrote that after he had rowed the chiefs to shore in one of the pirogues:

> three of their young men Seased the Cable of the Perogue [...in which we had presents &c.], the Chiefs Soldr. ...Huged the mast, and the 2d Chief was verry insolent both in words & justures...declareing I Should not go on, Stateing he had not recved presents Suffient from us, his justures were of Such a personal nature I felt my Self Compeled to Draw my Sword.[3]

In *Lewis and Clark among the Indians*, historian James P. Ronda discusses this and other confrontations between the expedition and the Teton Sioux during Lewis and Clark's stay among them in the fall of 1804. According to Ronda, competing Sioux chiefs like Black Buffalo and the Partisan, two of the chiefs involved in the incident described above, found Lewis and Clark's presence among them problematic. Ronda writes, "Teton bands had come to expect their headmen to obtain gifts from river traders. A chief who could not deliver was bound to have his authority openly questioned....At the same time...[i]f there was a bloody incident and Indian casualties were high, the chiefs would surely lose influence."[4] What Clark viewed as insolence and chicanery on the part of the chiefs had serious inter-tribal implications to the Teton Sioux—the chiefs sought to maintain their positions of authority within their band by demonstrating continued control over Missouri River traders.

In writing about the contact zone, explorers often employ the rhetoric of empire that literary critic David Spurr defines in his book, *The Rhetoric of Empire: Colonial Discourse in Journalism, Travel Writing, and Imperial Administration*. This rhetoric dominates certain kinds of travel and adventure writing, including writing in which the explorer surveys the landscape and people present (what Spurr calls the trope of surveillance). Spurr notes that

> [t]he ideology of the gaze takes on one of its clearest forms in the convention of the commanding view....it offers aesthetic pleasure on one hand, information and authority on the other....At the same time the commanding view is an originating gesture of colonization itself, making possible the exploration and mapping of territory which serves as the preliminary to colonial order.[5]

In his 1803 "Instructions to Captain Lewis," Jefferson directed Lewis and Clark to employ the commanding view in order to survey the newly purchased Louisiana Territory with the goal of discovering "for the purposes of commerce" a direct water route to the Pacific.[6] Jefferson also instructed the captains to literally survey (using compass, sextant, etc.) the entire route and note the people, soil, water, animals, fossils, minerals, and climate of the areas the expedition passed through.[7]

In mapping the West, Lewis and Clark followed orders given to them by Jefferson. They also followed geographical precedent in employing the trope of surveillance in their expedition journals. John Logan Allen, a geographer and the author of *Passage Through the Garden: Lewis and Clark and the Image of the American Northwest*, contends that most adventurers enter into their journeys with the ideological aims of "those who seek to have blank spaces on the map filled." Explorers, therefore, cannot "be separated from the greater historical realities of their time and place."[8] The greater historical reality of the early nineteenth century included fierce competition among Britain, France, Spain, Russia, and the United States for control of the lucrative fur trade in the American West,[9] and the equally competitive rush to discover an easy route across the continent in order to facilitate trade with the Orient.

With these pressures in mind, it is not surprising to find the trope of surveillance in Lewis and Clark's journals of 1804. During this period, although the expedition covered previously mapped territory, most members of the group experienced the region for the first time. Lewis spent this time identifying and describing the flora and fauna of the region, taking celestial readings, and fixing the expedition's longitude and latitude as the group proceeded up the river. In addition to assisting Lewis with these tasks, Clark wrote daily entries in the expedition journals describing the group's progress and activities; he also began work on a map of the Missouri River, its tributaries, and the adjacent lands. When the expedition halted on July 23, 1804, to refresh the men and dry some of the provisions, Clark reported that he "commenced Coppying my map of the river to Send to the Presdt. of U S."[10] Surveying was a requirement of the expedition, and both Lewis and Clark spent much time walking along the shore, later transferring what they saw into written and pictorial descriptions of the landscape.

In his discussion of surveillance as a mode of writing, Spurr recognizes that seeing and naming that which exists around you is less than an innocent act. Spurr writes, "It is, on the contrary, a mode of thinking and writing wherein the world is radically transformed into an object of possession.... The writer's eye is always in some sense colonizing the landscape, mastering and portioning, fixing zones and poles."[11] In a sense, Lewis and Clark undertook this very task as they moved north and west against the current of the Missouri River. In many journal entries they succeed in colonizing the landscape, reconceptualizing unfamiliar territory into organized, familiar, pastoral scenes. On June 19, 1804, Clark noted that "the Lands on the North Side of the river is rich and Sufficiently high to afford Settlements,"[12] and on July 2, he reported that "The french formerly had a Fort at this place, to protect the trade of this nation, the Situation appears to be a verry eligable one for a

Town, the valley rich & extensive, with a Small Brook Meanding [meandering] through it and one part of the bank affording yet a good Landing for Boats."[13] Several days later, on July 7, 1804, Clark remarked that the expedition "passed a butifull Prarie on the right Side which extends back, those Praries has much the appearance from the river of farms, Divided by narrow Strips of woods;"[14] and previously, on June 16, he had taken note of "a Kind of Grass resembling Timothey which appeared well calculated for Hay."[15] In organizing the landscape this way, Lewis and Clark succeed in producing a perceptual map of the area, a map filled with towns, farms, and fields suitable for cultivation.

Lewis and Clark's journals of this period also reflect their tendency to survey the area with a view toward establishing commercial and military structures. On June 28, 1804, Clark wrote that the "the high lands Coms to the river Kanses on the upper Side at about a mile, full in view, and a butifull place for a fort, good landing place."[16] Similarly, on July 4, 1804, Clark noted that they encamped in an area once occupied by a large group of Kansas Indians. He wrote, "I observed Spring braking out of the bank, a good Situation for a fort on a hill at the upper part."[17] Four days earlier, in describing the Little Shoal River in present-day Platte County, Missouri, Clark envisioned the area's potential for commercial success. He reported that "this river is about 70 yds. Wide and has Several rapids & falls, well Calculated for mills."[18]

Jefferson initially planned to designate the lands west of the Mississippi River an extensive reservation for eastern Indians. Here they would settle into farming communities and "become civilized, so that they could be incorporated into the body politic."[19] According to historian Stephen Ambrose, Jefferson envisioned only eventual white, agrarian settlement in the area.[20] Jefferson took it for granted that whites already living west of the Mississippi River would gladly move east and that Native Americans both east and west of the Mississippi would not resist this imposition of "order" upon their land and way of life. It was this vision of a settled, agrarian West policed by the military that Lewis and Clark had in mind as they surveyed and mapped this section of the Missouri River and its adjacent lands.

In *Imperial Eyes*, Pratt also discusses the trope of surveillance, or what she terms the "monarch-of-all-I-survey" scene, found in much mid-nineteenth century travel and adventure writing. When recording the landscape, the explorer (or "monarch-of-all-I-survey") generally employs three different types of descriptions, which, combined, create measurable meaning and value for future readers of the explorer's account. First, the writer draws the scene in painterly terms. The view brings such delight to the writer (and to the reader) that the voyage is rendered worthwhile simply for the pleasure of seeing (or reading about) the scene. Second, the scene is infused with meaning—the lens (in modern terms) fills with lush images conveyed in writing through excessive use of adjectives to modify the objects viewed. Third, the writer commands the view—the images the writer conveys through words and how the writer orders the landscape represent the extent of the scene's meaning. As far as the reader knows, the writer's account represents all that exists in the landscape.[21]

Although Lewis and Clark wrote their journals a half century before those of the adventurers Pratt cites (in addition to Richard Burton, she also cites examples from his partner and rival, John Speke), this "rhetoric of presence" is evident in their field notes written during the summer and fall of 1804. In this passage dated July 4, 1804, Clark looks out over the landscape and describes the following scene:

> We camped in the plain one of the most butifull Plains, I ever Saw, Open & butifully diversified with hills and vallies all presenting themselves to the river...a handsom Creek meandering thro at this place....the Plains of this countrey are covered with Leek Green Grass, well calculated for the sweetest and most nourishing hay—interspersed with cops [copses] of trees, Spreding their lofty branchs over Pools Springs or Brooks of fine water. Groops of Shrubs covered with the most delicious froot is to be seen in every direction, and nature appears to have exerted herself to butify the Senery by the variety of flours Delicately and highly flavered raised above the Grass, which Strikes and profumes the Sensation, and amuses the mind throws it into Conjectering the cause of So magnificent a Senery...in a Country thus Situated far removed from the Sivilised world to be enjoyed by nothing but the Buffalo Elk Deer & Bear in which it abounds &...Savage Indians.[22]

Clark asserts that this is the most beautiful plain he has ever seen, a meaningful utterance when one considers that almost daily during the summer of 1804 Clark remarked on the natural beauty of the landscape adjoining the Missouri River. In this passage Clark personifies nature as putting forth extra effort in order to "profume the Sensation, and amuse the mind." In wondering why this splendid scene is wasted on the beasts and the "Savage Indians," he communicates his good fortune at having happened upon the scene (not being a beast or a savage) and arouses the reader's desire to participate in the splendor. Clark, therefore, accomplishes the first mode of description in Pratt's "monarch-of-all-I-survey" scene—he offers an aesthetic representation and suggests that experiencing such a scene is well worth the trip.

In describing this experience, Clark spares no modifiers. He crowds the landscape with lofty trees, handsome waters, delicious fruits, and delicate flowers; this overabundant landscape cries to the "sivilized" world to experience it. Also reflected in Clark's reading of the landscape are the values the explorer brings to his enterprise. He laments that "nothing but" the overabundant wildlife and the Indians can experience such a scene every day. What Clark is privileged to see and enjoy, one assumes, cannot be seen or enjoyed in the same way by the natives of the region. Ironically, Pratt points out that aside from the effort expended to reach a natural wonder, the act of "discovering" really consists of a rather passive experience—seeing. Only in writing down their observations and publishing them back home do explorers truly "discover."[23] And the thing discovered consists, in most cases, of something the natives have known for years, something they had "discovered" long ago.[24] In the "monarch-of-all-I-survey" scene, then, "the esthetic qualities of the landscape constitute the social and material value of the discovery to the explorers' home culture, at the same time as its esthetic deficiencies suggest a need for social and material intervention by the home culture."[25] The above example from Clark's notes reveals both the beauty of the Missouri River plains and the need for someone to appreciate that beauty—specifically, civilized, white Americans.

And so by simply writing these words, Clark goes far toward appropriating the landscape he surveys. Spurr points out that "nomination and substantivization may...be seen as grammatical forms of appropriation: by naming things we take possession of them."[26] This rehearses Pratt's definition of the "monarch-of-all-I-survey," who fills his description of the landscape with named objects for the consumption of the home culture. Clark's rapturous July 4, 1804, description (a clear example of the "monarch-of-all-I-survey" scene) names the abstractions in order to make them real to the reader. Grass is leek green and fruits delicious. Flowers are described as both delicate and highly flavored. Identifying (surveying) the scene as beautiful and naming its components leads Clark to wonder who could best value such a land. According to Spurr, "the colonizing imagination takes for granted that the land and its resources belong to those who are best able to exploit them according to the values of a Western commercial and industrial system."[27] The abundance which confronted Lewis and Clark as they ascended the Missouri seemed naturally to belong to them. Geographer John Logan Allen, who also quotes extensively from Clark's July 4, 1804, journal entry, concludes that "Clark's words...more than adequately express the nature of the region and the potentialities for the American agriculturalist as seen by Lewis and Clark."[28] From their perspectives as captains in the United States Army and as leaders of an expedition to map the West for eventual American use, the U.S. legally owned the West and Jefferson had specifically instructed Lewis and Clark to inscribe an American presence on this territory through their maps and journals, and literally, on rocks, trees, and landmarks.

Lewis and Clark consciously surveyed the landscape during their expedition. As explorers, they naturally considered this voyage "the ultimate adventure"[29] and hoped to make great discoveries. They also had explicit, almost unrealistically ambitious, instructions from Jefferson to note and record everything they saw.[30] However, employing the trope of surveillance in their field notes was an unconscious effort, a result of their status as leaders of an expedition sent to establish U.S. authority in the region. Similarly, Lewis and Clark's writing unconsciously appropriated an obviously inhabited landscape for the United States. As Spurr points out, "Colonial discourse is not a matter of a given ideological position, but rather of a series of rhetorical principles that remain constant in their application to the colonial situation regardless of the particular ideology which the writer espouses."[31] The rhetoric Lewis and Clark employ in their field notes, then, does not necessarily suggest that they were ideologically motivated. Rather, the tropes of surveillance and appropriation that they use stem from assumptions about who is to dominate and control the land. In *Exploration and Empire: The Explorer and Scientist in the Winning of the American West*, historian William Goetzmann writes the following about nineteenth-century exploration in general:

> The nineteenth-century confrontation of the unknown was almost uniquely a Western phenomenon, and as such was primarily important because it helped to create in the centers of dominant culture a series of images which conditioned popular attitudes and public policy concerning the new lands. Out of the charts and the travel literature, the scientific reports...emerged a series of impressions—often a series of first impressions unconsciously conditioned by the established culture of the time—which became a crucial factor in shaping the long-range destiny of the newly discovered places and their peoples, and which at the same time altered forever the established culture.[32]

Goetzmann then goes on to discuss Lewis and Clark specifically, and in doing so articulates the broader implications of the rhetoric of imperialism. Lewis and Clark, Goetzmann writes, "succeeded in making the West itself an object of desire—a virgin wilderness that formed a thousand mile vacuum between the great powers of the world and the United States, and into which, by whatever laws of imperialistic physics prevailed, they must inevitably rush."[33] Lewis and Clark's depiction of this particular contact zone as a place to be surveyed and appropriated by the United States helped, then, to encourage its eventual appropriation and domination.

We Proceeded On—Without a Doctor: A Combat Flight Surgeon Comments on the Medical Aspects of the Lewis and Clark Expediton

Jerry L. Simmons

Preparing to proceed

I was born within twenty miles of the site of the very important but somewhat obscure Battle of Fallen Timbers. This battle turned out to be very important to those interested in the Lewis and Clark expedition. Following the Revolutionary War, under the Articles of Confederation, the new nation's territory expanded to the Mississippi River to the west and the Great Lakes to the north. The British were supposed to leave the area and go to Canada, but they did not. The fur trade was too lucrative and the alliance with local Indian groups too strong. In 1778 the passage of the Northwest Ordinance allowed ten thousand American settlers a year to pour into the Ohio territories. Weakness of the Articles of Confederation led to the ratification of the new constitution in 1788. The Indians strongly resisted the influx of the new settlers, and soon desperate requests for protection flowed in to the government.

A large group of soldiers was sent to punish the Indians. Brigadier General Harmer and 1,133 Kentucky militiamen, 320 regular troops, and a battalion of Pennsylvania infantrymen were ambushed and soundly defeated by Chief Little Turtle on October 22, 1790. This embarrassing humiliation resulted in the dispatching of a much larger group of men under General Arthur St. Clair to attempt to defeat Chief Little Turtle's band. In November 1791, a surprise attack by Little Turtle and his confederation of Indian warriors killed 700 Americans, including 56 women who had journeyed to Ohio with their men. This little-known battle at Fort Defiance, Ohio, was one of America's worst defeats during the Indian wars. The much more widely known Battle of the Little Bighorn resulted in fewer than 300 men killed. Our citizens and foreign powers alike began to wonder if the new nation was able to defend the new territory.

President Washington, in near despair, selected General Anthony Wayne to lead the new "legion," so called because many Americans did not believe the new nation should have a standing army. In July 1792 General Wayne began to train his men at Pittsburgh, Pennsylvania, and a year later he moved his well-trained men to Cincinnati, Ohio. Washington tried to negotiate with the British-Indian coalition but the negotiations failed. Just before Christmas Wayne moved his men to an area just north of the site of St. Clair's defeat and built Fort Recovery. In the summer of 1794, a force of 2000 Indians attacked the fort. In spite of being vastly outnumbered by their Indian attackers, Wayne's well-trained soldiers and well-built fort defeated the enemy. Captain William Clark was one of the combatants. After this crucial loss, Little Turtle gave up his leadership, the Indians' confidence was greatly eroded, and many warriors abandoned the confederation and returned home.

General Wayne traveled further north and built Fort Defiance in August 1794. He proceeded on and met another large group of 1,300 Indians near Fort Miami. The battle was called the Battle of Fallen Timbers because it took place in an area just north of the Maumee River where large numbers of trees had been felled by a tornado. Clark was an officer under General Mad Anthony Wayne and fought in this battle near Toledo, Ohio, on August 20, 1794. The Indians were quickly defeated by superior training and tactics and ran to the British fort at present-day Detroit. The British would not let them in nor would they help them or support them, an action that resulted in diminishing the trust of the British by the Indians. The British agreed to abandon their fort and leave the area in exchange for their lives. This battle for control of the Northwest Territories really opened the West and resulted in the signing of the Treaty of Greeneville on October 20, 1795. If the Americans had not prevailed, the United States of America may have been limited to the eastern part of the country and the Lewis and Clark voyage of discovery might not have occurred.

During this military operation and subsequent Ohio territory forays, Clark and Lewis met for the first time. Lewis did not fight in the Battle of Fallen Timbers but he did serve under Captain William Clark and Mad Anthony Wayne at Fort Greeneville. Lewis and Clark are both depicted in the background in an etching on the monument marking the spot where the treaty was signed. Later Lewis was a military paymaster and traveled extensively in the Ohio territory. This acquaintance led to his choice of Clark to help lead the Lewis and Clark Expedition. Lewis's second choice for a fellow commander was Lt. Moses Hooke (Chuinard). We could be celebrating the anniversary of the Lewis and Hooke Expedition! Only recently has the Battle of Fallen Timbers site been recognized and preserved by the Toledo metroparks system. The interested reader should look on the internet at the Battle of Fallen Timbers website.

Twenty-eight years after the dedication of the Fallen Timbers site, I found myself on my own military adventure with the 101st airborne in Vietnam. As a flight surgeon I spent one year to the minute in the jungles and rice paddies, including the Ashau Valley and Hamburger Hill. I carried a seventy-pound pack of medical supplies, which was used to try to stabilize wounded soldiers and downed aircrews until they could be airlifted to combat hospitals by helicopter (medevacs). Lewis and Clark had to carry enough medicine to treat their men on the entire expedition. They had no helicopters or backup medical care.

Another activity I experienced in Vietnam similar to the Lewis and Clark experience was the medical civic action program. We would go to villages and hold medical clinics to treat the local Vietnamese. Flocks of people would come to see us because we were exotic-looking Caucasians and gave magic medicine to them. In return for our "clinics" they gave us protection. Similarly, Clark probably saved the corps of discovery expedition by treating native people and receiving desperately needed supplies in return.

Expedition medicine (wilderness medicine) is an unusual branch of medicine, which has a professional organization (The Wilderness Medical Society) that holds medical meetings and provides advice about wilderness medicine, including diagnosis and treatment in the field. Many of the members are doctors who go on expeditions. Medical situations can occur at any time, on a short hike or an expedition to Mount Everest. There is a thick, heavy, and expensive textbook on wilderness medicine that covers many aspects of wilderness emergencies, from altitude sickness to zebra bites. This book is available in most medical school libraries and contains many fascinating tidbits of information, including remarks about Lewis and Clark (Paton, *Wilderness Medicine*).

My family does some hiking and we primitive camp in semi-wilderness areas. My own expeditionary medical kit contains band-aids, moleskin for blisters, ace bandage for severe sprains, duct tape to fashion splints, splinter forceps, Pepto-Bismol, and aspirin or Tylenol for pain. I also carry a ballpoint pen that can be converted to a breathing tube with a penknife to treat a crushed larynx or laryngeal edema from anaphylactic shock from a bee or wasp sting. If anyone is allergic to bee stings, an epinephrine injection kit should be available. Each individual should carry sunscreen and insect repellent. Baby wipes can literally save your behind, and they are also are good to clean wounds and abrasions. Don't forget your cell phone; Lewis could not call 911 in the wilderness but in most cases you can.

A rush course in medicine

Benjamin Rush, the American Hippocrates and signatory of the Declaration of Independence, was selected by President Jefferson to provide medical advice for the expedition. Rush also founded the first post office, encouraged education for women as well as free education for poor children, and was a great proponent of programs for the mentally ill. He wrote *Directions for Preserving the Health of Soldiers* in 1777, a book widely used by the military to treat disease and maintain good hygiene in the field.

He gave directions to Lewis to keep his men healthy:

1. When you feel the least indisposition, do not attempt to overcome it by labour or marching. Rest in a horizontal posture—also fasting and diluting drinks for a day or two will generally prevent an attack of fever. To these preventatives of disease may be added a gentle sweat obtained by warm drinks, or gently opening the bowels by means of one, two or more of the purging pills.
2. Unusual costiveness (constipation) is often a sign of approaching disease. When you feel it take one or more of the purging pills.
3. Want of appetite is likewise a sign of approaching indisposition; it should be obviated by the same remedy.
4. In difficult and laborious enterprises and marches, eating sparingly will enable you to bear them with less fatigue and less danger to your health.
5. Flannel should be worn constantly next to the skin, especially in wet weather.
6. The less spirit you use the better. After being wetted or much fatigued, or exposure to the night air, it should be taken in an undiluted state. 3 table-spoons taken this way will be more useful in preventing sickness than half a pint mixed with water.
7. Molasses and sugar water with a few drops of the acid of vitriol will make a pleasant and wholesome drink with your meals.
8. After having your feet much chilled, it will be useful to wash them with a little spirit.
9. Washing the feet every morning in cold water, will conduce very much to fortify them against the action of the cold.
10. After long marches, or much fatigue from any cause, you will be more refreshed by lying down in a horizontal posture for two hours, than by resting a much longer time in any other position of the body.
11. Shoes made without heels, by affording equal action to all the muscles of the legs, will enable you to march with less fatigue than shoes made in the ordinary way.

Rush believed in bleeding and purging, especially with his favorite medication—his very own thunderbolts. These handmade rolled pills were a combination of mercury salts and Mexican morning glory. They quickly achieved the desired results. Today Lewis and Clark campsites are authenticated by the presence of mercury, which the men deposited in abundance at the latrine sites. Bleeding was a very common form of treatment for just about any symptom. Special lancets were purchased to open the veins of the hapless patients on the expedition. Most of these treatments did more harm than good, and today bleeding is used only for rare conditions in patients with iron overload.

Heeding the advice of Doctor Rush, Lewis purchased medicines from Gillaspay and Strong for about ninety dollars. They were placed in two multi-compartmental wooden chests, a pine chest measuring 16½ x 15½ x 14 inches and a walnut chest measuring 11¼ x 12¼ x 11 7/8 inches. These chests are similar to those used by Rush and Jefferson (Chuinard, Lentz, and Loge). Additional medications were stored with other provisions. By the way, the illustration of Jefferson's medicine chest in Elden Chuinard's book is upside down. This is the most scholarly of the books written on the medical aspects of the expedition and my favorite. Detailed accounts of the contents of the medicine chest are available in articles by Gary Lentz and Ron Loge. The following lists many of the medicines used by Lewis and Clark:

Peruvian Bark (Pulv. Cort. Peru)—Dried stem and root bark of cinchona (quinine). Used for the fever of malaria (ague) and as a poultice for snake bites and gunshot wounds when mixed with gun powder.

Jalap (Pulv. Jalap)—Root of the Mexican plant *Exogonium jalapa* (Mexican morning glory). Used as a laxative. It also increases the flow of bile.

Rhei (Pulv. Rhei)—Rhubarb root. Laxative, hemorrhoid ointment, astringent, and digestive aid.

Ipecacuan (Pulv. Ipecacuan)—Root of *Cephaelis ipecacuana*, a South American plant related to cincona, gardenias, and coffee. Syrup of Ipecac emetic (causes vomiting), diaphoretic (increases perspiration) and in low doses an appetite stimulant.

Cream of Tartar (Crem.Tart.)—potassium bitartrate. Laxative and diuretic.

Camphor (gum Camphor)—Gum of an evergreen native to China *Cinnamomum camphora*. Topical salve for rashes and applied to the chest to produce sweating.

Assafoetic—*Ferula foetida* (fetid gum). Unpleasant odor may keep infectious people away and reduce disease. Poultice or internal enema relieves colic. Some wags stated it was a foolproof way to identify the location of the medicine chest—just follow your nose.

Opium (Opii Turk. Opt.)—Poppy, *Papaver somniferum.* Pain relief and sleeping aid.

Tragacanth—Gummy sap from Asian shrub *Astragalus gummifer* Mixed with lard and other things and used as skin ointment.

Glaubers Salts (Sal Glauber)—sodium sulfate. Used as a laxative.

Saltpeter (Sal Nitri)—Potassium nitrate. Diuretic and diaphoratic.

Copperas (Green Vitriol)—no copper, ferrous sulfate. Anti-diarrhea medicine.

Lead Acetate (Sacchar. Saturn opt)—sugar of lead. Mixed with water used as eyewash or injected into the urethra for venereal disease. Mixed with alcohol used as topical poison ivy treatment.

Calomel (mercurous chloride)—Treatment for syphilis and other sexually transmitted diseases.

Tarter (Potassium tartrate)—Applied to boils.

White Vitroil (Vitriol Alb.)—zinc sulfate. Eyewash and tonic.

Root of Colombo (Colombo Rad.)—African plant (powdered root) Menispermium palmatum. Mixed with water to treat dyspepsia.

Sulfuric acid (Elix. Vitriol)—Mixed with alcohol, then neutralized with magnesia for colic and diarrhea

Laudanum (Alcohol diluted opium)—Pain killer and sleep aid.

Yellow Basilicum (Ung. Basilic Flav.)—Ointment from hog lard, pine resin, and beeswax. Ointment to treat skin conditions.

Calamine (Ung. E lap Cailmin)—Ointment from ferric oxide and calamine ore (zinc silicate and carbonate). Used on rashes. This is the calamine lotion used today, minus the antihistamine.

Epispastric (Red mercuric chloride)—Blistering agent.

Mercury Ointment (Ung. Mercuriale)—that old blue ointment. Mercury chloride in a salve used to treat sexually transmitted diseases.

Emplast (Emplast. Diach. S.)—Lead monoxide or carbonate in olive oil. Used on burns.

Wintergreen or Peppermint (Ess. Meth.pip)—Oil of wintergreen or peppermint used as topical cooling agent or stomach sedative.

Copaiboe—South American plant *Copaifera officinalis*. Dissolved in alcohol used for diaphoretic, diuretic, and expectorant.

Benzoin (Traumat.)—Tincture applied to skin .

Magnesia (Milk of magnesia)—Antacid

Nutmeg—Mild laxative.

Cloves—Oil of clove is a tooth-pain killer.

Cinnamon—Flavoring to mask the bitterness of other medicines.

Bilious Pills (Rush's Thunderbolts)—15 grains of calomel and jalap. Purgative; Lewis took 600 with him on the expedition.

Several instruments were taken on the expedition, including surgical and tooth-removal tools and syringes for giving medicines in both urethral and rectal avenues.

Lancets and tourniquets were used for blood letting, and patent lint was to dress deep wounds.

Lewis's mother, like many women of her time, was an expert herbalist, and Lewis remembered many remedies he learned from her. Some of these remedies were used on the expedition

Two other doctors taught Lewis in Philadelphia

Two other physicians, both of them doctors in the Revolutionary War, taught valuable lessons to Lewis in Philadelphia. Doctor Benjamin Smith Barton was the botanist who taught Lewis how to collect and describe plants. The collection of plants acquired on the expedition still exists in the Natural History Museum in Philadelphia, the most valuable scientific resource remaining from the adventure. The other mentor was Caspar Wistar, an anatomist and surgeon with a special interest in paleontology. He urged Lewis to look for fossils and signs of prehistoric animals. Jefferson and others thought Lewis might find living mastodons in the wilderness of the West.

The doctors that did not go

Two other doctors had the chance to go with Lewis and Clark (Chuinard). Dr. Ewing Patterson, from Wheeling, West Virginia, met with the men when they stopped at the Ohio River town. He was asked to go along on the adventure because his father was an outstanding professor of mathematics in Philadelphia. He would have had to be ready to leave the afternoon of the next day. The boats left on time that afternoon but he missed the boat. Later it was realized he had an alcohol problem and was not in physical or mental shape to withstand the rigors of the journey.

Dr. Antoine Saugrain of Saint Louis was an outstanding French doctor who was a friend of Captain Lewis. He was also asked to go with them. He would not leave his wife or his lucrative life in Saint Louis, but he did give the expedition useful advice and saw them off on their adventure. He made thermometers and invented sulfur matches; both went with the voyage of discovery.

A shot to the head—almost disaster

On an island just a few miles from Pittsburgh, a friend of Lewis asked to fire the famous air gun. Since he was not used to the weapon, it discharged accidentally and a woman in the crowd of onlookers fell to the ground, bleeding profusely from her head. After rushing to her side, bystanders found she had only a very superficial head wound. Her hat was ruined but not the expedition. This may be the first example of the wonderful luck Lewis and Clark enjoyed on their journey.

Malaria and smallpox

Malaria (ague) was very common along the waterways of the Midwest in the nineteenth century. Almost everyone had experienced the "shaking ague," and Patrick Gass was said to have it so severely he could not steer the keelboat (Chuinard). Synonyms for this malady thought to be caused by bad air include "autumnal, bilious, intermittent, remittent, congestive, miasmatic, malarial, marsh, chill fever, ague, fever and ague and lastly the fever" (Chuindard). The word *ague* is derived from French and means a sharp fever because malaria results in a very fast rise in temperature as the red blood cells are destroyed and release baby parasites.

Smallpox was a deadly disease for both Indian and non-Indian people. The smallpox vaccine was available in the early 1800s as the kinepox, which Jefferson advised Lewis and Clark to take with them and vaccinate their men. This may be the first instruction on preventative medicine given by a president. Unfortunately there was not enough vaccine to protect the Indian people along the journey (Chuinard).

Selected medical notations from the journals

The following episodes are examples of the medical challenges faced by the men on the journey. They appear in an article by Donald Snoddy published in *Nebraska History* in 1970. He went through the Thwaites edition of the journals and noted each time some medical aspect of the Lewis and Clark expedition occurred. The dates are the same in Moulton's more recent edition.

1. Snakebite

July 4, 1804: Fields got bit by a snake, which was quickly doctored with Bark by Capt. L.

Lewis used a poultice made of gunpowder and Peruvian bark to treat snakebite. We do not know if the snake was poisonous, and Fields apparently recovered. Today treatment is not much better. If the snake is poisonous, antivenom is available at most hospitals.

2. The abdominal catastrophe

Aug 19, 1804: Sergt. Floyd was taken violently bad with the Biliose Cholick.

Aug 20, 1804: Serj. Floyd Died with a great deal of Composure.

Floyd was miraculously the only one who died on this epic journey. Most authorities think this was a case of ruptured appendicitis, although bowel perforation or perforated gall bladder are also possibilities. Today surgery would probably be used and the sergeant's death avoided.

3. Arsenic and old lace, or was it moon goddess madness?

Aug 22, 1804: Capt. Lewis...was near poisoning himself by the fumes & taste of the Cabalt [Cobalt; this and other minerals found on a bluff]. Capt Lewis took a Dost of Salts to work off the effects of the Arsenic [or was it selenium?].

It is not clear what the fumes and minerals were at this location. Many of the banks of the river contain selenium, which could lead to similar symptoms. Some areas in this region may exude hydrogen sulfide fumes.

4. Shouldering too much responsibility

Nov 29, 1804: Sergeant Pryor in takeing down the mast put his Shoulder out of Place, we made four trials before we replaced it.

Replacing a dislocated shoulder can be a difficult task without anesthesia. Once dislocated, a shoulder tends to dislocate again, which did happen to this man.

5. Too hot—too cold

July 7, 1804: one man verry sick, Struck with the sun.

Hyperthermia in the summer in South Dakota can be a life-threatening condition. Most of the time the men were near water, which would reduce the possibility of heat stress and stroke.

Jan 10, 1805: boy about 13 years of age Came to the fort with his feet frosed....we had his feet put in cold water.

Jan 27, 1805: Capt Lewis took off the Toes of one foot of the Boy who got frostbit Some time ago.

Hypothermia in the winter in the Dakotas can be a real killer. One can die with short exposure in the very dangerous wind chills that commonly occur in this part of the country. Frostbite is very common and slow rewarming is the best treatment.

6. The Mandan memories

Jan 21, 1805: one ban [man] verry bad with the pox.

Sexually transmitted disease is very common when people are on expeditions or at war. Syphilis and gonorrhea were rampant on this expedition. Mercury and lead salts were somewhat helpful, but today penicillin or other antibiotics would cure these diseases. The men lived a most enjoyable life that winter with the Mandans (Ronda).

7. Sacagawea—Pompey's birth and the sins of the fathers

Feb 11, 1805: about five oclock this evening one of the wives of Charbono was delivered of a fine boy. After a tedious labor she rapidly delivered after a dose of rattlesnake rattle.

Labor and delivery can be hazardous, especially away from definitive medical care. Many women died in childbirth or from infection afterwards. Ground rattlesnake rattle is not used very much today.

June 16, 1805: the Indian woman extreemely ill. I caused her to drink the water altogether [from the sulphur spring]. I...continued the cataplasms of barks and laudnumn.

June 19, 1805: the Indian woman was much better this morning.

Sacagawea most likely had pelvic inflammatory disease from gonorrhea. Antibiotics would have been very useful if used early.

8. Bumps and runs

July 31, 1805: we have a lame crew just now, two with tumers or bad boils.

Boils, bumps, and bruises were probably so commonplace they were not mentioned very often in the journals. Some of the tumors were enlarged lymph nodes from infections.

Sept 19, 1805: several of the men are unwell of the disentary

Gastrointestinal disturbances are very common on expeditions. Many bacteria, parasites, and viruses are present in the environment and food. New bacteria that the men were not used to may have caused disease even though the local people were immune to them. Pepto-Bismol or Lomotil is now taken on every trip by most savvy travelers.

9. The red-headed medicine show saves the day

May 5, 1806: [An Indian man] brought forward a very eligant Gray mare and gave her to me....I gave him a phial of Eye water [a combination of zinc sulfate and lead acetate].

Clark was a favorite medicine man among the tribes. His red hair and professional demeanor were magic to them. They were especially fond of eyewash, which soothed their irritated and inflamed eyes. Clark's services were so much in demand he probably saved the expedition by trading his skills and medicine for provisions and horses.

10. Lewis gets shot in the behind

Aug 11, 1806: I was in the act of firing on the Elk a second time when a ball struck my left thye about an inch below my hip joint.

Lewis was shot in the buttocks by a near-sighted companion. The bullet penetrated the flesh and was found in his pants. The wound bled and was fairly clean. Lint was used to pack the wound, allowing it to heal from the inside out, avoiding infection. Modern medicine could do no better.

11. Eye, eye, sir

Sept 20, 1806: three of the party was unabled to row from the State of their eyes.

This condition was undoubtedly due to ultraviolet uveitis (inflammation of the inner eye). Modern sunglasses could help prevent this painful situation.

Home at last

Sept 23, 1806: decended to the Mississippi and down that river to St. Louis at which place we arrived about 12 oClock.

Home at last and unbelievably lucky. An epic journey and only one man died.

Afterword

Yes, Lewis and Clark were unbelievably lucky, but luck favors the prepared. Jefferson made sure Lewis received the best medical advice from one of the leading physicians of the day. Some of the medicines he used actually worked, a few are still in use today. The men (and woman) on the expedition were young, healthy, hardened woodsmen or soldiers who could withstand the rigors of their wilderness experience. With the exception of the winter encampments, the party was always on the move. They seldom stayed more than a few days in any location, thus avoiding unsanitary conditions that could affect the health of the men. Lewis and Clark were both experienced military officers who were used to caring for their men. Their cordial friendship and leadership played a major role in the success of the voyage of discovery as they proceeded on to the Pacific Ocean and back without a doctor.

Sexual Relations of the Lewis and Clark Expedition

Brad Tennant

On June 20, 1803, President Thomas Jefferson wrote a formal letter to Captain Meriwether Lewis outlining his expectations for the exploration of the American West to the Pacific Ocean. After months of informal discussions and planning between the two, Jefferson instructed Lewis as to the specific military, commercial, and literary objectives of the expedition then being organized. In doing so, Jefferson explained that, in addition to other objectives, it was important to gain knowledge of the native nations whom the expedition would meet along the way. Consequently, Lewis was informed that the expedition should become acquainted with the nations as well as "acquire what knolege you can of the state of morality, religion, & information among them."[1] In many cases, this information was best reflected in the sexual relations between expedition members and the native peoples. As a result, the Lewis and Clark Expedition is credited with recording some of the most important ethnographical information in the history of the American West.

James Ronda, author of *Lewis and Clark among the Indians*, stresses that, from a strictly sociological viewpoint, the men of the expedition who recorded their observations were ethnographers, not ethnologists. Whereas ethnologists critically examine a culture and its social structure, ethnographers are content to describe the more obvious cultural traits seen in a given society. Unfortunately, there are notable shortcomings associated with recording what a person generally observes in a foreign culture, and the Lewis and Clark Expedition was certainly no exception. For example, while Lewis and Clark and other members of the expedition may have recorded in detail what they observed, they were often not qualified to fully understand the norms and values of a given society. In reality, they were often more intent on *describing* a culture than *examining* it. In addition, as ethnographers, Lewis and Clark did not always describe a culture as impartial observers. Rather, they were often biased by their non-Indian standards while observing and judging Indian cultures.[2] Likewise, it would be unfair to judge by today's standards the way of life of people who lived two hundred years ago.

It was not until the expedition made its way to the upper Missouri River valley that they began receiving offers of sexual favors. Among many of the tribes of the northern plains, sexual relations outside of marriage were not considered promiscuous as much as they were held to be culturally significant. Some sexual favors were offered for the simple purpose of gaining trade items, while some people believed that sex was a medium by which certain mental or physical powers could be transferred. The fact that many tribes practiced polygamy is also noteworthy. Since it was common for a man to have several wives, it was socially acceptable for him to offer one of them to an important guest.[3]

Many people who are unfamiliar with the Lewis and Clark journals are often surprised by the references to sex. For example, on October 12, 1804, Clark recorded that "a curious Cuistom with the Souix as well as the reckeres [Arikaras] is to give handsom Squars to those whome they wish to Show Some acknowledgements to."[4] A little over a year later, on November 21, 1805, Clark reported that several young Chinook women arrived toward nightfall to "sport openly with our men."[5] Such boldness was characteristic of the social attitude of many of the tribes toward sex.

According to journal entries, members of the Sioux (Lakota) nation were the first to offer the expedition sexual favors. Although it was reported that the men politely refused the offers, two women continued to follow the expedition up the Missouri River. Eventually the women overtook the expedition, but, according to Clark, the men held firm in their refusal. Upon reaching the Arikara nation, Clark also mentioned that, like the Sioux, the Arikara felt despised if their offers were not readily accepted.[6]

The Arikara, however, apparently did not have reason to feel rejected for long. During their stay with this tribe, the expedition began taking full advantage of the opportunities afforded them for female companionship. As stated earlier, a variety of motives caused tribes like the Arikara to pursue sexual relations with the men of the Lewis and Clark Expedition. In many cases, sex was considered to be either an act of hospitality or a means by which goods could be gained in return for services rendered. Both of these were considered to be quite acceptable according to societal norms. Furthermore, there was the shared belief among the Plains village tribes that intercourse was the means by which special powers, or medicine, could be transferred from a highly respected man through a woman to her husband. For many of the Arikara tribesmen, the white members of the expedition, and especially Clark's servant York, were held to have such powers. As a result, many of the Arikara men offered their wives to the men of the expedition without hesitation. Since the Indians of the northern plains had never seen a black man before, York was considered to be more than a curiosity. He was, in fact, considered to be Big Medicine. Not only did the Arikara husbands openly encourage such sexual relations, but one husband even served as a sentry while York was with his wife.[7]

Unfortunately, such sexual practices, regardless of the reason, also created an increased likelihood of contracting sexually transmitted diseases. As a result, during the expedition's first winter, the men were not only sexually active, but they also experienced their first bouts of venereal disease. When the expedition left the Arikara villages, it was already well into the month of October, and they were ready to establish a residence for the winter. By the time the expedition settled into its winter quarters near the Mandan villages, the men had been offered female companionship by the Teton Sioux (Lakota), Arikara, Hidatsa, and now the Mandan. On January 14, 1805, Clark indicated that several of the men were suffering from venereal disease, which was transmitted by the Mandan women.[8]

Indeed, the winter of 1804-1805 with the Mandans resulted in the men's suffering greatly from venereal disease. Since the long stay allowed the men to engage in repeated sexual encounters over several months, the winter was marked by recurring outbreaks of syphilis among the men and the Mandan population. Consequently, it was common that, as symptoms began to improve, a new outbreak would cause yet another wave of pain and suffering.[9]

In early January 1805, expedition members were invited to participate in the Mandan Buffalo Dance, a religious ceremony that had two main objectives. The first was to transfer the hunting skills and knowledge of the older men to the next generation. As a result, it is sometimes referred to as the Medicine Dance. The second objective is identified by the ceremony's more common name, the Buffalo Dance. It was believed that this ceremony would cause buffalo herds to come near the villages. When the buffalo did in fact return, their arrival, which was sooner than expected, was attributed to the participation of the expedition's members in the ritual.[10]

The Mandan performed the Buffalo Dance for three successive nights in early January 1805. Whereas other sexual encounters were private affairs between a man and a woman, the Buffalo Dance was much more public. On January 5, 1805, Clark described the ritual in his journal:

> a curious Custom the old men arrange themselves in a circle & after Smoke a pipe, which is handed them by a young man, Dress up for the purpose, the young men who have their wives back of the circle go to one of the old men with a whining tone and [request] the old man to take his wife (who presents necked except a robe)...the Girl then takes the Old man...and leades him to a Convenient place for the Business .... (we Sent a man to this Medisan Dance last night, they gave him 4 Girls)

It is interesting to note that, because Clark's description was so risqué, Nicholas Biddle and Elliot Coues, who published the first edited versions of the Lewis and Clark journals in 1814 and 1893 respectively, translated Clark's account into Latin for the sake of modesty.[11]

The fact that the Mandan appeared to be very open in their sexual relations does not mean that there were never problems with jealousies. Within a month of establishing the expedition's winter quarters, Sergeant John Ordway found himself in a volatile love triangle. A jealous husband had beaten his wife and stabbed her three times for being with Ordway. The woman then left her husband and was staying with the wives of the interpreters. Given the seriousness of the situation, the captains ordered that no member of the expedition should have intercourse with the woman on pain of severe punishment. When her husband arrived at Fort Mandan on November 22nd threatening to kill her, Clark intervened by instructing Ordway to present the husband with some trade items. Clark then told the man to take his wife home and be reconciled with her.[12]

It was not until April 1805 that the main party of the Corps of Discovery left the Mandan villages and headed west toward the Pacific Coast. The next Indian nation that they expected to encounter was the Shoshone, the people from whom Sacagawea came. It was hoped that, with Sacagawea's assistance, the expedition could procure horses for crossing the continental divide.[13] Unfortunately, it would be more than four months before the expedition finally met with the Shoshone tribe.

During the expedition's time with the Shoshone, Lewis noted that their women were more actively involved in tribal matters than were women in previously encountered Indian nations. Nonetheless, Shoshone women participated in sexual relations with strangers in a fashion similar to other tribes. There were, however, specific conditions under which such relations were acceptable. As with previous tribes, a refusal on the part of the guest to accept a man's wife could be grounds for considerable resentment by the husband. When a guest accepted such hospitality, it was quite common for the husband to guard the entrance to his lodge so that the couple would not be disturbed. Such arrangements were apparently dictated by the will of the husband, and when a woman secretly engaged in sexual relations without his consent, she would be considered a disgrace to her husband if she was discovered. The severity of such a public disgrace often resulted in the woman's being exiled, beaten, or in some cases punished by death.[14]

It was, therefore, extremely important that the men of the Lewis and Clark Expedition became familiar with the social customs of each tribe. Although Lewis often reminded the men just how serious it could be should these social norms be violated, he also recognized that it would be difficult to prevent all sexual contact by his men. On August 19, 1805, Lewis recorded:

> I have requested the men to give them no cause of jealousy by having connection with their women without their knowledge, which with them, strange as it may seem is considered as disgracefull to the husband as clandestine connections of a similar kind are among civilized nations. to prevent this mutual exchange of good officies altogether I know it impossible to effect, particularly on the part of our young men whom some months abstanence have made very polite to those tawney damsels. No evil has yet resulted and I hope will not from these connections.[15]

In this same entry, Lewis reported that he asked his interpreter if the Shoshone suffered from "the venereal." The interpreter stated that they sometimes suffered from it. Although Lewis acknowledged the fact that smallpox had been introduced by whites and, passing from tribe to tribe, had eventually reached the Shoshone, he concluded that both gonorrhea and syphilis were "native disorders of America."[16]

The journals do not mention any violations of social norms by the expedition members during their stay with the Shoshone, and it is probably safe to conclude that any sexual relations were according to local native customs. About a month later, as the expedition followed the Lolo Trail across the Bitterroot Mountains, the men were reported to suffer from "irruptions of the Skin," which historian Stephen Ambrose assumed to have been the result of venereal disease transmitted from the Shoshone women.[17]

Lewis's references to venereal disease are found scattered throughout the journals. The greatest sufferings, however, appear to have been associated with the Mandan, Shoshone, and Chinook Indians. The Chinook were not encountered until November 1805 as the Lewis and Clark Expedition neared the Pacific Coast. On November 21, 1805, Clark reported that an old Chinook woman had brought six of her daughters and nieces to the camp to oblige "the passions of the men" in return for various trade goods. Clark continued, "Those people appear to View Sensuality as a Necessary evel," and they sell sexual favors with the approval of their friends and relatives. Clark further noted that "[t]he young females are fond of the attention of our men," and unlike other tribes that they had met, the Chinook did not seem to care if the women were unmarried.[18]

Once again, the men enjoyed immediate gratification only to pay for their sexual encounters at a later date. On January 27, 1806, Lewis recorded that he treated Private Silas Goodrich's symptoms of "Louis Veneri which he contracted from an amorous contact with a Chinook damsel." What Lewis meant to write was *lues venera*, which was the Latin terminology for syphilis. He further mentioned that his use of mercury to cure Goodrich was similar to his treatment of Private George Gibson during the previous winter with the Mandans.[19]

On the following Ides of March, the expedition was visited at Fort Clatsop by the six young women who had appeared the previous November. This time, a Chinook chief escorted them. It was quite apparent that the Chinook were interested in some new trading for sexual favors. Lewis, however, ordered the men to refrain from engaging in any sexual bargaining. Given the fact that trade items were now in very limited supply and that the men did not want to experience a new bout of venereal disease, the men gave Captain Lewis their word.[20]

The fact that only a few men suffered from syphilis during the 1805-1806 winter as compared to the year before can be attributed at least in part to the unappealing appearance of the Chinook women. Consider, for example, the following general descriptions of women from other Indian nations followed by a description of Chinook women.

- Clark described the Teton Sioux (Lakota) women as having a good appearance with good teeth and high cheek bones.[21]
- Sergeants Patrick Gass and John Ordway both referred to Arikara women as being clean and handsome.[22]
- On October 24, 1804, Sergeant Ordway noted that the first group of Mandans encountered by the expedition "had Some handsome women with them."[23]

In contrast, Nicholas Biddle included the following description of Chinook women in his 1814 edition of the journals:

> Their broad flat foreheads, their falling breasts, their ill shaped limbs, the awkwardness of their positions, and the filth which intrudes through their finery; all these render a Chinnook or Clatsop beauty in full attire, one of the most disgusting objects in nature.[24]

While this description may seem cruel, it is perhaps best understood as a classic example of Lewis and Clark as ethnographers. What they were actually describing was how a society's values, including attractiveness, can vary from those of other societies.

Despite the generally unfavorable perception of the Chinook by expedition members, the fact remains that at least a few of the men willingly engaged in sexual relations and suffered later. Four days after Goodrich was declared recovered from his case of venereal disease, Lewis diagnosed Private Hugh McNeal as having syphilis.[25]

Lewis's medical supplies reflect anticipation that venereal disease would be a likely problem for the expedition. Syphilis was certainly the main ailment attributed to the expedition's sexual activity; however, Lewis was also prepared to treat gonorrhea if necessary. Although Lewis often made general references to his use of mercury in treating the men, it is more likely that he used a mercury ointment, a calomel pill, or both. While the mercury ointment could have been applied directly to sores, it would also have been commonly administered by a process known as inunction, in which the salve was rubbed into the skin of the left forearm. Meanwhile, the calomel pill would have been carefully administered over a period of time until all sores were gone. Unfortunately, although Lewis may have treated the early symptoms of syphilis, the tertiary stage of the disease may not have become apparent until long after it was first contracted. As a result, Lewis mentioned in a couple of instances that outbreaks of the "pox" reappeared several months after the initial treatment. For instance, Lewis recorded at one point that he had cured Goodrich only to record six months later that Goodrich was once again "unwell with the pox."[26]

The journals do not mention that any of the men were treated specifically for gonorrhea, although there were numerous references to eyesight complications suffered by many Indians. Some of these cases of blindness may have been due to gonorrheal conjunctivitis. Should Lewis have had to treat the men for gonorrhea, he was prepared to do so. Saltpeter, zinc sulfate, lead acetate, and four penis syringes were included in his medicine chest. The saltpeter would have been used as a diuretic to increase urination, while the zinc sulfate and lead acetate would be used in an eyewash. The penis syringes would likely have contained a lead acetate solution that was used for urethal irrigation.[27]

If the men contracted sexually transmitted diseases through their sexual encounters, one cannot help but wonder about the possibility of the Indian women becoming pregnant by members of the expedition. It is interesting to note that, while many journal entries mention the sexual encounters of the expedition, the journals do not specifically mention that either Lewis or Clark actually accepted any sexual offers themselves.[28]

Historian Bernard DeVoto refused to speculate whether Lewis and Clark took part in the same sexual activities as their men; however, DeVoto noted that there have been a number of people who claimed to be descended from Meriwether Lewis.[29] One such claim was recorded in 1872 in an Episcopal baptismal register. Joseph DeSomet Lewis, a Sioux man who was then sixty-eight years old, was baptized at St. Philip the Deacon Chapel, White Swan, Dakota Territory. He listed his father's name as Captain Meriwether Lewis although no verification has ever been made. Nonetheless, his headstone in St. Alban's Cemetery on the Lower Brule Reservation identifies him as the "son of Meriwether Lewis."[30]

In contrast to the paternity claims made against Lewis, DeVoto mentioned that he had never met a person who claimed to be a descendant of William Clark.[31] In 1955, however, *Montana, Magazine of Western History* published a short article addressing the possibility that a Nez Perce man of mixed descent was fathered by Clark. The article included a circa 1866 photograph of a man with the caption, "Son of Captain William Clark of the Lewis and Clark expedition of the years 1804-05-06." Yet another photograph shows a woman who claimed to be Clark's "quarter breed" granddaughter. The woman, known as Mary Clark, was reported to have been the daughter of a half-breed Nez Perce Indian with reddish hair who was "the reputed son of Wm. Clark."[32]

Perhaps the most common paternity claims have been made against York. According to Clark's journal entry for December 8, 1804, York suffered a mild case of frostbite on his penis. His suffering was apparently short-lived as E.G. Chuinard, who wrote on the medical aspects of the Lewis and Clark Expedition, wrote that York's "kinky-haired progeny were traceable among the Indian tribes contacted by the Expedition all the way to the Pacific."

Furthermore, other historians noted that African-American physical characteristics were observed among the Mandan nation well into the late 1880s.[33]

With the 2004-2006 bicentennial commemoration of the Lewis and Clark Expedition, we can reflect upon and continue to better understand its significance to the ethnography of the American West. The sexual relations of the Lewis and Clark Expedition, however, should not be regarded by the standards of today's society. Rather, they should be interpreted in the context of young frontier soldiers, explorers, and traders as well as the societal norms and values of American Indian cultures in the early nineteenth century.

Honoring and Gift Giving among the Lakota and Dakota: An Interpretation of Two of Lewis and Clark's Encounters with the Sioux

Laurinda W. Porter

Introduction

The journals of Lewis and Clark provide valuable information on geography, weather, navigation, and natural history, as well as detailed descriptions of their meetings with various Indian bands. During two extended encounters in 1804 with bands of Nakota and Lakota Indians—whom most Americans would recognize by the name "Sioux"—Lewis and Clark took part in a series of Indian cultural activities which can be recognized today as *honoring* and *gift giving*. In this paper, I will describe and explain honoring and gift giving—cultural customs important to all Lakota, Dakota, and Nakota, which form bases for much communication within tribal communities and between tribal communities and representatives of the Euro-American world. First, I will provide historical background on Lakota, Dakota, and Nakota encounters with Euro-Americans. Second, I will explain the concept of honoring as it is known to Euro-Americans today and then as it is known to the Lakota, placing it within a context of Lakota behavior today and in the past. Finally, I will discuss the descriptions of honoring given in two journal accounts of meetings between Lewis and Clark's expedition and bands of Sioux and interpret these incidents using Lakota cultural concepts.

Historical Background

The Lakota are one of three closely related native groups—the Dakota, Lakota, and Nakota—whose distinctiveness is often overlooked in the historical literature. Although they speak different dialects, they share a common language, spiritual tradition, and way of life.[1] The Lakota were the westernmost group, traditionally inhabiting areas of North America now known as North Dakota, South Dakota, Nebraska, Wyoming, Montana, and southern Canada. They are the group identified in American popular thought with fine horses, buffalo culture, and courage in battle. The Nakota lived in the middle, between the Missouri and Big Sioux Rivers, and the Dakota lived in the eastern part of the territory, in south central Minnesota and western Wisconsin.

The Lakota, Dakota, and Nakota encountered Euro-American explorers and traders during the seventeenth, eighteenth, and nineteenth centuries. Spanish explorers were probably the first Europeans to meet the Lakota, perhaps Coronado in the mid-1500s, or Oñate in 1601. Scholars indicate it is unlikely that regular trade between Lakotas and Spaniards took place until after 1739.[2] It is significant that in 1804, when Lewis and Clark first encountered a band of Lakota (whom they called Tetons), that band had two "flags of Spain" displayed prominently in their council lodge.[3]

Other Euro-American travelers reached the Great Plains after about 1600. English fur traders and explorers from the Hudson's Bay Company, chartered in 1670, traveled throughout what is now Canada and down into the Dakotas and Montana. Lewis and Clark reported that some of the Indian bands they met in what are now North and South Dakota and Montana traded regularly with the English.

Between 1634 and 1742, French explorers and traders traveled west to reach the Sioux, beginning with Jean Nicolet. He started west from Quebec in 1634 and reached Lake Michigan and Green Bay. In 1673, Louis Joliet and the Jesuit priest Jacques Marquette followed the route of Nicolet and reached the Mississippi River. Robert Cavalier, Sieur de La Salle, conducted many explorations of the Ohio and Mississippi Rivers beginning in 1669. During the winter of 1679-80, La Salle sent his friend Father Hennepin to explore the Mississippi River further. In 1681, Daniel Greysolon, Sieur du Luth, claimed to have "taken formal possession of the country of the Sioux. He was thereupon named commandant of this extensive region and spent the next ten years exploring and trading with the Indians."[4] Between 1731 and 1738, La Verendrye traveled west, exploring and trading, building forts, and trapping until in 1738 he reached the Plains tribes. In 1742, two of the sons of La Verendrye set off west, moving from Indian camp to Indian camp, reaching the Missouri river at the present Fort Pierre and probably journeying as far as the Black Hills.[5]

During the time of French exploration, thousands of voyageurs were traveling and trading in the Indian country. Grace Nute reports that in "1777, for example, 2,431 voyageurs are recorded in the licenses obtained at Montreal and Detroit. Add to this number the men already in the interior as [winter traders], the employees of the Hudson's Bay Company, and the traders from the new states on the coast, and five thousand is a conservative estimate of the men who were sprinkled from Montreal to the Rocky Mountains, from Hudson Bay to the Gulf of Mexico."[6] Thus one can conclude that the Lakota, Dakota, and Nakota had heard about and probably seen Spanish, English, and French explorers and traders more than 100 years before they encountered Lewis and Clark.

The Concept of Honor

Honoring among Euro-Americans. Before discussing the Lakota concept of honoring, it is useful to establish what is familiar about honoring among Euro-Americans, as a kind of touchstone.

Dictionary definitions of the English word "honor" as a noun include ideas like "esteem paid to worth; high estimation; reverence; veneration; any mark of respect or estimation by words or actions; dignity."[7] As a verb, " to honor" is "to regard or treat with honor; to revere; to reverence; to bestow honor upon; to elevate in rank or station."[8] These definitions apply to the word as used today in honoring activities.

In contemporary Euro-American culture, honoring someone might mean giving a dinner for him or her to recognize a personal achievement or change in status, e.g., a promotion at work, the conferring of a degree, the winning of an award, or an impending marriage. Honoring someone could also be done by the presentation of an award in recognition of an achievement or important deed, e.g., giving a plaque to a citizen who enters a burning building to rescue someone, or a medal to a police officer who shows extra bravery, or a financial award to someone who has discovered an important scientific or medical principle, as in the Nobel Prize for economics, physics, or medicine. In Euro-American culture, people give gifts to the honoree as a reward for what he or she has done. Parents might give a substantial gift, such as a car, a sum of money, or jewelry to a son or daughter upon graduation from high school or college, "in honor of" that achievement. A family might hold a large party to recognize their grandparents' 50th wedding anniversary and honor their long commitment to marriage. Further, in Euro-American culture, different gifts have different meanings and social value, depending upon a person's age, gender, and economic status, and the occasion. For example, it would be appropriate to give a girl graduating from high school a gift of jewelry, such as a string of pearls or a pin, but it would be inappropriate to give a boy a string of pearls or a pin. It would be appropriate to give a police officer who performed a heroic deed an engraved plaque to hang on his or her wall; the plaque would have to be no larger than twelve inches square. To give a police officer a huge plaque, say two feet wide and made of marble or gold, would be overdoing it. Finally, the person being honored in Euro-American culture must behave in a culturally approved way. The person must express appreciation at being honored and thank the people who organized the occasion for honoring. In some situations the person must express humility, as in "Many others helped me with this" or "I could not have done this alone" or "Only with the help of God and my family could I have managed this."

Honoring among the Lakota. To explain the Lakota concept of honoring, I will present cultural definitions, examples of honoring activities today and those from the old times, and a discussion of the expected behavior of an honoree. My information was obtained from three native informants.

During the pre-reservation period, Lakota, Nakota, and Dakota people traditionally lived in small bands of grandparents, their adult children, spouses, and grandchildren, all of whom were related by kinship. Usually, one man who showed leadership, generosity, protectiveness, and courage was recognized as the head of the band. The people hunted and gathered their food; they did not grow crops. They moved among several camping spots during the year, according to the movements of the buffalo, ceremonial activities, and the ripening of natural foods that needed to be gathered. At certain times during the year the bands would meet other bands and hunt and camp together, hold ceremonies, play at sports, and share food. The bands shared a common language, spiritual tradition, and way of life.[9] Although the Lakota, Nakota, and Dakota no longer follow the buffalo today, many still live in small communities in their traditional geographic areas and try to maintain their cultural traditions.

One of the most basic cultural skills in the Lakota way is honoring. This concept among the Lakota is visible in actions—basically doing and singing.[10] Singing is the culturally appropriate way to express most emotions and acknowledge most situations, whether good or bad. Honoring someone in the Lakota culture means acknowledging them or some act that happened.[11] It is done in a semi-public way. For example, today a family might wish to honor an achievement or event involving their child, as explained by Severt Young Bear:

> This could be graduating from high school, going into the service, getting an Indian name, being honored as a committee member or because of something bad such as a death in the family or remembering a deceased veteran. You don't just celebrate or bring something sad before the public and forget your obligation to say thank you to people—with words, by feeding, and by giving away. If you do the best you can, the people will then remember that child in a good way because they'll think of that feast and that giveaway. In this way the parents have paid or provided for the child's status in the community. Their preparation and their willingness to plan for this day and sacrifice what they can shows their child as well as the community how much they love and think of their child, but also what they think of themselves.[12]

This is the way an honoring would be planned today. A singing group would be asked to sing[13] about someone or something or some act that occurred. A feast would be organized and people would be invited to it. After the feast, an elder, community leader, or other person with high status would explain the situation, then ask the singing group to sing the "honor song" that tells about the person, object, or event to be acknowledged. Then there would be a giveaway. Prior to the giving of the gifts, the honoree would ask someone to speak for him or her and explain to the community about the situation that led to the honoring, thank people, and thank the singing group. If the honoree is an elder, then he or she could speak for him or herself. At a giveaway, as part of the Lakota concept of honoring, gifts are given to others, either by the honoree or on his or her behalf by someone else. If the gifts are given on behalf of the honoree, then the honoree, the person about whom the song is sung, must also give back—must give to the person who organized the honoring and to the singing group. If the honoree is giving the gifts, then the recipients simply shake his or her hand and that is considered an acknowledgment of the gift at the time. On another occasion, the people receiving the gifts today will themselves be giving away, and so there is a cycle of giving. Honoring happens "when someone gives back."[14]

According to Severt Young Bear, "The traditional way of thinking tells us that when you have material possessions, the best thing you can do with them is to give them away, especially to those who are without or who are having a hard time. A leader is not the guy who can store up and keep lots of things but instead someone who will share them with the people. We are taught as young boys and girls that in order to honor ourselves and our relatives, we should always be ready to share."[15] Young Bear, a gifted Lakota singer who was known all over Indian country, died in 1993. One of the songs he knew had words that explained the Lakota attitude toward giving: "'There isn't anything I won't give away because my parents are still alive.'" He went on to explain, "The ones we love are so much more important than material objects. Also, we believe that when you give, you create good feelings and harmony in your community. If you keep everything, you are inviting envy and jealousy."[16]

Gifts that are appropriate at a Lakota honoring today include blankets, beadwork, quillwork, clothing, household items, food, and cash. In the old times, gifts would have been tanned hides, beaded or quilled clothing and moccasins, horses, meat, weapons, and tools.[17] "The most prized possession to be given away was a horse. It showed our respect for the person we gave it to and also our willingness to give not just little things but also things that meant a lot to us, to give all that we could," recalled Young Bear. "There is even a special honor song for a guy who gives a horse away.... Also, they would sing a *wopila* (thanksgiving) song like this one: 'Whatever you possess, give it away to the needy. You will have it again!' Those are powerful words that encourage people to give away shawls and material, wagonloads and pickuploads of goods, or a team and wagon, horses and saddles. There are always special honor songs for those kinds of people."[18] In the old times, guests were honored by being asked to smoke with their hosts, by the preparation of a meal for them by their hosts, by the performance of dancing for guests to observe, and particularly by special foods offered at a meal.

The person being honored must behave in a culturally approved way. In the Lakota culture, humility is the most important characteristic. The Lakota person being honored should feel unworthy and should express in some way, verbally or nonverbally, that he or she does not deserve the honor. A person might be afraid to attend an honoring because that might indicate to others that the person felt entitled to the recognition that honoring brings. In the

Lakota culture, it is considered wrong to seek recognition. The term *osica* (pronounced 'oh-SHE-cha'), "not to feel bad," is connected with honoring. A person may feel *oscia*, meaning that he or she is happy about the honoring but still has humility, and the person shows the humility by "giving away" to others at the conclusion of the honoring ceremony.[19] Those receiving the gifts do not show emotion but accept them calmly. Food offered to people must be eaten. It is considered rude for people to refuse to eat something that is prepared for them. The speeches must be courteously attended to, although it is improper to look at the speaker. Lakota listeners should look straight ahead or at the ground. Sounds of agreement and acknowledgment, such as "Hunh," may be made to the speaker.

According to Lakota spiritual helper Roger Thundershield, a member of the Standing Rock band of Hunkpapa, honoring is in one way like a vision quest (the Lakota rite during which a person seeks a vision or message from the spirits to guide his or her life path). In an interview, Thundershield explained that honoring "comes from somebody being chosen by the spirits to have those thoughts, so that is sort of like a vision. That person would interpret what he would like to do and then that is how an honoring thing starts."[20]

> "In the old days, honoring...was done by doing it. Wives and mothers would without even asking cook and then give the food to all the people. Some people honor by showing someone how to dance, teaching someone about singing, by namegiving. Honor was given the best by the father's uncles to the father's sons (their nephews). For example, an uncle would take his brother's son and teach him things, like to hunt, etc.
>
> Some ways to honor a man are by giving a gift, asking him for advice, asking that person to interpret a vision, asking him to help chop wood, help with a ceremony, etc. Honoring old men is done when a camp leader or a holy man asks an old man for advice, or to pray, or to help name someone, or to explain something, like "How do you cook dog?" Old men like to talk about things like that.
>
> In the old times, the warriors were honoring the people by going out to fight and protect them. Honoring has to do with everything. Some lady who made you something, or your wife is giving you children, cooking things for you—you don't want them to die, so you try to use the wisdom of your fathers and uncles to help protect the people. When the warriors returned to the camp, the camp criers would come around to announce what had taken place, e.g., "Shoots Himself in the Toe has counted coup on the enemy." They try to let the people know the important things. The criers are known as people who are quiet. So when they say something, it is true. They were selected to tell the people the important things.
>
> Giving gifts would take place after the criers announced something. The people would honor those warriors who did something important by having a feast, giving gifts to them, etc. Gifts could be feathers, arrows, a new bow, a blanket.[21]

Ella Deloria was a university-trained Yankton Nakota scholar born in 1889 who worked with Franz Boas and Ruth Benedict in the 1920s, '30s, and '40s. She lived among the Lakota on the Standing Rock reservation where her father was an Episcopal missionary and made it "her lifelong quest to preserve traditional Sioux language and culture,"[22] but only one of her manuscripts was published during her lifetime. In an unpublished manuscript located in the South Dakota State Historical Society Archives in Pierre, South Dakota, she wrote about honoring among the Lakota:

> *Tiyospaye*[23] loyalty and interdependence were desirable as marks of group solidarity and stability, and consequently were good to foster. They could be demonstrated in various ways, all of which were for honoring one another. A family preparing a feast to memorialize a dear one who had died, or to accompany some child's rite, were made proud and happy by the assistance of their relatives, whose gesture was heart-warming to them, no matter how well able they might be to stand the cost independently. More than once I have seen this happen: A feast all set to be served, and a big circle of guests waiting for the preliminary speeches to commence—and then some relatives arriving with huge kettles of cooked food to add to the menu.
>
> And it was not the extra food—there was plenty, already—but what it revealed; that the spirit of mutual dependence among *tiyospaye* relatives, and of a mutual readiness to meet that dependence, was healthily present there. That lively awareness of mutual obligation to honor relatives was what men were judged by. For, to be generous in behalf of relatives was essential in Lakota society. People were lauded for it. "How well those relatives treat one another!...So should all men do. It is the Dakota way!"[24]
>
> Another and even more spectacular way of honoring a relative was not to give him something, directly, but to cause him to give to someone else at the give-away ceremonies. During the festivities there, a man (or woman) gave away a horse or something of comparable value, with the public announcement that "My relative (naming man, woman, or child) gives this!" The official drummers and singers immediately raised a song of praise in which they named the one who had been honored, as though he had personally parted with something valuable. The honor to him was multiple. He had been honored by a relative, he had been lauded in song, and presently the lucky recipient came to thank him "by stroking his face." That was the traditional thank-you gesture on such an occasion. The recipient knew who it was who provided the gift, of course; but he had benefited from the one in whose name it had been given. Thus was goodwill spread far around, to include, the real giver, the one caused to give, and the one who received.
>
> To give at the give-away is to *ituh'a*. It literally says, "To act in vain." That is idiomatic, of course, for "To give freely, gratuitously," without proper stipulation; without prior agreement as to what one would get out of it, and when. To honor another by giving in his name as though he had given was to *ituh'a-kiya* [to cause (him) to give]. (93-94) [25]

These details from Young Bear, Thundershield, and Deloria present honoring and gift-giving customs that are different from Euro-American customs but common among North American Indian nations. These customs would have been unknown to early explorers meeting Lakota and Nakota tribes unless the explorers had experience with Ojibwa, Cree, or other bands who had similar ways.[26] Through trial and error and through information given them by interpreters and traders, early explorers probably learned to become more competent in Lakota honoring and gift giving customs. In the accounts left by Lewis and Clark, we can see how they perceived and responded to the honoring and gift giving they experienced on their journey.

Lewis and Clark's accounts of Lakota, Dakota, and Nakota honoring activities.

Excerpts from Journals of Lewis and Clark.[27] Lewis and Clark have left us two extensive descriptions of their meetings with Lakota and Nakota bands of Indians during their trip west in 1804. On August 27, 1804, three months after they left St. Louis, Lewis and Clark made contact with a band of Sioux Indians camped near the mouth of the Yankton River, now the James. They sent word to invite the "principal chiefs" to council with them, and two days later they saw Indians camped by the Missouri shore. Clark described what transpired:

> At four o'clock, P.M., Sergeant Pryor and Mr. Dorion [an old white man, who had lived for many years with the Sioux, and had agreed to interpret for Lewis and Clark and arrange this meeting], with five chiefs and about 70 men and boys, arrived on the opposite side. We sent over a pirogue, and Mr. Dorion and his son, who was trading with the Indians, came over with Sergeant Pryor, and informed us that the chiefs were there. We sent Sergeant Pryor and young Mr. Dorion with some tobacco, corn, and a few kettles for them to cook in, with directions to inform the chiefs that we would speak to them tomorrow....
>
> Sergeant Pryor informs me that when they came near the Indian camp, they were met by men with a buffalo robe to carry them. Mr. Dorion informed they were not the owners of the boats and did not wish to be carried.... A fat dog was presented as a mark of their great respect for the party, of which they partook heartily, and thought it good and well flavored. (56)

The next day, Lewis and Clark sent a boat over to the opposite shore to bring over the chiefs and warriors to a meeting at noon:

> At 12 o'clock we met, and Captain Lewis delivered the speech; and then made one great chief by giving him a medal and some clothes; one second chief and three third chiefs, in the same way. They received those things with the goods and tobacco with pleasure. To the grand chief we gave a flag, and the parole [certificate] and wampum with a hat and chief's coat. We smoked out of the pipe of peace, and the chiefs retired to a bower, made of bushes by their young men, to divide their presents, and smoke, eat, and council. Captain Lewis and myself retired to dinner, and to consult about other measures.

On the third day, August 31, 1804, after breakfast, the meetings began again:

> After the Indians got their breakfast, the chiefs met and arranged themselves in a row, with elegant pipes of peace all pointing to our seats. We came forward, and took our seats. The great chief, The Shake Hand, rose, and spoke at some length, approving what we had said, and promising to pursue the advice.

The four additional chiefs also spoke, and then one man representing the warriors promised to support the chiefs. They agreed to go to Washington, D.C., in the spring and see the President,

> and to do all things we advised them to do. And all concluded by telling the distresses of their nation by not having traders, and wished us to take pity on them. They wanted powder, ball, and a little milk [rum: "milk of Great Father" means spirits.].
>
> Last night the Indians danced until late in their dances. We gave them some knives, tobacco, and bells, tape, and binding, with which they were satisfied
>
> We gave a certificate to two men of war, attendants on the chief. Gave to all the chiefs a carrot of tobacco....
>
> This great nation, whom the French have given the name of Sioux, call themselves Dakota....Their trade comes from the British, except this band and one on Des Moines who trade with the traders of St. Louis....In the evening, late, we gave Mr. Dorion a bottle of whiskey, and he, with the chiefs, and his son, crossed the river and camped on the opposite bank. (56-59)

This concludes Lewis and Clark's first meeting with the Sioux from August 27 to 31, 1804.

In the description by Clark quoted above, one can identify several honoring activities: (1) the gifts given by Lewis and Clark to pave the way for contact, (2) the invitation given by Lewis and Clark to the chiefs to meet on the next day, (3) the offer from the Indians to carry Pryor and Dorion in a buffalo robe, (4) the meal of cooked dog given to Pryor and Dorion at the Indian camp, (5) the medals, clothing, and other gifts given by Lewis and Clark to the men whom they decided to designate as "chiefs," (6) the ceremony of smoking the pipes together, (7) the speeches made by the "chiefs" in response to the speech of Captain Lewis, (8) the promise by the Indians to do as Clark asked, (9) the holding of a dance by the Indians at the meeting site, (10) the gifts given by Lewis and Clark in response to the dance, (11) the certificate and tobacco given to the Indians by Lewis and Clark. There is a rhythm and a reciprocity of honoring and gift giving going on between the Indians and Lewis and Clark that made their intercultural encounter proceed successfully. Each group seemed aware of the major expectations of the other and tried to meet those expectations.

The second encounter with the Sioux lasted from September 23 to 30, 1804. On September 23rd, after the Lewis and Clark group had been traveling up the Missouri for several more weeks, the expedition was approached by "three Sioux boys," who swam out to the boats to tell Lewis and Clark "that the band of Sioux called the Tetons, of 80 lodges, were camped at the next creek above; and 60 lodges more a short distance above. We gave those boys two carrots of tobacco to carry to their chiefs, with directions to tell them that we would speak to them tomorrow" (p. 66). The Tetons would today be called Lakota. In getting ready for the anticipated visit with this band, Lewis wrote:

> We prepared some clothes and...medals for the chiefs of the Tetons' bands of Sioux, which we expect to see today at the next river....Prepared...for action in case of necessity. Our pirogues went to the island for the meeting....
>
> We soon after met 5 Indians, and anchored out some distance, and spoke to them. Informed them we were friends, and wished to continue so, but were not afraid of any Indians....Came to about 1 1/2 miles above [an island], off the mouth of a small river about 70 yards wide called by Mr. Evans the Little Missouri River. The tribes of the Sioux called the Tetons are camped about two miles up on the N.W. side; and we shall call the river after that nation....
>
> The French pirogue came up early in the day; the other did not get up until the evening. Soon after we had come to, I went and smoked with the chiefs who came to see us here. All well. We prepare to speak with the Indians tomorrow, at which time, we are informed, the Indians will be here. (67)

The meeting with the Lakota the next day, September 25, 1804, did not go well. Lewis and Clark tried to start things correctly by having the men set up an "awning" or "shade" under which the meeting would take place, as it was the custom of the Indians to meet under some sort of shelter. When the first few Indians arrived, everyone smoked together and Lewis gave a speech which had to be short because there was no interpreter. Next all present introduced themselves and then the men of the expedition put on a military parade. Lewis and Clark gave out a few medals, invited the chiefs on board the boat, and served them a small glass of whiskey. Then some trouble started, as a couple of the chiefs began to behave badly. Clark took three soldiers and two Indians back to shore and then an incident took place which ended with Clark drawing his sword and calling for a dozen armed men to rescue him. He tried to end the situation by offering to shake hands with two of the chiefs, but they refused. Clark and the armed men started back to the boat, and then two chiefs and two warriors followed in friendship; he took them with him and they all boarded the boat (68-69). On the third day, September 26, the expedition continued upstream with the four Indians accompanying them. After a while they landed "at the wish of the chiefs" so that the women and children now lining the river banks could see the boat and "suffer them to treat us well" (69). After they landed, Lewis and five men "went on shore with the chiefs, who appeared disposed to make up and be friendly." Clark sent a man to see how Lewis was doing, and he reported that the Indians were preparing for a dance that evening. "They made frequent solicitations for us to remain one night only and let them show their good disposition toward us. We determined to remain" (70). After Lewis came back to the boat, Clark went on shore:

> On landing, I was received on an elegant painted buffalo robe, and taken to the village by 6 men, and was not permitted to touch the ground until I was put down in the grand council house, on a white dressed robe.... I was in several lodges, neatly formed, as before mentioned as to the Bois Brule—Yankton tribe.
>
> This house formed a 3/4 circle of skins well dressed, and sewn together, under this shelter. About 70 men sat, forming a circle. In front of the chiefs, a place of 6 feet diameter was clear, and the pipe of peace raised on forked sticks, about 6 or 8 inches from the ground, under which there was swansdown scattered. On each side of this circle, two pipes, the two flags of Spain and the flag we gave them in front of the grand chief. A large fire was near, in which provisions were cooking. In the center, about 400 pounds of excellent buffalo beef as a present for us.
>
> Soon after they set me down, the men went for Captain Lewis. Brought him in the same way, and placed him also by the chief. In a few minutes an old man rose and spoke, approving what we had done, and informing us of their situation, requesting us to take pity on them and which was answered. The great chief then rose with great state, speaking to the same purpose as far as we could learn, and then, with great solemnity, took up the pipe of peace and, after pointing it to the heavens, the four quarters of the globe and the earth, he made some dissertation, lit it and presented the stem to us to smoke. When the principal chief spoke with the pipe of peace, he took in one hand some of the most delicate parts of the dog which was prepared for the feast, and made a sacrifice to the flag.
>
> After a smoke had taken place, and a short harangue to his people, we were requested to take the meal, and they put before us the dog which they had been cooking, and pemmican, and ground potato in several platters.... We smoked for an hour, till dark, and all was cleared away. A large fire made in the center. About ten musicians playing on tambourines (made of hoops of skin, stretched), long sticks with deer and goats' hoofs tied so as to make a jingling noise, and many others of a similar kind. Those men began to sing and beat on the tambourine. The women came forward, highly decorated in their way, with the scalps and trophies of war of their fathers, husbands, brothers, or near connections, and proceeded to dance the War Dance. (70-71)

Four chiefs stayed on the boat with Lewis and Clark that night. The following day, September 27th, Lewis and Clark prepared to take leave of the Teton Sioux, but this ended up being more difficult and drawn out than they imagined. First, Lewis and Clark "gave the chiefs a blanket apiece, or rather, they took off, agreeable to their custom, the one they lay on; and each, one peck of corn" (72). After breakfast, Lewis and the chiefs went ashore, seeing a large number of their band members gathering there. Later, Clark went with the men to three of the important men's lodges and spoke there. Then another dance started. When they returned to the larger boat, a chief and a warrior accompanied them. On the way to the larger boat, there was a problem with steering the smaller boat and Clark barked some orders which the Indians apparently interpreted as threatening. Within ten minutes, there were 200 armed warriors on the river bank, led by a chief. Soon they dispersed, but about 60 remained on the bank all night. On the morning of September 28th, the expedition decided to get going on its upriver journey once again, and they

> with great difficulty, got the chiefs out of our boat; and when we were about setting out, the class called the soldiers [camp police] took possession of the cable. The 1st chief, who was still on board, intended to go a short distance with us. I told him the men of his nation sat on the cable. He went out and told Captain Lewis, who was at the bow, the men who sat on the rope were soldiers and wanted tobacco. Captain Lewis would not agree to being forced into anything. The 2nd chief demanded a flag and tobacco, which we refused to give....After much difficulty, which had nearly reduced us to the necessity for hostilities, I threw a carrot of tobacco to 1st chief.... The chief gave the tobacco to his soldiers, and he jerked the rope from them, and handed it to the bowman. We then set out under a breeze from the S.E. About two miles up, we observed the 3rd chief on shore beckoning to us. We took him on board. He informed us the rope was held by the order of the 2nd chief, who was a double-spoken man. Soon after, we saw a man coming full speed through the plains; left his horse, and proceeded across a sand bar near the shore. We took him on board and observed that he was the son of the chief we had on board. We sent, by him, a talk to the nation, stating the cause of our hoisting the red flag under the white. (73-74)

The following day, September 29th, the seventh day since meeting the Teton Sioux boys, the expedition set out early. But their encounter with the Tetons was not yet over. Clark writes:

> At 9 o'clock we observed the 2nd chief and 2 principal men, one man, and a squaw on shore. They wished to go up with us as far as the other part of their band, which, they said, was on the river ahead not far distant. We refused, stating very sufficient reasons, and were plain with them on the subject. They were not pleased....They proceeded on. The chief on board asked for a twist of tobacco for those men. We gave him 1/2 of a twist, and sent one by them for that part of their band which we did not see, and continued on....The 2nd chief came on the sand bar and requested we would put him across the river. I sent a pirogue and crossed him and one man to the S.S., and proceeded on. (74-75)

The next day, September 30, the boats set sail again. Later that day, the last chief asked to get off the boat. He was given a blanket, a knife, and some tobacco. Lewis and Clark smoked a pipe with him and he set off (76). This ended the second encounter with the Lakota.

In interpreting this material, it is necessary to refer to the honoring and gift giving discussion presented earlier. Certain activities like smoking, giving gifts, accepting gifts, making speeches, responding to speeches, offering food, and eating food that is offered are behaviors essential to the Lakota notions of cultural competence. In Lewis and Clark's second encounter with the Sioux, this one with a Teton (or Lakota) band, some attempts at honoring and gift giving were successful and some were not. One of the difficulties that can be noted in the eight days of contact with this band is the problem Lewis and Clark experienced in dealing with multiple "chiefs." Euro-Americans impose on Indian bands the requirement that one leader, or a few leaders, speak for, or represent, all the Indians in that band, because Euro-Americans are accustomed to speaking for or representing their constituents as councilmen, mayors, congressmen, and senators. But Indian bands do not have the custom of appointing someone to represent them. Indian bands are composed of loosely allied family groups who choose to stay or go every day. Each Indian is an individual who makes personal decisions about daily living. [28] There is no person "in charge" of other persons, who can speak for other persons without their direct and immediate consent via a council meeting. When Indians meet in council, it is to discuss an existing situation and potential responses to it. If an enemy is approaching, each warrior decides for himself whether to fight and under whose leadership. Several warriors might offer to lead war parties and would announce their intentions to the community. If other warriors wanted to go with a warrior who was leading a party, they would speak to that leader. Older people were recognized as having wisdom from long years of living and survival. They would be called upon to share their wisdom, but they did not order anyone to do anything. Someone whom European Americans perceived as a "chief" because Indians seemed to respect his word was a leader on that day through community respect that had to be constantly renewed. But Lewis and Clark were following an American tradition that they had learned from others when they "made" chiefs or bestowed power and authority on certain Indian men of their choice. They thought, as most American government messengers or emissaries have thought, that it would simplify things to identify one or two Indians with whom they could deal, and ignore the rest. To do this, Lewis and Clark, like many before them and many who would come after them, presented medals, certificates, wampum, and gifts and smoked with the chosen men of whatever tribe they met. With the Sioux, Lewis and Clark also presented the medals, certificates, wampum, and gifts, smoked, made speeches and listened to responding speeches, ate meals, and so on. Lewis and Clark thought that they were appointing these men to positions of authority which their Lakota community would acknowledge and follow; however, they were mistaken. The three or four "chiefs" were probably heads of family groups, meaning that they were older than young warrior age, had wives and children, had demonstrated success in hunting, and had earned influence by these means. Certainly the "2nd chief" had also made a reputation for himself as dishonest, since he is called "a double-spoken man" by one of the other chiefs in an attempt by that chief to apologize to Lewis and Clark for the bad behavior of the "2nd chief" and his followers. Clark's perception of danger from this man and his followers led him to draw his sword and order his men to arm themselves. At this point, the meeting with the Teton Sioux almost ended. But Clark extended his hand to the chiefs. Although they refused to take it, they quickly changed their minds and set off after him to try to communicate again.

Once the 1st and 3rd chiefs decide to go ahead with the planned meeting, the series of honorings and gift givings resumes. (1) The chiefs stay on the boat with Lewis and Clark all night; this honor indicates that the chiefs are willing to put their lives in the Americans' hands. (2) When Lewis leaves in the morning with the chiefs and five men from the expedition to attend preliminary meetings, that honor indicates that Lewis and Clark would put their lives in the hands of this band. (3) When Lewis returns, Clark goes ashore and is carried in a buffalo robe to the camp. Then Lewis is carried to the camp. This honoring recognizes them as men of high stature. (4) Two important men of the tribe, elders, rise and address them, say prayers, and smoke the pipe with them. All of these things indicate a willingness to accept the Americans. (5) An offering of dog meat is made to the American flag, and then a feast is served to the Americans, including dog meat, which is the most sacred meat the Sioux had. (6) More pipe smoking takes place after the meal. (7) A dance is held, and Lewis and Clark observe dancing and singing. (8) Four chiefs return with Lewis and Clark to the boat for the night and sleep there, indicating their trust in Lewis and Clark. (9) Lewis and Clark give each chief a blanket and a peck of corn. (10) Lewis and Clark make separate farewell visits to important men's lodges. (11) Another dance is held. (12) Lewis and Clark start back to the boat for the night, accompanied by the 2nd chief and a warrior. This is when the misinterpretation of the sailing mishap occurs and the 2nd chief calls for 200 warriors. In the morning the 2nd chief directs his men to prevent the boat from sailing. The 1st chief solves the problem by calling for tobacco to be given to the 2nd chief's men. The boat sails and this encounter with the Tetons ends.

The actions of the 1st chief in calling for tobacco to be given to the men of the 2nd chief, even though they were engaged in wrongdoing, is an example of another Lakota custom—intervening in disputes and trying to end them. Ella Deloria writes that one way the Sioux solve interpersonal conflicts is by a third party giving gifts to those who are in conflict, in effect asking them on behalf of the community to stop fighting. In the following excerpt from one of her unpublished manuscripts on Lakota customs, Ella Deloria explains this practice:

> Serious open quarrels among persons of consequence were rare, though they did occasionally take place. And whenever two men or two women had a quarrel it could not remain their private affair for very long. It became the concern of the entire community, for everyone was a kinsman, however indirectly or remotely. Not that they all needed to take sides and implicate themselves, but the atmosphere of possible tragedy made for general uneasiness.
>
> At such times, prominent men who were accustomed to peace-making once again decided to interfere and try to restore friendship between the ones at enmity, for their sakes and for the community's as well. The peacemakers...used an approach somewhat like this:
>
> "Alas, my relative, it grieves me to see you in this unhappy state. You wrong not only yourself but also all your kinsmen and friends. As long as you are at odds with another, we all go about with heavy hearts. For daily we are apprehensive because of you. We fear what this could lead to.... Come, then, my relative, before it is too late." (52)

If that persuasion was not sufficient, the speaker would continue to make appeals, based on the fear of murder taking place. If this failed, the speaker would resort to kinship appeals:

> "I plead with you, my nephew (or whatever the relationship.) I even humble myself to beg of you!" So he would talk and then pause between arguments. He might add, "You know I am not a man of property. I have no worthy gift with which to beguile you... But, at least, I offer you these words of entreaty...and a little food...and a little tobacco...." Gently, soothingly he would talk. If on the other hand he was able to make a gift he said, "Out on the hillside a horse is grazing.... He shall cool off your heart. Take him, and so live happy in our midst again."(52-53)[29]

In offering tobacco to the men of the 2nd chief, the 1st chief persuaded them to stop holding Lewis and Clark's boat rope and to let the boat sail. In this way, the 1st chief demonstrates his understanding of Lakota honoring. He does not offend his relatives holding the rope, and he does not insult the 2nd chief.

Conclusion

To assure success in intercultural encounters, the participants must know as much as possible about one another's ways. Lewis and Clark apparently knew a few of the elements of honoring and gift giving that they were obliged to take part in if they wanted to meet in friendship with the Lakota and Nakota bands: offering gifts, accepting the offer of being carried in a buffalo robe, smoking the pipe, listening and responding to speeches, eating the meal prepared for them, and accepting gifts. But they did not know some of the other requirements: how to solve a dispute without violence by giving additional gifts to the parties, how to deal simultaneously with the heads of several family groups and keep all of them satisfied, and how to avoid showing favoritism. Americans today also need to learn about the Lakota customs of honoring and gift giving so that they can communicate successfully with their relatives, the Lakota. The writings and oral histories of traditional people help Americans to understand the differing expectations and ways of Indian tribes. Study of these materials will greatly improve Americans' interactions with the Lakota and other Indian nations.

Native American Trade from the Great Plains to the Interior Plateau Encountered by Lewis and Clark

Ralph J. Coffman, Jr.

The purpose of this study is to examine two types of Indian trade institutions, the trade center and the rendezvous, and their associated social institutions and religious ceremonies as they are presented in the journals of Lewis and Clark, recorded along the Missouri and Columbia Rivers in 1804 and 1805. Because their accounts became definitive in the establishment of U.S. Indian policy in the Trans-Mississippi West, they became a basis for nineteenth-century U.S. Indian policy. Therefore, it is crucial to compare these accounts with those of their contemporaries and with other ethnographic material in order to elucidate their accuracy.

The first aspect of Trans-Mississippi Indian trade to keep in mind is that it had developed over many centuries of prehistoric gestation. Networks had evolved among a variety of Indian trade entities ranging from the most permanent to the seasonal. Many commodities were exchanged either close to their sources, as was the case with utilitarian goods such as Knife River flint, obsidian, leather, corn, and pemmican, or through down-the-line exchange hundreds of miles from their sources, as was the case with ceremonial objects such as pipe bowls made from Minnesota pipestone or other exotic rocks, California and Gulf marine shell beads, breast plates and gorgets, and southeastern galena mirrors.

A second aspect of this trade was the need to establish peace among the participants, who might be either potential enemies or speakers of diverse languages and who gathered together in order to socialize, gamble, trade goods, and vie for marriage partners. Basic to this trade was the calumet ceremony and various fictive adoption rites designed to ritually establish peace among neighbors and enemies alike. A third aspect of trade was to provide a context for marriage outside one's tribe or clan, an arrangement that was deemed to be critical to raising healthy families, so partners were often sought in the course of trade.

Of the two types of trade and exchange that characterize the Trans-Mississippi West, the trade center and the rendezvous, the more permanent was the trade center, which was associated with sedentary villages that had developed as a result of either corn horticulture along the Mississippi River and its tributaries or salmon fishing along the Columbia River. (See Map 1.) The largest and most important of these were the *primary* trade centers of the Arikara near the mouth of the Grand River in South Dakota, of the Mandan

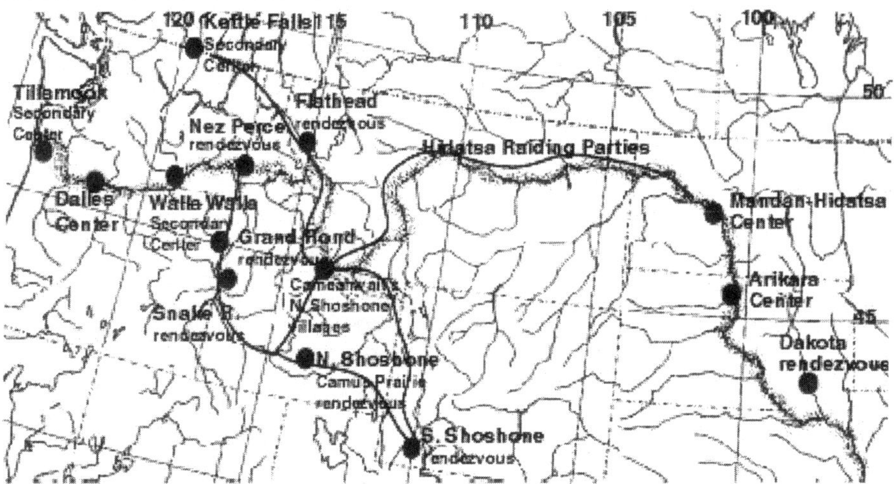

Map 1. The Indian trade network in the Trans-Mississippi West, ca. 1805. Stippled line indicates the Lewis and Clark Expedition route to the Pacific Ocean.

and Hidatsa near the mouth of the Knife River in central North Dakota, and of the Chinook near the Great Dalles in south-central Washington. *Secondary* trade centers, which were similar in mechanism but smaller, were those located at the Walla Walla and Tillamook villages in Washington.

The other most significant trade mechanism was the rendezvous, an eighteenth-century French fur-trapper concept involving an impermanent but predictable seasonal trade fair that attracted nomadic and semi-nomadic hunting bands. One of the largest and most significant of this type was the Dakota *primary* rendezvous on the upper James River in north-central South Dakota. Lewis and Clark did not attend this primary rendezvous, but Lewis gathered information about it from a French fur-trader. *Secondary* rendezvous in the Trans-Mississippi West included those of the Flathead, Nez Perce, and Northern Shoshone, and although Lewis and Clark did not visit them, traders from these gatherings crossed the expedition's path.

The mandate for Lewis and Clark to seek out Native American traders and gain their confidence was occasioned by the Louisiana Purchase. In 1801 Spain retroactively acknowledged a secret agreement of 1800 by which it had supposedly ceded the Louisiana territory to France. The U.S. viewed this larger presence of Napoleon I in North America with suspicion since it was thought he might continue to expand his conquests or curtail U.S. trade on the Mississippi River. Consequently, President Jefferson resolved that the U.S. must control the mouth of the Mississippi River at the "Isle of Orleans" (i.e., New Orleans) in order to protect U.S. trade. He empowered the American minister to France, Robert R. Livingston (1746-1813), and minister-extraordinary James Monroe to offer France $2 million to secure the port. Meanwhile, Napoleon I had been stymied by a recent revolt on Hispaniola (Haiti) and by an impending war with Great Britain. On April 11, 1803, in need of funds, he instructed his foreign minister, Charles Maurice de Talleyrand, to begin negotiations with the U.S. to secure a bid on the entire Louisiana territory. Eighteen days later a U.S. offer of $15 million was accepted, a treaty was dated April 30, 1803, and it was ratified by the U.S. Senate in October. When the U.S. flag was raised over New Orleans on December 20, 1803, Lewis and Clark's expedition was given the implicit mandate to seek out Native American traders and win them over to the U.S (Hosmer 1902; Robertson 1910-1911; Brown 1920; Whitaker 1934). Consequently, the expedition's route along the Missouri River was designed to examine locations that English, Spanish, and French traders had frequented. The prime targets were the Dakota rendezvous on the James River and the Arikara and the Mandan and Hidatsa centers in the Dakotas, where Lewis and Clark spent the winter of 1804-05. What lay beyond was unknown.

Indian trade in the Trans-Mississippi West involved intricate social institutions that had taken centuries to develop in the context of several degrees of sociability, ranging from the most amicable to the most pugnacious. Among friends and kinsmen, trade was unrestrained and fictive relationships and inter-tribal marriages were endorsed. Among more distant relations and neighbors as well as among Euro-American traders, reciprocity remained balanced and fair but impersonal, yet fictive relationships were still endorsed. Among those who were socially and culturally removed, even potentially hostile, social behavior was often fickle and unpredictable, subject to subterfuge and force. Finally, among strangers and enemies, risky behavior, including looting and taking of captives, was common (cf. Sahlins 1965). Yet, regardless of the degree of sociability, a ritually established temporary peace was a pre-condition for trading. The rite that invoked this temporary peace was the offering of the calumet in an elaborate ceremony.

"Calumet" is derived from the French *chameau*, meaning "hollow reed," which was a "breathing" shaft that among many Native Americans was used in shamanic healing rituals, where the illness was literally sucked out of the afflicted person. This sacred shaft (without a pipe bowl affixed) had a long history prior to its being used as a smoking device. Among the Natchez, Osage, and Pawnee, two dancers, with feather-adorned calumets and with arms outstretched, simulated the soaring flight of mating eagles in an eagle dance. This dance was intended to establish a state of protection from evil, including all forms of violence, prior to trading or the exchange of gifts or partners

The culmination of the calumet ceremony was ritual adoption, which could take many forms. Among the eastern Siouan Tutelo of the Piedmont of Virginia, who are thought to be related to the Plains Siouan Mandan, fictive adoption was practiced when a deceased person's identity was assumed by an individual of another band. After the ceremony, the sticks, or calumets, were committed to the flames since their efficacy had ceased with the last song, which sealed the bond between the deceased and the adopted one (Speck 1942, 26). The Rev. James Owen Dorsey recorded the adoption ceremony (*ciegithe*) of another Siouan-speaking group, the Omaha, which was applied not to the deceased but "to take a person instead of one's own child."

Similarly, the Caddoan Pawnee celebrated the Hako ceremony, in which a visitor from another band would volunteer to become a fictive "Father" and adopt a child of the host village as a son. The "Father" would carry two calumet stems decorated with brown and white eagle feathers, respectively symbolizing the mother and father eagle powers. Next to him walked the chief with a Mother Corn medicine bundle that "leads and we follow on,…/ She leads us as where our fathers led/ Down through the ages" (Fletcher 1904, 300). As they marched across the prairie to the receiving village, they were followed by two medicine men waving eagle wings to dispel evil, and these were followed by thirty chanting drummers and the villagers with ponies loaded with gifts and trade items. The adopted son was usually a small boy who was painted with vermilion and given the Mother Corn medicine bundle. Meanwhile, the Hako priest and his assistant danced and waved the feathered calumets over him to establish a solemn condition of peace under the aegis of the Supreme Being "behind the sun," to whom the calumet was raised. Clearly, the earliest calumet ceremonies did not involve smoking.

The eagle-feathered calumet stem served as a baton of peace and could also be interpreted as a disarmed weapon, such as the atl-atl or throwing stick, the ancient hunting weapon that preceded the bow and arrow in North America, *ca.* 300 A.D. (Hall 1983). When the calumet was finally surmounted by a stone pipe bowl and *kinnikinnick* was used as the smoking mixture, the symbolism of a disarmed weapon was complete. *Kinnikinnick* was a combination of bearberry (*Arctostaphylos uva-ursi* L. Spreng) and red osier dogwood (*Cornus sericea* L.) shavings, the remnants left after a spear or arrow shaft was smoothed. If potential enemies smoked the remnant of a disarmed projectile through the stem of a disarmed throwing-stick, the act could be interpreted symbolically as disarming the weapon of mutual destruction and hence invoking peace (Gilmore 1922; Gilmore 1977, 56; Densmore 1928, 287).

However, the calumet ceremony was only the first half of the peace-inducing ritual. The second half was the adoption ceremony. Captain Clark tersely recorded that after he had participated in the calumet ceremony on the afternoon of November 13, 1804, with the chief of the Siouan-speaking Assiniboines, *Che Chark*, or The Crane, "a Dance at the Village" was followed by "a Serimony of adoption and interchange of property, between the Ossiniboines, [and] Christinoes" [i.e. buffalo-hunting Plains Cree] (Lewis and Clark 1983-2001, 3:236). To Euro-Americans, trade was the most important part of the ceremony, but to the Native Americans it was only incidental to the calumet ceremony, the dance, and the adoption ceremony. The Assiniboine were Yanktonai Siouans who had earlier established close relations with the Algonquian Cree, when they had been both located at the headwaters of the Mississippi River in Minnesota. Their invocation of the calumet and the adoption ceremonies on the northern Plains suggests a renewal of their ancient friendship (see Ronda 1984, 130).

Euro-Americans also misunderstood the parlance of fictive adoption. When Lewis and Clark invoked the relationship term of "Children" with regard to their Native American hosts, they were unknowingly invoking the language of fictive adoption that they had heard repeated in these ceremonies but did not understand. In attempting to establish their hegemony over the Native Americans they encountered, Lewis and Clark could superficially refer to Indians as their "Children," while Native Americans could refer to the President as their "Father." However, no fictive relationship was intended by Lewis and Clark. This is made clear in the bestowal of symbolic peace medals. Shell or stone gorgets, analogous to the Euro-American peace medals, had originated among horticultural Mississippian cultures in the period A.D. 800-1300, suggesting that fictive relationship ceremonies had originated with them as well (Brain and Phillips 1996). Euro-Americans, without knowledge of this cultural tradition, began bestowing silver "peace medals" not only to acknowledge an outwardly peaceful relationship but also to symbolically establish political sovereignty over the recipient. When a Euro-American donor gave a medal with the likeness of his ruler to a Native American, it was interpreted by the latter in terms of a fictive "Father-Son" relationship, but to the Euro-American it was perceived as a recognition of political authority.

Another form of fictive adoption was the Mandan *Okipa* rite of "Walking with the Buffaloes," which re-enacted the origin of human society. A senior man who was the owner of a buffalo medicine bundle was invited by a younger man to become his "Father." He would transmit the buffalo power he had acquired to the young man through his spouse in ritual intercourse, and thus married women became the conduit for renewal (Bowers 1950, 117-22; 336-37). The Hidatsa developed a similar ceremony in which a fictive "Father" would sell his buffalo bundle to an adopted "Son," and its power was transferred through the "Son's" wife in a similar ritual act of physical union (Lowie 1917, 40). Among Algonquian-speaking bands such as the Atsina, this power transfer was metaphorically ritualized as love medicine, enabling a young man to purchase the power of the buffalo for "two horses" from his wife's "adult male [fictive] kin [father]" (Kroeber 1908, 224). Among the Arapaho, the elder sponsor of the previous Sun Dance was the fictive "Grandfather," who took the current younger sponsor's wife at midnight to a ceremonial spot (a symbolic buffalo wallow) where symbolic intercourse was offered to a number of supernatural beings. The "Grandfather" then had symbolic intercourse with the woman, in which he transferred a medicinal root to her mouth from his, which she then gave to her spouse (Dorsey 1903, 173-76). The Cheyenne also engaged in a similar ritual in which the "priest lays with the woman underneath a buffalo robe which traps the sweet grass smudge and its sacred powers of transference of his powers" (Dorsey 1905, 130-31).

Lewis and Clark encountered the *Okipa* ceremony and permitted their enlisted men to act as "Fathers" in the Buffalo Calling ceremony during the Fort Mandan winter of 1804-05. The *Okipa* ceremony was already being transformed in response to contact with the Corps because the enlisted men were considered "Fathers," probably in light of their superior weapons that empowered them as though they owned buffalo bundles. Lewis and Clark also allowed their men to exchange sexual favors with village women even when it was not ceremonially sanctioned. However, once the Corps crossed the continental divide and reached the Interior Plateau culture groups, this activity would be sharply curtailed by Lewis and Clark, demonstrating their altered social interactions with these Chinook groups.

Not all groups of Native Americans were appreciated equally by Lewis and Clark. This is graphically evident in Lewis's account of the Dakota rendezvous. The upper James River was so well known to so many different bands, it was known simply as "the River" in Dakota—*wakpa* or *watpa* (Ehrensperger 1941, 148; Riggs 1992, 516, 540) and in Cheyenne, "Chansansan" (Frémont 1970-1980, 1:60). Three thousand lodges were annually erected by the Yankton, Yantonai, and Sisseton at a spot called by the Lakota, Otuhu Oju, "the giving away of the harvest" (Nicollet 1843; Buechel 1983, 410, 381).

Euro-Americans dismissed the figurative Lakota terminology and settled for a descriptive name. French fur traders called it Talle de Chênes, "a clump of oaks which was the rendezvous" (Frémont 1970-1980, 1:60), and the English called it the "Grove of Oaks" that became "Oak Wood Settlement" by 1843 (Nicollet 1843). It is located near Armadale, a small settlement near the village of Mellette on the James River in northern Spink County, South Dakota (Ehrensperger 1941, 79; Ramsey 1849, 88). The Scotsman William Dickson, who had represented the Fort Pierre traders "at the annual round up of the Sioux on the James River" in 1832, had erected a trading post there by 1843 (Fort Pierre *Journal*, April 7 and 13, 1832, in Robinson 1904,171).

The Native American purpose of the rendezvous was, according to Dakotas like Mrs. Joseph Renville, a full-blood Sisseton, who had accompanied the Frémont-Nicollet party in 1839, "more for...bringing the young men and women of the different bands together than for any other purpose" (Robinson 1904, 194 n., 341). Sitting Bull, a Sioux, agreed: "The Dakotas quite understood the degenerating influences of incestuous marriages, and as most of the persons in any one band were related, these summer visits among the tribes were encouraged to offer opportunities to the young people to marry outside their own bands" (Sitting Bull's "Memoirs" in *Sports Afield*, January 1904, extracted in Robinson 1904, 194 n. 341).

Even though there were some tensions displayed from time to time at the Dakota rendezvous, it was generally peaceful: "Although very often this general meeting produces disturbances among tribes already unfriendly, *it serves more commonly for their reconciliation and for peace*. The tribes of the St. Peter's River [i.e., the Dakota], more powerful though less numerous, but *far more enlightened through their association with the whites, become mediators among our fierce hordes and make them see the necessity of unity among them*. It is certain that *these savages urge them above all to treat the French kindly as they are the only people from whom the redskins can derive real advantages*" (Tabeau 1939, 122-3, italics added).

In the eyes of the Euro-Americans, the overwhelming attraction of the Dakota rendezvous was the prodigious quantity of goods exchanged, although the role of the rendezvous as a social institution to bring young together did not go unnoticed. For instance, John C. Frémont perceived that the rendezvous was a friendly gathering convened to exchange prized goods, but he also noted the level of conviviality among the young people who sought partners (being himself the love child of a runaway southern belle and a French tutor): "The next day they made their surround. This was their great summer hunt when their provision of meat was made for the year, the winter hunting being made in small parties. The meat of many fat cows was brought in and the low scaffolds upon which it was laid to be sun dried were scattered all over the encampment....[T]he liberal gifts distributed through the village heightened their enjoyment of the feasting and dancing, which was prolonged through the night. Friendly relations established, we continued our journey" (Fremont 1887, 49).

French voyageurs, who often married prominent Indian daughters to secure their pre-eminence in the fur trade, were generally more pecuniary in their appreciation of the Dakota rendezvous. For instance, Jean Baptiste Truteau of St. Louis noted the large stores of furs the Dakota annually raised, both from their own trapping and by acting as middlemen. He was also careful that the French maintain friendly trade relations with the Dakota since they were aware that the French had allied with their mortal enemies, the Ojibwa, in the Great Lakes. Without Sioux allies, the French could not establish safe storehouses of trade wares on the Missouri River without fear of molestation: "The Sioux nations are the greatest hunters of beaver and other good furs on the upper Missouri. They traverse all the rivers and streams without fearing anyone. Every spring they raise a great quantity [of furs] from our territory, which they go to exchange for merchandise with other Siouan people located on the St. Peter's River and less frequently by the trade with Canada. It would be easy to establish on the Missouri [River] storehouses of merchandise in order to furnish them with their needs and to have the trade of their furs" (Truteau in Tabeau 1939, 121-22 n.69a, my trans.). The activity of the Dakota as middlemen in the fur trade was also substantiated by Francois-Marie Perrin du Lac (1766-1824), a trader who had ascended the Mississippi, Ohio, and Missouri Rivers from 1801 to1803. He had noted that the Dakota bands who attended the rendezvous arrived not only with their own pelts but also those they had acquired as middlemen, and in return received muskets, lead, and gunpowder as well as vermilion paint and beads: "The Sioux who return every year after their hunt, bring not only their own pelts but also those of the northern peoples, which they exchange for gunpowder, lead bars or balls, some muskets, some vermilion, and other trinkets of which they are very fond" (Perrin du Lac 1805, 196, my trans.).

The variety of goods exchanged at the Dakota rendezvous was another attraction. They were acquired from near and far, as French fur trader Pierre-Antoine Tabeau (d.1820), who traded on behalf of the Spanish, noted: "Much trading is done there. Each man brings different articles according to the places he has wandered. Those who have frequented the St. Peter's River and that of the Mohens [Des Moines] furnish guns, kettles, red [catlinite] pipes, and bows of walnut. The Titons give in exchange horses, lodges of leather, buffalo robes, shirts and leggings of antelope-skin [*mitasses de peau de cabril*]" (Tabeau 1939, 121-2).

Meriwether Lewis included an account of the Dakota rendezvous in his manuscript to President Jefferson drawn up in the winter of 1804-05, but because he had not visited it personally, he had to rely on Tabeau's favorable first-hand account gleaned either from his lost journal or from himself when he visited Fort Mandan. Lewis altered Tabeau's relation to make the Dakota appear hostile to U.S. interests because the Dakota were perceived to be allies of either the French or Spanish and hence enemies by political affiliation: "The Siouxs annually hold a fair on some part of this river, in the latter end of May. [T]hither the Yanktons of the north and the Sissetons, who trade with a Mr. Cameron, on the head of St. Peter's River bring guns, pouder & balls, Kettles, axes, knives and a variety of European manufactures, which they barter to the Tetons and the Yanktons Ahnah, who inhabit the borders of the Missouri & the upper part of the River Demoin, and receive in exchange, horses, leather lodges, and buffalo robes....This traffic is sufficient to keep the Siouxs of the Missouri tolerably well supplied with arms and ammunition, *thus rendering them independent of the trade of the Missouri, and enableing them to continue their piratical aggressions on all who attempt to ascend that river, as well as to disturb perpetually the tranquility of their Indian neighbours"* (italics added; Lewis and Clark 1983-2001, 3:356).

Lewis then inserted his military recommendations for managing the perceived Sioux menace: "I am perfectly convinced that until such measures are taken by our government as will effectually prohibit all intercourse or traffic with the Siouxs by means of the rivers Demoin and St. Peters, that all *citizens of the United States can never enjoy, but partially* the advantages which the navigation of the Missouri now presents" (italics added; Lewis and Clark 1983-2001, 3:356-7). Lewis then recommended to Jefferson that four garrisons of U.S. cavalry be established at St. Louis, Chicago, at the mouth of the Wisconsin River, and at Sandy Lake on the Mississippi in Minnesota so that the Sioux would be prevented from trading "through the St. Peters and the Demoin for a few years" in order to reduce them "to order without the necessity of bloodshed." Interestingly, the spurious American edition of the *Travels of Capts. Lewis and Clarke* edited by William Fisher, originally published in Philadelphia in 1809, toned down Lewis's negative characterization of the Dakota: "This country abounds more in the valuable fur animals, the beaver, the otter, the martin, than any portion of Louisiana yet known. This circumstance furnishes the Sissetones with the means of purchasing more merchandise, in proportion to their number, than any nation in the quarter. A great proportion of this merchandise is reserved by them for their trade with the Tetons, with whom they annually meet at some point previously agreed on, upon the waters of the James river, in the month of May. The Indian fair is frequently attended by the Yanktons of the north and Ahnah. The Sissetones and Yanktons of the north here supply the others with considerable quantities of arms, ammunition, axes, knives, kettles, cloth, and a variety of other articles; and receive, in return, principally horses, which the others have stolen or purchased from the nations of the Missouri, and west of it. *They are devoted to the interests of their traders*" (Fisher 1813, 148, 151, italics added). However, to Lewis and Clark the "traders" were hostile foreign powers to be resisted at all costs.

The trade centers that Lewis and Clark next encountered on the Missouri River were multilingual (Ewers 1968; Wood 1980, 98-109). Most resorted to commonly understood lingua francas or trade languages. The Caddoan Arikara near the mouth of the Grand River understood the multilingual bands to the south with whom they traded by using lingua francas appropriate to each region. Uto-Aztecan Comanche (a lingua franca of the southern plains in the nineteenth century) may have been used by the Algonquian Cheyenne and Arapahoe, the Tanoan Kiowa and Kiowa-Apache and the Siouan Crow and Uto-Aztecan Shoshone. Similarly, Siouan Assiniboine was used as the lingua franca by the Siouan Mandan and Hidatsa (Minataree) near the mouth of the Knife River, while further north Algonquian Plains Cree was used by the

Siouan Hidatsa and the Algonquian Blackfoot (Mithun 1999, 322-23). To the west, Shoshone was apparently the lingua franca across the continental divide down to the Columbia River. Sign language supplemented these lingua francas, especially when these various groups came in contact with exotic languages such as French or English, so that the Euro-American perception of sign language as being the only means of communication was vastly exaggerated.

The Mandan were the pre-eminent trading middlemen with whom the Euro-American powers had to come to terms. Prior to the smallpox epidemic of 1780-81, they had flourished in seven villages along the Missouri River with a combined population of about 6,000, nearly double the contemporary population of Washington, D.C. However, the smallpox epidemic and Sioux raids reduced them to two villages of 1,500. Not to be defeated, they strategically consolidated upstream at the confluence of the Knife and Missouri Rivers with their Siouan kinsmen, the Hidatsa, and by 1804 they had recouped their primacy as trading middlemen, as nomadic plains Indians gathered annually near their villages to exchange dried meats for corn and British traders from the Assiniboine River valley exchanged guns for Spanish horses from the southwest.

Since the British had already established trade relations with the Mandan, Lewis and Clark were eager to establish similarly amicable trade relations for the United States. When they disembarked at the Mandan village of *Mitutanka* on October 26, 1804, they were greeted cordially. Lewis confided his elation to his mother that the Mandan were "the most friendly and well disposed savages that we have yet met with." Consequently, Lewis and Clark constructed Fort Mandan two miles south of *Mitutanka* on the left bank of the Missouri River, where "there was an extensive and well timbered bottom," christening it in honor of their "friendly neighbors" on Christmas 1804 (Jackson 1978, 222). Lewis and Clark had managed to achieve two prime objectives: the establishment of both an American alliance with the powerful Mandan and a zone of American sovereignty symbolized by their fort to counter further European fur trade intruders from the north.

Knowledge of a lingua franca was essential to success in establishing trade relations. On the Missouri River many lingua francas were in use, as Clark noted in the Fort Mandan Miscellany during the winter of 1804-05:

> In all the languages of the Different nations on the Missouri maney words are the Same. The Osage, Kanzas, Mahars [=Omaha (Hodge 1912, 2:1085)] & Poncars [=Poncas] speak the Same language with different pronounciatian and Some words Different. The Pania [=Ponca (Hodge 1912, 2:279)], Loups [="wolf" in French, probably Skidi Pawnee (Hodge 1912, 2:1083) and probably not the eastern Algonquian languages referred to by Mithun (1999, 329)], Republican, Pania Pickey, and Ricaras [=Arikara] Speak the same language with much [Corruption?]. The Sioux &

> Assiniboins the Same Language-The Mandans some fiew words of Several language (They lern with great facility) The *Minitarres* [=Hidatsa (Hodge 1912, 2:2091)] *Ma har ha* [=Omaha (Hodge 1912, 2:1085)] Crow & fall [=Atsina (Hodge 1912, 2:1054)] Indians Speake the Same language The Ottoes Missoures Ayuwuais [=Iowas (Hodge 1912, 1:1123)] Speake the Same Language. (Lewis and Clark 1983-2001, 3:490-91)

Therefore, Lewis and Clark anticipated that for the next leg of their journey across the Bitterroot Mountains into Shoshone territory they would need not only horses but also a Shoshone interpreter since that was the lingua franca of the continental divide. When on November 4, 1804, they met French fur trader Toussaint Charbonneau at Fort Mandan, who had two Shoshone wives whom he had purchased as captives from the Hidatsa, Clark immediately realized that these women could be the solution to their linguistic requirement. On that day Clark recorded that he interviewed "A french man by Name Chabonah, who Speaks the Big Belley [i.e., Gros Ventre, or Hidatsa] language…, he wished to hire & informed us his 2 Squars were Snake [i.e., Shoshone] Indians, we engage him to go on with us and take one of his wives to interpret the Snake language."

One was named *Sacagawea*, recorded by both Clark and Sergeant Ordway with a hard "g," which was the Hidatsa for "Bird Woman." She had been born about 1788 in a Northern Shoshone village, possibly of the Agaiduka or Salmon Eater band in the Lemhi River valley, seven miles north of Tendoy, Montana. "Bird Woman" could have referred to the bird that guards the corn fields, just as one might place an owl effigy in a garden to protect it from crows. She also had another reputed Shoshone name, *Bo-i-naiv*, which meant "Grass Woman." If so, this may have alluded to the Shoshone womanly craft of weaving buffalo grass into exquisite, colorful, and durable carrying baskets, hats, water bottles, and food containers, as well as house mat coverings (Mason 1904, 489-91; Schlick 1994; Strong et al. 1930-32, 39-40). Another reputed Shoshone name was *Sacajawea* (Shoshone because of its soft "j"), which means "travels with the boat that is pulled" or "boat launcher," according to Rees (1958). This may have been given to her by the Shoshone when she returned to them with Lewis and Clark in 1805, if they tried to interpret her Hidatsa name in terms of Shoshone. If we pair her other reputed Shoshone name *Boinaiv* with her reputed later Hidatsa name *Sacagawea*, they can be viewed as a pair with a double entendre as "grass woman, craftsperson" or "bird woman, protector of the yellow grass," i.e. corn.

The most important function for Charbonneau's wives was to barter for horses on the continental divide. The second most important function was to quell suspicions by any Indians encountered since "a woman with a party of men is a token of peace," and Sacagawea may have been slightly favored because a nursing mother provided even more assurance of the peaceful intent of the mission to wary Indians along the way. When Sacagawea was later afflicted with "a verry bad" illness that lasted from June 10 to 16, 1805, Lewis was concerned less for her health than "from the consideration of her being our only dependence for a friendly negociation with the Snake [Shoshone] Indians on whom we depend for horses to assist us in our journey from the Missouri to the Columbia river." Lewis gave her a decoction of some bark, opium, and sulphur water, and she recovered to complete her task.

The Northern Shoshonean villages were finally reached on April 7, 1805, after the Corps had plied their six smaller canoes and two larger pirogues up the Missouri River to Three Forks and set up Camp Fortunate at the head of the Jefferson branch on the Beaverhead River. As Sacagawea walked with her son in a cradleboard on her back and Charbonneau by her side, they suddenly found themselves surrounded by mounted Indians, but behind the line was a face she recognized, her old girl friend who had escaped capture. These people were her family! A council was called and Sacagawea was given the honored position of interpreter. As she turned to initiate the proceedings, she recognized the chief of the Northern Shoshones with a buffalo blanket over one shoulder as her lost brother, Cameahwait, and he in turn embraced her, promising to help her and her companions.

Lewis and Clark noted that the Shoshone "maintain a partial trade with the Spaniards, from whom they obtain many articles of cloathing and iron-mongery, but no warlike implements (Fort Mandan Miscellany, Lewis and Clark 1983-2001, 3:436), referring to the main *historic* Shoshone rendezvous located in southwestern Wyoming, where the mountain men of the mid-nineteenth century traded. There is no documentary evidence that indicates where the *proto-historic* rendezvous actually took place (Ewers 1968, 17), but it may have been closer to the Northern Shoshone rendezvous west of Cameahwait's villages. In any event, Cameahwait demonstrated that he was well versed in the calumet ceremony, which he performed for Lewis and Clark on Aug. 13, 1805 (Appleman 1975, 270), and although they did not have the corn, buffalo hides, and pemmican of the Mandan, they did have horses and a modicum of foodstuffs:

> In an old leather lodge...we were seated on green boughs and the skins of Antelopes. one of the warriors pulled up the grass in the center forming a small circle of about 2 feet in diameter the chief next produced his pipe and native tobacco and began a long ceremony of the pipe when we were requested to take off our mockersons, the Chief previously having taken off his as well as all the warriors present. this we complied with; the Chief then lit his pipe at the fire kindled in his little magic circle, and standing on the opposite side of the circle uttered a speech of several minutes in length at the conclusion of which he pointed the stem to the four cardinal points of the heavens first beginning at the East and ending with the North. He now presented his pipe to me as if desirous that I should smoke, but when I reached

my hand to receive it he drew it back and repeated the same ceremony three times, after which he pointed the stem first to the heavens then to the center of the magic circle smoked himself with three wifs and held the pipe until I took as many as I thought proper; then he held it to each of the white persons and then gave it back to be consumed by his warriors. the pipe was made of a dense semitransparent green stone very highly polished about 2 1/2 inches long and of an oval figure, the bowl being in the same direction with the stem. a small piece of burned clay is placed at the bottom of the bowl to separate the tobacco from the end of the stem and is of an irregularly rounded figure not fitting the tube perfectly close in order that the smoke may pass. this is the form of the pipe. (Lewis and Clark 1983-2001, 5:80-81)

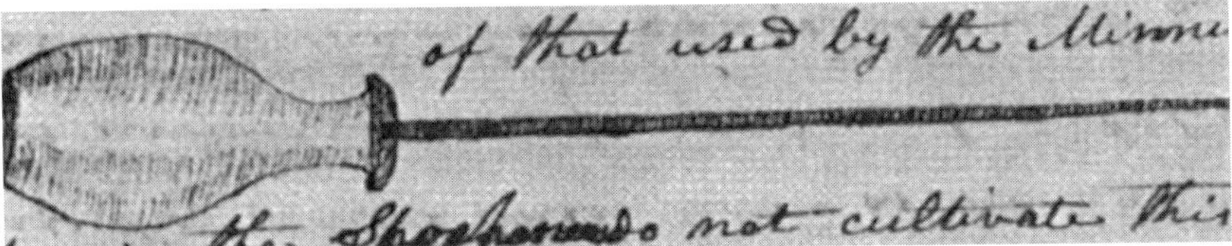

Fig. 1. Tube pipe, 2.5 inches (63.5 mm.) long, sketched by Lewis in Codex F, p. 99. Note the resin applied to the collared mouthpiece in order to secure the reed.

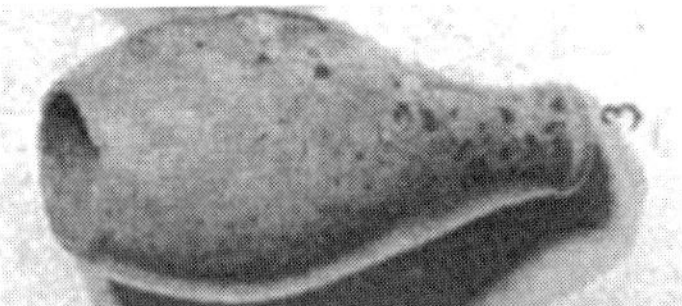

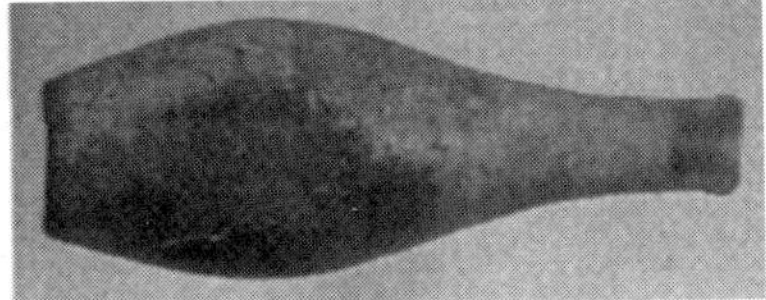

Fig. 2 (left). "Green steatite Tube [pipe], polished. Bowl somewhat enlarged by gouging. Bowl polished for about 25 mm. down the cavity. L. 63 mm. Coll. John J. Hughes, from Adams Co.", Ohio (Ohio State Museum Cat no. 1046-16, after West 1934:149, 562, pl. 41, no. 3).

Fig. 3 (right). Limestone tube pipe, 3.5 inches long (88 mm.). Found by Chris Barr in a fire pit, perhaps a grave, near Ashville, Ohio, where it had been subjected to intense heat and charcoal staining (after Converse 1994:19).

The three tube pipes illustrated above are nearly identical and have an unusual "cigar-shape" that is much smaller than most tube pipes. They also have a distinctive, enlarged bowl, a constricted stem, and a tip encircled by an expanded collar to facilitate securing a reed or bone pipe stem as Clark sketched it. The pipe that Clark recorded from the Lemhi village is nearly identical in shape, color, polish, size, and construction to the Ohio specimen from the Ohio State Museum. Other similar forms of the cigar shape have been found in Washington state (West 1934, plate 13 nos. 2-4, plate 15 no.5), but they are not nearly as close matches as those from Ohio. In the eastern United States the first cigar-shaped pipes appear in New York about 1000 B.C. and are found in Adena sites in the central Ohio River valley 800-100 B.C. (Ford 1969, 83). According to Olaf Prufer (1961, 630), it is possible that this Adena cigar-shaped tube design evolved into the early Hopewell diagnostic platform pipe *ca.* 100 B.C.-A.D. 300. The Hopewell Interaction sphere extended west into the Kansas City area, where it may have diffused along the

Missouri River and possibly to the Three Forks, Montana, area. Susan Vehik provides some data to suggest such a route (Vehik 1990, 1994), and Brad Lepper et al. (1997) provide data on the flow of Wyoming obsidian to the eastern woodlands in the Hopewell period. Hatch et al. (1990) summarize recent studies to support this east-west route of Hopewell trade.

The design of the pipe from the Shoshone village of Lemhi that Lewis so accurately sketched suggests an Hopewellian design and a possible ancient northerly trade and exchange route between the eastern woodlands and the plateau. Since the Shoshone pipe was used in the calumet ceremony, it is possible that the Hopewellian pipe was also used in a similar ceremony, suggesting a much earlier date for the calumet ceremony than has heretofore been acknowledged. This route also supports John Ewers' contention that pre-contact pedestrian trade routes provided the basis for later horse-back trade routes.

Native American east-west trade is also supported by the occurrence of other materials on the northern Plains and the Plateau, such as catlinite from Pipestone quarries in southwestern Minnesota. However, trade also flowed from the Pacific coast as well. Pacific coast marine shells, *Olivella* and *Dentalium*, have been excavated at Wilson butte cave in south-central Idaho (Borden 1962, 582) as well as the Middle Missouri Huff village dating to the mid-1400s. This establishes a route from the Columbia River near the Dalles to the northern Plains. Furthermore, trade also flowed from the south as well. Ann Ramenofsky (1987, 132) found that the vectors of the 1780-81 smallpox epidemic emanated from Mexico, suggesting a route whereby maize and conch shells found their way from Mexico to the horticultural Plains Woodland villages before the Mandan entered the area and usurped this trade (Jelks 1962, 71).

When Cameahwait, Sacagawea's brother, vowed to provide the expedition with horses and guides to continue the journey across the Bitterroot Mountains and through the Salmon River country to the Columbia River, he acknowledged the ancient east-west trade route that had been used by Native American pedestrians for centuries. To Euro-Americans, horses were paramount to the success of the mission. Therefore, when Cameahwait initiated plans for a winter buffalo hunt, Lewis and Clark intervened because this would have deprived them of the horses that they desperately needed to cross the mountains. After much cajoling, Cameahwait upheld his word to delay the hunt until the Corps had their horses and were on their way.

Knowledge of the route to the Columbia River was essential to the Shoshone, as Sacagawea demonstrated as the expedition's guide and interpreter. Her uncanny familiarity with the route even as a nursing mother was admired by Lewis, who secured a horse for her even though Charbonneau regarded it a disgrace for his wife to ride while he walked.

The eastern perimeter of Great Dalles trade center was reached by the Corps on October 22, 1805, at Celilo Falls, near Wishram, Klickat County, Washington, and Celilo, Wasco County, Oregon, and extended for 12 miles downstream,[1] amidst rushing rapids and warm dry winds. Instead of buffalo as the chief animal and maize as the chief grain, salmon was the prized fish and "*wappatoo*" (*Saggitaria variabilis*), or camas root, was the prized vegetable root, and both were traded in three seasonal rendezvous, of which the one in September and October was the largest. Although Lewis and Clark were in time to witness only the last two weeks of the fall rendezvous, even so, Clark estimated that there were 10,000 pounds of dried salmon stored at the Wishram village of Nixluidix, which translated as "the trading place" (Lewis and Clark 1983-2001, 5:335), and Clark called it a "great mart of trade" (Jackson 1978, 2:527). At the peak of trading some three weeks earlier, this trade center attracted some 3,000 Indians, according to Alexander Ross (1923, 127-128), who visited the area soon after Lewis and Clark. The Chinookan bands of the Wishram and Wasco on the north and south banks of the Columbia, respectively, acted as the trade middlemen with the nearby Yakima and Tenino and the more distant Umatilla, Walula, and Nez Perce.

This primary trade center had ancient origins, based on archaeological excavations, as groups from the Plains, the Northwest Coast, and the Plateau traded, among other commodities, durable obsidian and marine shell for perishable dried salmon and buffalo-grass basketry. This distinctive basketry, in its variety of shapes and sizes, embodied images of mythic figures that are also found in prehistoric rock art panels along the Columbia River opposite the modern town of Roosevelt and the mouth of the John Day River. The Corps' canoes evidently passed by these petroglyphs without comment (Keyser 1994).

The Great Dalles trade center was the scene of social activities that included the calumet, giving gifts, gambling, and ceremonial exchanges between the sexes, which Alexander Ross alluded to when he noted that it "is the great emporium or mart of the Columbia and the general theatre of gambling and roguery" with as many as 3,000 in attendance (Ross 1923, 127-128).

On October 24, 1805, Clark recorded the visit by "The principal Chief from the Nation below with Several of his men [which] afforded us a favourable opportunity of bringing about a Piece and good understanding between this chief and his people and the two Chiefs who accompanied us which we have the Satisfaction to Say we have accomplished....gave this Great Chief a Medal and Some other articles, of which he was much pleased. [Pierre Cruzatte] played the violin and the men danced which delighted the natives, who shew every civility toward us. we smoked [the calumet] with those people until late at night, when everyone retired to rest" (Lewis and

Clark 1983-2001,5:335-336). On October 25, 1805, Lewis and Clark "met with our two old [Nez Perce] Chiefs who had been to a village below to smoke a friendly pipe, and at this place they met the Chief....we landed to Smoke a pipe with this Chief whome we found to be a bold pleasing looking man of about 50 years of age in a war jacket a cap Legins & mockersons. he gave us some meat of which he had but little....we gave this Chief a Medal, &c. a parting smoke with our two faithful friends..." (Lewis and Clark 1983-2001, 5:338-39). Then on Oct. 26, 1805, the Corps again entertained "in the evening two Chiefs and 15 men....those Chiefs proved to be the two Principal Chiefs of the [Wishram and Wasco] tribes above at the [Celilo] falls....we gave each Chief a Meadal of the Small Size a red silk handkerchief, arm band, Knife & a piece of Paint, and acknowledged them as chiefs; [to...son {of the first} a Piece of riben tied to a tin gorget and 2 hams of Venison (5:341)] as we thought it necessary to treat those people verry friendly & ingratiate our Selves with them, to insure us a kind & friendly reception on our return....[Pierre Cruzatte] Played on the violin, which pleased those natives exceedingly (Lewis and Clark 1983-2001, 5:342-43).

However, for all the Chinooks' apparent similarities with the Mandan and Hidatsa social institutions, Lewis and Clark could not comprehend the intention of what they perceived to be the Chinook habit of stealing. This was perplexing, because for miles along the Columbia River lay Chinook private property in the form of piles of dried salmon. How was it that the Chinook apparently *deliberately* appropriated items from the stores of the Corps. How was this to be explained? The Chinook did not consider this appropriation from the Corps as wanton theft, because they regarded the taking of an article from what seemed to be an endless supply inoffensive, and furthermore, the Corps were intruders into their sovereign territory so that permission to descend the Columbia River entailed due payment, which they routinely exacted (Ronda 1984, 172). Taking of tribute was a symbolic gesture of establishing sovereignty over intruders, but Lewis and Clark, who operated from a Judaeo-Christian framework and from a position of perceived cultural superiority, could not possibly understand this custom, which was intensified when Clark's ceremonial calumet tomahawk was taken by a Skilloot in November 1805. He summarily ordered sentries to shoot would-be looters on sight, but from the point of view of the Chinook, this was an overt challenge and a violation of their sovereignty.

To compound matters, gone were the days of the friendly attitude that Lewis and Clark and their men had displayed to the Mandan and Hidatsa women in sexual relations, ceremonial and otherwise. Instead of condoning relations between the Corps and Chinook women, Lewis and Clark now colored their perceptions with a racial tinge, regarding Chinook women as prostitutes who sold their "badly clad and illy made" bodies for trinkets. Now they felt trapped in a land of theft and subterfuge in which native traders demanded high prices for goods that Lewis and Clark had earlier traded for trinkets. This trade center had proved to be a painful reminder that they were, indeed, intruders in a foreign, sovereign nation that was not about to capitulate for a trinket or a peace medal.

Therefore, the encounters of Lewis and Clark with the two different forms of trade and exchange institutions across the Trans-Mississippi West, the trade center and rendezvous, provided a context for U.S. interaction with specific bands for the next half century, a context that was conditioned by different degrees of sociability. Those bands who were accorded a place of high sociability (Mandan, Shoshone) were regarded as allies, but those whose customs were either not understood and deemed fickle (Chinook) or whose former political allegiances were deemed unreliable (Dakota) were considered as hostile. Lewis and Clark's assessment of these groups, for better or worse, helped establish the path of U.S.-Indian relations as they would unfold for the next half-century and beyond.

Fulfillment of Jefferson's Expectations

Tim S. Beck and Brad Tennant

The exploration of the American West was not a novel consideration for Thomas Jefferson when he thought of sending Lewis and Clark west. In fact, Jefferson contemplated explorations into the western regions of North America on several occasions even before he became president of the United States. As his interest in the West grew, so did his plans and objectives for an American expedition to explore this mysterious land. His rise to the American presidency and the windfall purchase of the Louisiana Territory allowed Jefferson to solidify his plans for an expedition. Consequently, the task of fulfilling Jefferson's expectations would fall upon the shoulders of the Lewis and Clark Expedition.

In 1783, Jefferson became concerned about the potential British expansion into North America. At this point, he attempted to enlist the services of the American Revolutionary War hero George Rogers Clark in a privately financed exploration. Upon learning that the British were financing an exploration of the lands west of the Mississippi River, Jefferson expressed his concern to General Clark in a letter dated 4 December 1783. In this letter, Jefferson was skeptical of the stated intentions of the British to explore the region just for the sake of knowledge and feared that their real motive was "colonising into that quarter." As a result, Jefferson asked Clark if he would be interested in leading an American expedition to similarly "search that country." Although Clark agreed with Jefferson on the need for such an expedition, he declined the offer to serve as its leader, and plans were temporarily postponed.[1]

With perhaps the same intentions as the British, the French also planned an expedition to the Pacific Northwest. Although the French expedition was declared to be scientific in nature, Jefferson was fearful of the French establishing commercial connections and viewing the area with visions of colonization. In 1786, Jefferson, perhaps feeling desperate because America's expansionist hopes were slipping away, embraced the somewhat eccentric plan of one John Ledyard. Ledyard's plan was to proceed east from Europe through Russia to the east coast of Siberia, cross the Bering Strait to Alaska, and then walk from the Pacific Coast to the Mississippi River, eventually entering the nation's capital city to boldly report on the nature of his findings. While Ledyard had high aspirations for completing his route as planned, his adventure ended abruptly when Catherine the Great had him arrested in Siberia.[2]

Jefferson's third attempt to explore the American West came in 1793 when French botanist Andre Michaux was contracted for an expedition to "seek for and pursue that route which shall form the shortest and most convenient communication between the higher parts of the Missouri and the Pacific Ocean." Michaux's effort was brought to a sudden end near the Ohio River when Jefferson learned that Michaux was working as a French agent.[3]

With each planned expedition, it became increasingly apparent what expectations Jefferson had in mind. Over the years, Jefferson visited with experts in many fields whose advice and input he openly received. This is especially obvious in the 1793 contractual agreement between then Secretary of State Jefferson and his colleagues at the American Philosophical Society and Michaux. Dated 22 January 1793, the agreement stated:

> Whereas Andrew Michaux, a native of France, and inhabitant of the U.S. hath undertaken to explore the interior country of North America, from the Mississippi along the Missouri and Westwardly to the Pacific ocean, or in such other direction as shall be advised by the American Philosophical society, and on his return to communicate to the said society the information he shall have acquired of the geography of the said country, it's inhabitants, soil, climate, animals, vegetables & minerals, & other circumstances of note....[4]

In 1803, undaunted by the failure of his three previous undertakings, Jefferson, as the president of the United States, once again attempted to secure an expedition to the West. On 18 January 1803, Jefferson delivered a confidential message to the members of the United States Senate and House of Representatives officially requesting $2,500 for an expedition to the Pacific Ocean.[5] While awaiting approval of his request, Jefferson began to make plans in earnest for his long-desired expedition into the American West. Shortly after delivering his message to Congress, Jefferson began communicating with a number of scholars who shared his enlightened curiosity. It was through these communications that Jefferson's final instructions to Lewis were developed.

In a letter to Bernard Lacepede, a noted French naturalist who was living in Philadelphia at the time, Jefferson wrote of the future expedition's objectives. He not only talked of gaining knowledge about the West's geography, population, natural history, soil, and climatic conditions, but he also specifically mentioned hopes of gaining further information regarding such intriguing creatures as the mammoth, the Megatherium (giant ground sloth), and the Megalonyx (grizzly bear). Jefferson's interest in such mammals, whether extinct or not, reflected his newfound curiosity about mammalian paleontology, which was then emerging as a completely new field in science.[6]

It was of course vital to the success of the expedition that Meriwether Lewis be able to fulfill Jefferson's expectations in many fields of study. On this point, Jefferson was confident that Lewis was indeed the man for the job. On 27 February 1803, Jefferson wrote to Benjamin Smith Barton, a noted

Philadelphia naturalist and medical doctor, reiterating his confidence in Lewis's ability to lead the expedition. He also asked Barton to prepare a list of questions for Lewis in the areas of botany, zoology, and American Indian history that he thought "worthy of inquiry and observation." Barton was to have his notes prepared and to share them with Lewis upon Lewis's arrival in Philadelphia. A similar letter was sent on 28 February to Caspar Wistar, an anatomy professor at the University of Pennsylvania. Jefferson once again asked the favor of writing out any information that might assist Lewis in meeting Jefferson's ever growing list of objectives.[7]

A third letter was written to Dr. Benjamin Rush, a well-known physician and professor of medicine at the University of Pennsylvania. Rush agreed to share his medical training with Lewis, and he also prepared a list of questions regarding medical and ethnographic information he wished Lewis to answer during the expedition.[8]

Because the above letters were dated the latter part of February, which was before the purchase of Louisiana had been completed, Jefferson asked that the matter be kept confidential, as he was still planning a rather secretive expedition. In all likelihood, however, Jefferson's growing excitement over the expedition was causing it to be a topic of conversation in many political and scientific circles.

During the time that Jefferson was asking experts to help prepare Lewis, he was also making arrangements to procure passports for the expedition from the British and the French. The British passport stated that the expedition was to be "undertaken with a scientific motive only." This broad objective was repeated in Lewis's French passport, which stated that Captain Meriwether Lewis was "setting out on a voyage of discovery with the purpose of exploring the Missouri river and the western regions of the Northern Continent." Furthermore, the passport explained that "Lewis has no purpose other than the above,...his voyage being of a purely scientific nature, and in its end of equal interest to all the civilized world."[9]

As the groundwork was being laid for the expedition, Jefferson's instructions were being finalized. On 20 June 1803, Jefferson forwarded his instructions to Lewis. By the time the news of the Louisiana Purchase arrived on 4 July 1803, the expedition's objectives were well established. Foremost among his intentions was to gain a geographic perspective of the territory:

> The object of your mission is to explore the Missouri river, & such principal stream of it, as...may offer the most direct & practicable water communication across this continent for the purposes of commerce.[10]

The annexation of Louisiana Territory doubled the size of the young United States; however, its vast expanses were largely unknown. Lewis and Clark would be the first to describe and map in detail the void that was the Louisiana Territory and the Pacific Northwest.

The main responsibility for recording distances and mapping the region fell into the hands of the capable but untrained cartographer William Clark, who was asked by Lewis to assist him in leading the expedition. Clark's use of the technique of dead reckoning, that is, estimating the distance from one point to another, was remarkably accurate. For example, his reckoning of the distance from St. Louis to the Mandan villages at 1,400 miles was short a mere one hundred miles.[11]

While spending the winter of 1804-05 at Fort Mandan, Clark completed a large map he titled a "Connection of the Countrey." Based on his own recordings and observations as well as a wealth of knowledge supplied by traders and Indians, Clark produced what many geographers consider to be one of the most important maps made during the expedition. In addition to geographic features, Clark also included demographic information on the locations of significant Indian tribes and a census of native populations.[12]

Lewis's own geographic contribution included his "Summary View of the Rivers and Creeks which discharge themselves into the Missouri." In accordance with Jefferson's objective to explore the Missouri River, Lewis's summary included a detailed study of the principal waterways between St. Louis and the continental divide.[13]

In retrospect, Lewis and Clark did indeed find "the most direct and practicable water communication" across the continent although it certainly was not the Northwest Passage that Jefferson had hoped. In addition, they

- discovered that two mountain systems, the Rockies and the Cascade Range, separated the upper reaches of the Missouri River from the Pacific Ocean;
- disproved the mistaken idea of a southwestward flowing Missouri River;
- detailed the previous void with extensive physiographic descriptions of Louisiana Territory and beyond; and, in the process,[14]
- named and mapped hundreds of geographic features. Today, geographic places named for Lewis and Clark rank among the most common in America. Furthermore, of the thirty-three individuals who traveled from Fort Mandan to the Pacific coast, each person's name was given to at least one physical feature. Fifteen names were used twice, while Lewis's name was used three times and Clark's four.[15]

While Lewis and Clark named a number of geographic places, many of these already bore names given by the native peoples of the regions. Herein lies a second of Jefferson's major objectives—to take notes on the people encountered along the way. The tribes of the West were not as well known as Jefferson desired. Therefore, he gave Lewis the following instructions:

> The commerce which may be carried on with the people inhabiting the line you will pursue, renders a knolege of those people important. You will therefore endeavor to make yourself acquainted...with the names of the nations & their numbers.[16]

The Corps of Discovery encountered nearly fifty tribes, including such important ones as the Mandan, Shoshone, Flathead, Nez Perce, Pawnee, Clatsop, and the Sioux. During the preliminary planning stages of the expedition, President Jefferson, Dr. Rush, and others submitted a detailed list of questions regarding ethnological data. They covered a wide array of topics including the tribes' physical history, customs, language, and economic activities.[17]

Of these tribes, Jefferson gave Lewis specific instructions pertaining to one particular band, the Teton Sioux. Jefferson told Lewis, "On that nation, we wish most particularly to make a favorable impression, because of their immense power."[18] Lewis and Clark were made well aware of the Teton's power and role in controlling trade up the Missouri River. Later, after spending four days with the Teton and averting a disastrous end to the expedition, Clark characterized the Teton as "the vilest miscreants of the savage race, and must ever remain the pirates of the Missouri."[19] Nonetheless, true to Jefferson's instructions, Lewis and Clark came away from the encounter with many notes regarding the Teton's way of life.

Despite being faced with literally dozens of questions to answer and confusing language barriers, Lewis and Clark made many notable contributions to American ethnography. Today they are credited with:

- initiating formal relations between the United States government and the tribes of the Missouri Valley, Rocky Mountains, and the Columbia watershed;
- being the first to provide detailed physical descriptions of tribes existing in the three cultural areas of the West—the Plains, Plateau, and Northwest Coast;
- conducting the first language studies of at least six linguistic groups including Siouan, Shoshonean , and Chinookan; and
- providing the basis for an understanding of the intertribal trade network of the upper Missouri valley.[20]

Lewis and Clark rightfully deserve a tremendous amount of credit for their work in American Indian studies conducted during the journey. And yet, in considering their contributions, they must be viewed from three perspectives. The first concerns what they saw and fully comprehended. In this respect, Lewis and Clark described in detail cultural elements such as housing, food, clothing, and weapons. On the other hand, there were many customs and practices they witnessed and described but did not fully comprehend. Many of the observations recorded in this category involved religious practices that were simply too foreign for them to understand (e.g., the Mandan buffalo-calling ceremony). Finally, there were many cultural events that they simply did not see first hand; therefore, they were unable to note them in their journals, for example, certain seasonal events such as trade fairs and religious practices that were kept private from outsiders.[21] Regardless of these shortcomings in some of their observations, Lewis and Clark's overall success in meeting one of Jefferson's foremost objectives is certainly one of their major accomplishments.

In accordance with the scientific theme of the Corps of Discovery, Meriwether Lewis contributed greatly to the development of American zoology and botany. Included among Jefferson's instructions to Lewis was the directive to observe "other objects worthy of notice [such as] vegetable productions [and] the animals of the country generally, & especially those not known in the U.S." Using the training gained during the time spent in Philadelphia, Lewis made detailed observations of 122 species and subspecies of animals and 178 plants never before recorded.[22] These included such namesakes of the explorers as Lewis's Woodpecker and Clark's Nutcracker as well as two plant species named *Lewisia* and *Clarkia*.[23]

The following journal entries represent a small sampling of some of the animals first recorded by members of the expedition.

> Discovered a Village of Small animals that burrow in the gro…covers about 4 acrs of Ground…and Contains great numbers of holes on the top of which those little animals Set erect, make a Whistleing noise and whin allarmed Slip into their hole…those animals are Called by the french Petite Chien.
>
> —*William Clark's journal entry on prairie dogs*[24]

> [Clark] had killed a curious annimil… The legs like a Deer, feet like a Goat; horns like a Goat, only forked…Such an animil was never yet known in U.S. States.
>
> —*John Ordway's journal entry on the antelope*[25]

> John Shields…killed a verry large white rabbit or haire…of a different description of any one ever yet seen in the States.
>
> —*John Ordway's journal entry on the white-tailed jackrabbit*[26]

> George Drewyer killed a prairie woolf. Some larger than a fox; long teeth & of a different description from any in the States …. The Bones of the woolf was taken apart and Saved, as well as the Skin…in order to send back to the States next Spring, with the other curiousities we have.
>
> —*John Ordway's journal entry on the coyote*[27]

> We saw also many tracks of bear of enormous size …. We have not as yet seen one of these anamals, tho' their tracks are so abundant and recent. The men as well as ourselves are anxious to meet with some of these bear. [After meeting several members of this ferocious species, Lewis ironically expresses the company's respect for this beast.]
>
> I find that the curiossity of our party is pretty well satisfyed with rispect to this anamal.
>
> —*Meriwether Lewis's journal entries on the grizzly bear*[28]

After spending the winter of 1804-05 at Fort Mandan, Lewis and Clark prepared to ship their written report, Clark's map, and various animal, plant, and mineral specimens by keelboat back to St. Louis and eventually to President Jefferson. Included in this shipment were the skeletons or hides of antelope, squirrels, a weasel, coyote, badger, fox, and jackrabbit and the horns of elk, mule deer, and bighorn sheep. In addition, live specimens of a prairie dog, a grouse hen, and four magpies were sent back to Jefferson. Only the prairie dog and one magpie actually survived the trip.[29]

In the area of botany, Lewis collected, preserved, and returned over 240 plant specimens gathered during the course of the expedition, including the ragged robin (*Clarkia pulchella*), bitterroot (Lewisia *rediviva*), lodgepole pine, ponderosa pine, and prairie turnip.[30] Today, over 200 of these specimens can still be found at the Lewis and Clark Herbarium in Philadelphia's Academy of Natural Sciences. Other highlights of Lewis's contributions to zoology and botany include:

- his extension of the ranges of animals and plants not known to exist west of the Mississippi;
- the first written descriptions of a variety of fish, reptiles, birds, and mammals resulting in the development of American zoology; and
- descriptions of how various plants were used by American Indians both nutritionally and medicinally.[31]

Considering the fact that Jefferson was often criticized for not appointing a trained naturalist to lead such a scientific venture, Lewis's remarkable success in each of these areas certainly speaks for itself.

In the final analysis, did Lewis and Clark in fact fulfill Jefferson's expectations? In Lewis's letter to Jefferson dated 23 September 1806 from St. Louis, Lewis reported that they successfully carried out Jefferson's orders. By exploring the interior of the country, Lewis and Clark found the most practical route to the Pacific coast, thereby accomplishing Jefferson's main objective. Although Lewis attempted to sound positive, he later wrote in the same letter that the route was not what was ideally anticipated. Nonetheless, Lewis did highlight some of the expedition's major successes.[32]

It is true that Lewis and Clark did not discover a true Northwest Passage as hoped; however, their real discovery was the land itself. A wealth of knowledge was acquired during the expedition that broadened the scope of geography, geology, ethnography, botany, and zoology in the American West. In short, Lewis and Clark not only fulfilled Jefferson's expectations, but they exceeded them, thus establishing the Corps of Discovery as one of the most ambitious and successful undertakings in American and world history. Without question, the legacy of Lewis and Clark is their successful fulfillment of Jefferson's expectations.

The Lewis and Clark Expedition Now: Contemporary Controversies and Critical Approaches

Meriwether Lewis and His Son: The Claim of Joseph DeSomet Lewis and the Problem of History

Harry F. Thompson

Sixty-eight years after the Corps of Discovery ascended the Missouri River through the Dakotas, a Yankton (or possibly Teton) Sioux man, claiming to be the son of Meriwether Lewis, was baptized at St. Philip the Deacon Chapel, White Swan, Dakota Territory. As recorded in the Yankton Mission registers of the Diocese of South Dakota (Episcopal), Joseph DeSomet Lewis (also spelled "DeSomit" in the register) and his wife, Annie Tamakoce, their sons, Francis Saswena Lewis (age twenty-one) and Joseph Wanikiya Lewis (age nineteen), and two of their grandchildren by another son, John DeSomit Lewis, presented themselves for baptism on June 18, 1872.[1] Joseph DeSomet Lewis (age sixty-eight), gave as his place of birth Yankton Agency, his father's name as "Capt. Meriwether Lewis (of Lewis & Clarke's Exp.)," and his mother's name as "Winona." Annie (no age indicated) gave "Ft. Pierre, Dakota" as her birthplace and the names of her parents as Hunkanwicasa and Wisdo.[2]

No biographer of Meriwether Lewis credits or even acknowledges the assertion of Joseph DeSomet Lewis (hereafter called "DeSomet") regarding his paternity, yet, today, along the Missouri River that Lewis and Clark traversed two centuries ago, live several people who claim direct descent from the leader of America's most famous expedition. Without arguing either for or against the claim of DeSomet and his descendants, an examination of the conflicting evidence in this matter serves as a way to consider how we write history. It may also suggest ways to negotiate the limits of research protocols, which can sometimes be exclusionary and self-imposed. Confronted, on the one hand, by DeSomet's claim in the Episcopal church registers and the claims of his descendants, and, on the other, by the scarcity of corroborating evidence, the historian faces a vexing problem concerning one of the nation's defining events. Use of the parish registers as "evidence" of paternity raises fundamental questions about the nature of documentary, or source-based, history.

Baptism record of Joseph DeSomet Lewis and his family, Yankton Mission Register, Volume 1. Courtesy Diocese of South Dakota (Episcopal) Archives, Center for Western Studies, Augustana College, Sioux Falls, South Dakota.

Since the early nineteenth century, documents have been the principal tool by which we have constructed our understanding of the past. As historian James Wilkinson notes, the definition of what constitutes acceptable historical evidence has been altered over time to include new forms:

> Yet as the breadth of the potential evidence has grown, so have doubts about its interpretation....meanings remain elusive, conferred by the interpreter rather than imposed by the evidence. Never have historians had so much evidence at their disposal; never has there been so much mistrust about what the evidence shows. How do the multiple pieces of the past cohere?[3]

To begin to answer these questions, we must examine the conventional evidence that might corroborate or at least lend credibility to Joseph DeSomet's claim that Meriwether Lewis was his father.

The DeSomet Family

Joseph DeSomet's grave is located on the western bank of the Missouri River in St. Alban's Cemetery at Fort Hale, on the Lower Brule Reservation. There are two markers identifying the grave, the inscriptions on which read: "Joseph 'DeSmet' Lewis, 1805-1889" (copper plate) and "Joseph Lewis, 'DeSmet,' 1805-1889, son of Meriwether Lewis of the Famed Lewis & Clark Expedition" (stone marker).[4] In all, a dozen descendants of DeSomet, and possibly Lewis, are buried at St. Alban's, including his son, John DeSmet, John's wife, Henrietta, and grandson, Mose DeSmet.[5] Mose DeSmet was born in 1891 at Fort Hale, where his father was a civilian employee of the fort and subsequently caretaker of the buildings after the army abandoned the fort.[6] One of the fort buildings later became the DeSmet residence. DeSmith Creek, which runs just below Fort Hale, is believed to have been named after Joseph DeSmet.[7] Granddaughter Amy DeSmet Carpenter was responsible for erecting Joseph's gravestone in St. Alban's Cemetery.[8]

In addition, the standard history of the county in which DeSomet's descendants live, *Early Settlers in Lyman County*, identifies Mamie DeSmet Thompson and Amy DeSmet Carpenter as the "great-great-granddaughters [great-granddaughters]" of "Merriwether Lewis" and their grandfather as the son of "Merriwhether [*sic*] Lewis."[9] The various spellings of the DeSomet name are puzzling, but based on an interview with Mose DeSmet, historian Merrill J. Mattes suggests that the "DeSmet" name is derived from Joseph DeSomet having been baptized by the Belgian priest Father Jean Pierre DeSmet around 1867.[10] Father DeSmet visited the Dakotas fourteen times between 1839 and 1870, ministering to traders, trappers, and soldiers, and was especially concerned with the mixed-bloods on the Upper Missouri.[11]

Apart from the parish registers and the testimony of his family, what do we know of Joseph DeSomet? He, or at least someone with his last name, appears in the journals of topographical engineer Lt. G. K. Warren, whose

Courtesy Mikkelsen Library, Augustana College

The gate to St. Alban's Cemetery and St. Alban's Church at Fort Hale, on the Lower Brule Reservation, located near the site where Lewis and Clark camped on September 16-17, 1804.

Photo by Gil Johnsson

Photo by Louis Leichtnam, courtesy of Lois Boe

Courtesty of Mikkelsen Library, Augustana College

The burial site for Joseph Lewis in St. Alban's Cemetery is marked with both a granite headstone and a copper plate.

three field surveys for the U.S. Army, conducted in the years 1855, 1856, and 1857, preliminary to the construction of a transcontinental railroad, produced what John L. Allen calls a "'master map' of the American West."[12] Warren drew this map based upon his own field surveys, but he also asked to have maps drawn for him by the mountain men, natives, and mixed-bloods whom he employed as guides. Among the guides who accompanied Warren on the survey expeditions, such as Jim Bridger, Alexander Culbertson, Colin Campbell, and Spotted Tail, was a man called Michael DeSomet. We can surmise that Michael DeSomet and Joseph DeSomet were the same individual because of the identifying description that Warren's assistant, W. H. Hutton, recorded in his report on the 1856 expedition. He wrote that Michael was a "hunter (a half breed Sioux who says that his father was *Lewis & Clarke* [*sic*])."[13]

In his "Survey of Military Reserve at Fort Pierre," dated August 7, 1855, Warren wrote to Major O. F. Winship that his party consisted of "six experienced men of the country, mostly half-breed Sioux, and Mr. Carrey and myself."[14] Warren specifically acknowledges the assistance of Michael DeSomet among those with whom he had "the benefit of consultation" for "information about portions of the country I have not visited."[15] DeSomet, in fact, played an important role in Warren's cartographic success.

In his journal for 1855, Warren explains how DeSomet came to join the expedition. Having reached Fort Pierre on July 16, 1855, Warren gave ten dollars to his assistant, Paul Carrey, to persuade some of the men near the fort to join the team for its journey, first to the Cheyenne River and then to Fort Kearney. The men refused. Carrey's second recruiting attempt—this time offering more money-was successful, for Warren writes in his journal entry for July 30 that the "men engaged were Benjamin Cadotte, Colime Larrive Lamont & Desomet. Campell & Descoteaux were engaged before."[16] Throughout his 1855 journal, Warren makes frequent reference to the "Indian guide" DeSomet.[17] We know, for example, that DeSomet worked closely with Carrey while the latter took measurements of the White River; that he identified the Calamus Creek (a branch of the Loup River); and, perhaps most important, made a map at Warren's behest of "Sioux Country" (the Missouri River from the Niobrara to the Powder River).[18] As William H. Goetzmann observes in *Army Exploration in the American West, 1803-1863*, the maps drawn by such guides as DeSomet "represented knowledge gained through experience and the sixth sense developed by these trappers which had kept them alive in that hostile country as late as 1855."[19]

On August 22, when Warren's survey team met up with General William Harney, who was in pursuit of the Brulé Sioux involved in the so-called Grattan Massacre, an attack upon the village of Conquering Bear in Wyoming in 1854 by troops under the command of Lieutenant John L. Grattan,

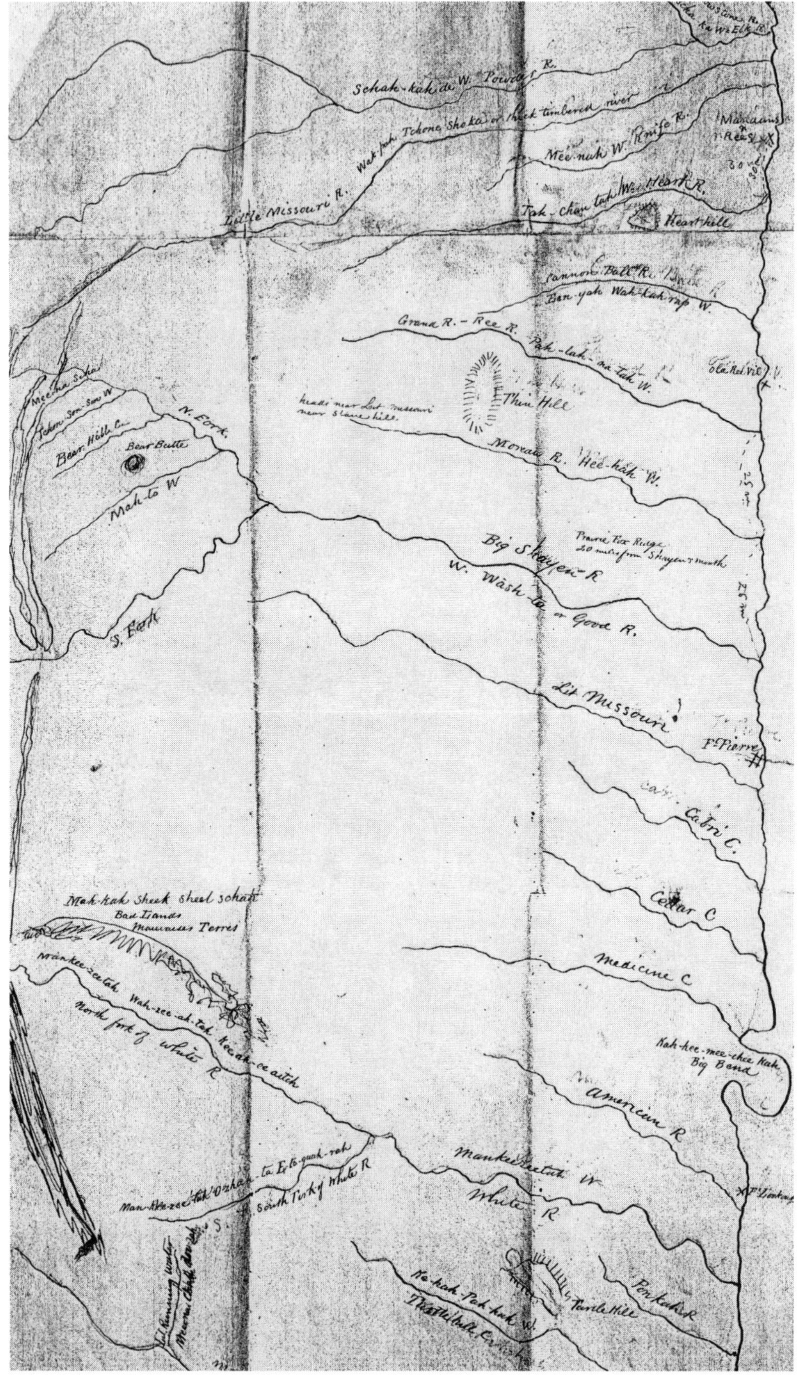

DeSomet Map of "Sioux Country," showing the Missouri River and its tributaries on the west, made by Joseph Lewis at the request of Lieutenant Warren, circa 1855. Courtesy G. K. Warren Papers, New York State Library, Albany, New York.

DeSomet was hired-probably as a hunter—by the quartermaster at $50 per month but soon "had a most narrow escape with his life."[20] Carrying Warren's shotgun during Harney's attack at Blue Water Creek, DeSomet was mistaken by the infantry for the enemy and "charged upon."[21] Warren explains that DeSomet "laid down the gun to show he was a friend (he could not speak English) and the arrival of some one who knew him saved his life."[22]

In preparation for Warren's 1856 expedition along the Yellowstone River, DeSomet was again hired at Fort Pierre, to begin his duties on July 1, but at half the salary of Colin Campbell, who was paid $100 per month as one of the guides, along with Jim Bridger. On this expedition, DeSomet's duties seemed to be principally those of a hunter, and, indeed, Hutton includes in his report for August 6 a dramatic account of a "Buffalo Run" at Charbonneau's Creek, in which DeSomet figures prominently.[23] Hutton's account for September 1 records the survey party's descent of the Missouri River: "For a week, we floated slowly down stream, Mr. Warren & Bridger & Desomet, hunting every point, & bringing in game in abundance."[24] Since no entries in Warren's 1857 journal mention DeSomet, we might reasonably conclude that the guide did not accompany Warren on his third expedition, which surveyed the valleys of Nebraska's Loup and Niobrara Rivers and entered into the Black Hills on the first military expedition.

DeSomet's involvement in events on the plains seems not to have begun with assisting Warren's expedition, however. In his notes to Warren's journals, James A. Hanson writes that DeSomet "apparently was the man who hauled trade goods from Ft. Pierre to the upper White River in 1837....Joseph Desomette was listed in the surviving Ft. Pierre accounts (1842-1848) in the Chouteau Accounts."[25]

In addition to DeSomet's name appearing in these accounts and in records relating to fur-trading activities at Fort Pierre in the 1830s and 1840s, it also appears, albeit in yet another variant, in the census of 1860. Its appearance there perhaps raises more questions than it resolves. In the 1860 census, a "Michael Derzannette" and family are listed as residents of Yankton Indian Agency (also known as Greenwood Agency), which had been established in 1858 by the Treaty of Washington. As a regional transportation center, the agency attracted permanent mission work, which was begun in 1869 by John P. Williamson under the American Board of Commissioners for Foreign Missions and by the Reverend Joseph Cook of the Episcopal Church.[26] Cook also opened the St. Philip the Deacon Chapel where he baptized DeSomet and his family in 1872. In the 1860 census record, DeSomet ("Derzannette") gives his age as fifty-eight, which does not accord with the age of sixty-eight that he gives in the parish registers twelve years later. Nevertheless, DeSomet's identity and presence in the region can be established with some degree of certainty.

The Reverend Joseph W. Cook (1836-1902) was a missionary at the Yankton Mission, Greenwood, Dakota Territory, 1870-1902; he officiated at the Lewis family baptisms recorded on June 18, 1872. Courtesy Diocese of South Dakota (Episcopal) Archives, Center for Western Studies, Augustana College, Sioux Falls, South Dakota.

Yankton Mission, Greenwood, circa 1886. Courtesy Diocese of South Dakota (Episcopal) Archives, Center for Western Studies, Augustana College, Sioux Falls, South Dakota.

do 5 Joseph Lewis (De Smet) 70
Annie Lewis Tamakoce)

Capt. Meriwether Lewis of Lewis & Clark's Exp.
Winona
Wm J. Cleveland. Mrs. Wm J. Cleveland.

Marriage record of Joseph Lewis and Annie Tamakoce Lewis, Yankton Mission Register, Volume II. Courtesy Diocese of South Dakota (Episcopal) Archives, Center for Western Studies, Augustana College, Sioux Falls, South Dakota.

Jefferson's Instructions to the Lewis and Clark Expedition

Before considering the evidence of Meriwether Lewis's paternity as found in the various journals of the Corps of Discovery, it is useful to examine the context in which the members of the expedition, particularly Lewis, had undertaken their mission. Jefferson's letters of June 20, 1803, and January 22, 1804, to Lewis, giving specific instructions regarding indigenous peoples, reveals three especially noteworthy points about Jefferson's conception of the expedition relative to native peoples. First, in contrast to the way it was later construed by Jefferson and others, the expedition was not originally intended as a scientific endeavor but as a reconnaissance mission to ascertain the commercial potential of the Louisiana Territory. Jefferson's primary goal was to learn what possible water route might exist between the Missouri River and the Pacific Ocean. Although Jefferson was personally curious about indigenous peoples, his interest in the expedition's scientific accomplishments was subordinate to his concern for the expedition's commercial success, which in turn depended on friendly relations with the native inhabitants. James P. Ronda has noted, "With its tangle of economic, military, and imperial interests, the Teton Sioux negotiation was perhaps the most demanding piece of Indian diplomacy assigned to Lewis and Clark."[27] Jefferson instructs Lewis to make friends with the natives so as to enhance the possibility of advantageous commerce between the two trading partners:

> In all your intercourse with the natives, treat them in the most friendly & conciliatory manner which their own conduct will admit; allay all jealousies as to the object of your journey, satisfy them of it's [*sic*] innocence, make them acquainted with the position, extent, character, peaceable & commercial dispositions of the U.S.[,] of our wish to be neighborly, friendly & useful to them, & of our dispositions to a commercial intercourse with them....[28]

The Indians with whom Jefferson was especially concerned and the only tribe about whom he specifically outlined a policy in his instructions to Lewis and Clark were the Sioux. In his letter of January 22, 1804, Jefferson writes, "On that nation [the Sioux] we wish most particularly to make a friendly impression, because of their immense power, and because we learn that they are very desirous of being on the most friendly terms with us."[29]

Second, Jefferson initially conceived of the expedition into Louisiana Territory as a journey into a foreign country under the sovereignty of France and in the immediate control of indigenous peoples. In his earlier instructions to Lewis, in a letter of June 20, 1803, he made a distinction between "your movements while within the limits of the U.S." and "your proceedings after your departure from the United states [*sic*]."[30] Even after settling the Louisiana Purchase, effective December 20, 1803, Jefferson continued to speak of the Sioux as a foreign nation through whose country the expedition must pass and whose trade the United States valued. In his letter of January

22, 1804, Jefferson writes what might be considered an addendum to his previous instructions: "Being now become sovereigns of the country, without however any diminution of the Indian rights of occupancy we are authorized to propose to them in direct terms the institution of commerce with them."[31] Such an acknowledgment of national identity in favor of the Sioux suggests, then, that Lewis and Clark were not so much explorers as trade representatives of the United States; as such, they should necessarily have understood their personal and official relations with natives as being of diplomatic importance.

Third, Jefferson expected Lewis to keep detailed notes about the expedition, even to the extent of making duplicate copies in case of their almost certain loss, an injunction that, unaccountably, Lewis largely failed to honor, both during and after the expedition. Jefferson was insistent that Lewis not only keep a record of his observations but that he also send "at seasonable intervals, a copy of [his] journal, notes & observations, of every kind, putting into cypher whatever might lead to injury if betrayed."[32] So concerned was Jefferson that a written record of the expedition be preserved that he suggests to Lewis that he employ traders and natives to convey the letters during the outbound journey and, upon reaching the Pacific Coast, "to send two of your trusty people back by sea…with a copy of your notes."[33]

On the basis of these injunctions—that the expedition was primarily a commercial endeavor requiring diplomacy (especially with the Sioux), and the keeping of detailed observations—we can begin to understand the nature of Jefferson's conception of the commercial primacy of the expedition and, therefore, Lewis's likely predisposition towards tribal people. Jefferson did not encourage him to establish personal/sexual relationships with native women as was the custom of fur traders of the time, nor did he offer an injunction against such relations.

The Journals of Lewis and Clark

Given Jefferson's instructions, one might assume that if there is any corroborative evidence for Lewis's liaison with a Sioux woman, it should be found in his or Clark's expedition journals. Perhaps more so than was the case with other expeditions of the time, the observations and activities of the Corps of Discovery were to have been recorded in writing. Donald Jackson calls Lewis and Clark the "writingest explorers of their time."[34] But as with all texts, the expedition journals pose several problems. In the introduction to his edition of the journals, Gary Moulton acknowledges that one of the most troubling problems in the journals concerns "when and how were the journals written."[35] His careful analysis of the manner in which the journals were constructed reveals that they are an amalgam of field notes and journal entries written at various times; some entries were, in fact, written well after the return of the Corps of Discovery, and some were copied by Clark into his journals from Lewis's field notes. In the journals, then, we have, at best, only a portion of what Lewis and Clark experienced and likely recorded.

Moulton points to the specific problem of Lewis's "journal-keeping procedure and particularly the large gaps in his writing, which raise the possibility of missing manuscripts."[36] The largest and most curious gap is the long hiatus from the start of the expedition in May 1804 until April 1805, so peculiar that some have speculated Lewis was probably keeping either field notes or journals that have since been lost.[37] Moulton, however, believes that there are no missing journals, characterizing Lewis, unlike Clark, as an undisciplined record keeper.[38] Popular Lewis and Clark author Dayton Duncan distinguishes between the writing abilities of the two captains by noting that Lewis "excelled at describing the different objects in an Indian village," whereas Clark "was better at deciphering Indian customs, particularly the rituals associated with the meetings of the chiefs."[39] Ronda states that "[w]hat Biddle finally brought to press in 1814 [the first edition of the journals] was essentially what Lewis had proposed as his first volume."[40] Stephen Ambrose, on the other hand, believes that there are missing journal entries by Lewis and holds out some hope that they may still be recovered.[41] In all, Lewis missed more than four hundred days of journal entries from May 1804 through September 1806, many of them during the time under examination in this study.[42]

Therefore, since Lewis did not keep a journal for most of the expedition's first year, we must rely on Clark's account of the expedition. Assuming that Clark recorded all the encounters between the Corps of Discovery and the Native Americans of which he was aware or that he wished to disclose, there are, in fact, four possible instances of contact between the corps members and the Sioux: August 28-31, 1804; September 17-23, 1804; September 24-27, 1804; and August 30-September 1, 1806. Ronda, however, offers a caution about what the journal entries do and do not tell us:

> No nineteenth-century American exploring party made a fuller and more intimate record of its daily doings than the Lewis and Clark Expedition. When expedition journal keepers encountered native women, the accounts they wrote revealed some things while concealing others. Journal entries made it plain that women were defined in terms of sexual identity, reproductive history, and domestic labor. Euro-American explorers were bound by those definitions and blinded to the other ways that native women might behave. What is either missing in or concealed by the journals are the ways native women explored the worlds beyond the sexual.[43]

Before examining Clark's journal entries for the above dates, we should review the way that this early period of the expedition has been largely mistreated and misunderstood by scholars.

Much attention has been given by scholars to the Corps of Discovery's contact with the western native tribes, but their encounters with the Plains

Indians in what became South Dakota are often overlooked, apart from the hyperbolic treatment accorded the incident with the Teton Sioux. Discussions of these encounters, in fact, often emphasize their "hostility" at the expense of their friendliness, however suspicious the parties were of each other. Bernard DeVoto's popular abridgement of the journals half a century ago devotes a mere thirty-two pages to encounters with Plains Indians out of nearly five hundred pages of journal excerpts, despite his acknowledgment that the journalists begin their most descriptive writing with the expedition's encounters with the Sioux:

> At Council Bluffs Clark had made only perfunctory ethnological notes. Now the expedition sees the cultures of the Plains Indians in detail and the notebooks fill with descriptions of Sioux, their costumes, weapons, language, tribal divisions, names, customs and beliefs. Nothing previously written about the Sioux was so accurate, thorough, or permanently valuable.[44]

Even as recently as 1998, John C. Ewers oversimplified the nature of the corps's encounters with the Sioux: "The explorers' brief contacts with the most powerful nomadic tribes of the Upper Missouri were hostile ones."[45] Close examination of the encounters of Lewis and Clark with the indigenous peoples along the Missouri reveals an almost entirely different situation. Although they traveled some distance inland to visit Spirit Mound on the Vermillion River on August 24-25, 1804, the corps did not encounter any Sioux. The entries for August 28-31, 1804, however, record an incident of sustained contact with the Yankton Sioux at Calumet Bluff on the Nebraska side of the Missouri River, across from present-day Yankton, South Dakota. Moulton identifies this encounter as "the first of this numerous tribe and the first of the truly nomadic Plains Indians they had met."[46] Clark's entries for this first encounter give no indication of fraternization between the Corps of Discovery members and the Sioux women, though meetings are extensive and friendly and include dances and speeches by Clark and the Yankton Sioux leaders.[47] At night, the two groups camped on opposite shores of the Missouri, though some Yankton males did sleep aboard the keelboat.

Contrary to the perception advanced by some Lewis and Clark popularizers, who seek to elevate the expedition to a mission of first contact, relations between Europeans and indigenous peoples had become common by the early nineteenth century, and these white explorers were by no means the first Euro-Americans that the Sioux or other natives, for that matter, had encountered. For example, the expedition's interpreter, the Frenchman Pierre Dorion, Sr., whom Clark instructed to make peace between the Sioux and other tribes and authorized to employ traders to take the Sioux chiefs to Washington, was married to a Yankton woman.[48] Ewers dispels any notion that this expedition should be understood as instigating initial contact with the Sioux:

> before the time of Lewis and Clark not only the Mandan and Arikara but all other tribes of the Upper Missouri had gained some knowledge of white

men. Furthermore, most if not all of these tribes knew from experience that white men were in competition for their trade. And they had no reason to believe that there were *any* whites who were not closely associated with the fur trade.[49]

Ronda notes further that "[b]y the time Lewis and Clark made their way upriver, there was already half a century of contact between plains people and the outsiders. Beginning in the 1730s, first a trickle and then a steady stream of European visitors came to call."[50] Relations between the Corps of Discovery and various Sioux tribes, then, would likely have been more advanced than the presumption of initial contact would suggest. To the Sioux, therefore, the explorers would be considered foreigners, but not aliens—and certainly not gods, as whites have flatteringly sought to portray themselves.

The only extant daily journal entries, as opposed to scientific notes, by Lewis between May 20, 1804, and April 7, 1805, are those of September 16-17, 1804, which are found in the fragmentary Codex Ba.[51] These entries, possibly written in the vicinity of the present-day home of the DeSomets, occur just previous to the corps' famous encounter with the Teton Sioux at Bad River. During these dates, the corps was encamped on Corvus Creek (American Creek), which is near the town of Oacoma, Lyman County, South Dakota. On September 17, 1804, Lewis records that "[h]aving for many days confined myself to the boat, I determined to devote this day to amuse myself on shore with my gun and view the interior of the country lying between the river and the Corvus Creek."[52] The passage reveals Lewis at his most effusive and descriptive, relieved to be off the boat and amidst the natural wonders of the Missouri River bottomlands, but he makes no mention of meeting any of the Yankton or Teton Sioux who lived in this area along the river.[53] In contrast, on September 22, 1804, Clark records seeing "a number of Indian Camps in a Conicel form," and on the following day he notes that "Capt Lewis walked on Shore this evening."[54] In the same entry, Clark records that his party was approached by three Sioux boys, who had swum across the river, indicating the proximity of two Teton Sioux encampments. Apart from Clark's reference to the native boys, neither Lewis nor Clark mentions making actual contact with the Sioux at this time, but Lewis's coming ashore puts him in geographical proximity to the traditional location of the DeSomet family.

The invitation by the three Teton youths resulted in a third contact with the Sioux, as the entries for September 24-27, 1804, record. This time, the encounter takes place with the Brulé Teton Sioux, led by Black Buffalo, at the mouth of the Bad River, near present-day Fort Pierre, South Dakota. Moulton characterizes this meeting as the corps's "first really hazardous and potentially violent encounter with Indians on the journey, arising from the arrogance of some of the chiefs, disagreements among the Sioux leaders, and very likely confusion resulting from the lack of a Sioux interpreter."[55] Seeking to heighten the drama of what was notably a peaceful expedition, some historians, such as Ambrose in his popular *Undaunted Courage*, choose to emphasize the potential for violence in this encounter. The captains, however, ever mindful of their diplomatic mission, displayed patience and remained with the Sioux three days, concluding their visit on relatively friendly terms, as Jefferson would have wished. They saw it as a characteristic attempt by the Brulés to wrest additional goods from the white foreigners. As James Ronda points out in his account of the standoff in *Lewis and Clark among the Indians*, with scores of women and children observing from the riverbank, there was no possibility that the Brulés would risk an attack on the corps. In fact, following Clark and Black Buffalo's diplomatic impasse, the parties resolved their differences amicably, providing repeated opportunities, as we shall see, for liaisons among the Brulés.

Aware that a show of force the previous day had proven counterproductive to their aim of controlling trade on the Upper Missouri, the Brulés invited Lewis and five of his men ashore on the morning of September 26, where they remained for about three hours. Fearing deception and becoming increasingly apprehensive about Lewis's welfare, Clark dispatched Sergeant Gass "to See him and know his treatment which he reported was friendly, & th[e]y were prepareing for a Dance this evening."[56] Lewis returned and Clark went ashore, having agreed to remain for one night with the Brulés as a gesture of goodwill, in response to their persistent solicitations. The Brulés carried first Clark and then Lewis into their village upon painted buffalo robes and seated them next to Black Buffalo. Clark makes no effort in the journals to explain Lewis's absence; perhaps Lewis did not share the experience, or he reasoned that Lewis would give his own account.

Clark records three separate occasions among the Brulés when he and Lewis were offered young women as sexual partners, concerning which Clark later wrote, "'a curious custom with the Souix as well as the rickeres [Arikaras] is to give handsom squars to those whome they wish to Show some acknowledgements to.'"[57] In his entry for September 26, for example, Clark provides this flattering description of the Brulé women:

> ther women appear verry well, fin[e] Teeth, High Cheek [bones] Dress in Skin Peticoats, & a Roabe with the flesh Side out and harey ends turned back over their Sholdes, and look well—they doe all the Laborious work, and I may say are perfect Slaves to thier husbands who frequently have Several wives.[58]

Later in this same entry Clark notes, parenthetically, that after the dance, which ended around midnight, "they offered us women, which we did not except [sic]."[59] Ronda comments that Clark was aware that such offers were made on behalf of the tribe and that to reject such hospitality, as Clark asserts that both he and Lewis did, "surely did not foster the friendship and trust

Jefferson was seeking" in the hope of establishing trade agreements with the Sioux.[60] The next day, in the afternoon of September 27, Clark records a second offer of a sexual partner: "They again offered me a young woman and wish me to take her & not Dispise them, I wavered [waived?] the Subject, at Dark the Dance began as usial and performed as last night."[61]

Moulton's editorial comment that Clark meant *waived*, not *wavered* in this passage may, in fact, reveal more about Moulton's presuppositions about Clark than Clark's own response to the Brulés' offer. Clark makes no reference this time as to whether Lewis was also offered a partner, nor do we know whether Lewis honored his hosts' expectations.

Regarding the third offer of sexual companionship, made on the morning of September 29, Clark provides only a brief notice. While aboard their boat, the explorers were hailed from shore by the second chief, who "offered us women we objected and told them we Should not Speake to another teton except the one onboard with us....[62] The plural pronouns "us" and "we" doubtless include Lewis, but Clark makes no distinction on this point.

The fourth possible opportunity for a sexual liaison occurred two years later, August 30-September 1, 1806, on the return journey of the corps down the Missouri, but the dates do not accord with the birth date given by Joseph DeSomet, nor did any of the exploring party camp with the Sioux. On August 30, below Oacoma, the Corps of Discovery exchanged taunting remarks with Black Buffalo's Brulé Teton Sioux band, whom they had first met in September 1804. This verbal exchange nearly caused a more deadly exchange two days later when, on September 1, 1806, the corps mistook Yanktons, who were shooting at a barrel floating down the river, for Tetons firing upon the rear canoe. Clark indicates that his party, including Lewis, came ashore ready to fight but, upon understanding the situation, stayed to smoke several pipes with the friendly Yanktons.

On the basis of the captains' journals, then, there is no record of a liaison between Lewis and a Sioux woman, although there appear to have been several opportunities. Of course, any one of the men could have identified himself as the leader of the expedition while on shore and, under this guise, fathered a child.

Sergeant John Ordway, Sergeant Patrick Gass, and Private Joseph Whitehouse also recorded their observations of the expedition. Ordway, the only member of the expedition to keep a daily journal, in fact, records no fraternization in his journal for August 28-31, 1804. Ronda notes that Ordway's significance "lies not only in his comprehensive coverage but in his keen eye for detail."[63] It is reasonable to expect that such a careful observer might have noted occasions if and when his superiors acceded to wishes of their hosts by taking partners among the natives. We know, for example, that Ordway found the Sioux women attractive, as revealed in the following description of the

Brulés, recorded for September 26: "Some of their women are verry handsome, & friendly....the Squaws formed on each Side of the fire & danced and Sang as the drum and other ratles &C. were playing....the womens voice Sounded one part of the tune delightful."[64] After the dance in Lewis and Clark's honor was performed, Ordway continues, "[t]he chiefs came on [board] & Selept with us in a friendly manner"—yet further confirmation of how quickly the hostility between the Tetons and the corps dissipated.[65] Gass's journals, which are, in fact, the writings of David McKeehan, based on Gass's notes, record no incidents of fraternization; indeed, he remarks in his entry for August 30, "No Squaws made their appearance among this party," in contradiction to Clark's account.[66] For September 27, Gass writes, "[The women] are the most friendly people I ever saw, but will pilfer if they have an opportunity. They are also very dirty...." [67] In his journal, Private Joseph Whitehouse offers no confirmation of fraternization, but, in his entry for September 28, he notes that the Sioux "are stout well made Indians and their Women are in general handsome, If I may be allowed to judge from those which I saw in the lodges that we left yesterday."[68] The other journalists on the expedition, then, do not provide any evidence that either of their commanders participated in the common practice among the men, nor, given military protocol, should one expect that they would, even if they had known about such incidents.

Apart from this concession, the various journals fail, then, to corroborate the assertions of Joseph/Michael DeSomet as recorded in Warren's and Hutton's journals and in the Yankton Mission registers. In the documentary-based model of historiography, the failure of documents to verify other documents presents significant problems for historians, as well as for genealogists. Genealogical research is based on the assertions of such authoritative sources as church and mission registers. In Native American communities, for example, mission registers are often the only evidence of birth and death dates. In the absence of birth records, the federal government accepts baptismal records, which include birth dates, for purposes of claiming Social Security benefits. To deny the legitimacy of DeSomet's claim solely on the basis of the absence of incontrovertible documentary evidence calls into question the principle of documentary historiography. The Episcopal priest officiating at DeSomet's baptism, the Reverend Cook, apparently did not object to DeSomet's claim, for he twice signed the baptismal record specifying Meriwether Lewis as the father, and in so doing also pledged the sanction of the Episcopal Church. In the case of Joseph DeSomet, then, is there any point in pursuing this inquiry, since a birth or baptism record cannot "prove" paternity? Does there exist any tool that we might employ in the hope of solving this puzzle?

A Possible Solution

There is a way in which our examination of DeSomet's claim might be of value in resolving this and another mystery associated with Meriwether Lewis: the long-standing controversy over the manner of his death, which occurred only three years after the expedition concluded. Whether the thirty-five-year-old Lewis was murdered or died of self-inflicted gunshot wounds at Grinder's Inn on the Natchez Trace in Tennessee is a matter of acrimonious debate among historians. It is, however, a debate that ultimately might expand the parameters of documentary-based historiography to include the methodologies of archeologists, pathologists, epidemiologists, geneticists, and forensic scientists. Epidemiologist Reimert Ravenholt, for example, speculates that Lewis's death was caused by depression, or dementia, resulting from an advanced stage of syphilis. Ravenholt finds a pattern in accounts of Lewis's increasingly strange behavior in the period following his return from the expedition, terminal illness, and death that he identifies as "pathognomonic for a much-dreaded infectious disease," convincing Ravenholt that "a strong fabric of evidence supports the diagnosis of *neurosyphilis paresis* as the underlying cause of the tragic death of Meriwether Lewis."[69] In his journal entries for the winter of 1804-5, when the Corps of Discovery was encamped at Fort Mandan, Clark records the medical battles that he and Lewis waged against syphilis among the expedition's men, many of whom, Clark alleges, had contracted syphilis from the Mandan women, who visited from their nearby village. Clark makes no mention of whether he or Lewis had also contracted the disease, and, again, there are no entries by Lewis from this period.

Stephen Ambrose, ever vigilant to maintain the heroic myth, finds that the possibility of Lewis's having syphilis is "more intriguing and speculative than convincing."[70] That Lewis may have been suffering from some form of dementia, whether induced by syphilis or by another disease causing depression, could possibly explain three of the persistent mysteries of Lewis's life: first, his peculiar behavior in the hours before he died; second, his failure to prepare his journals for publication; and, third, his apparent reluctance, despite repeated opportunities, to become engaged and to marry.[71] Along with Jefferson and Clark (though the latter at first dismissed suicide), Ambrose believes that Lewis committed suicide as a consequence of his dementia. Dillon, however, in his biography of Lewis, dismisses the suicide theory in favor of murder, pointing out the formidable inconsistencies in the suicide theory and noting that an 1809 inquest, the records of which are lost, concluded that Lewis had been murdered.[72] In his review of the conflicting evidence regarding Lewis's death, Vardis Fisher suggests that a stronger case can be made for murder than for suicide and concludes that "[p]erhaps the only lesson we can take from it all is an appalled sense of the way history usually gets itself written."[73]

In what way is it possible to alter the historiographic method by which Fisher and others are frustrated? The scope of this article does not allow for further consideration of the manner of Lewis's death, but, recent advances in genetics have afforded another tool for attempting to unravel historical puzzles.[74] Speculation about Lewis's health and the cause of his death could be addressed through exhumation and DNA testing of Lewis's remains, a possibility that has recently begun to attract attention, much of it decidedly negative. Further, such steps may also lead to a solution to the problem of Joseph DeSomet Lewis's claim to paternity. Appropriate to this discussion is the approach employed by historian Annette Gordon-Reed, in *Thomas Jefferson and Sally Hemings: An American Controversy*, which argues from circumstantial evidence that Jefferson fathered a child by his African-American slave, Sally Hemings.[75] Although vigorously attacked by several Jefferson scholars, Gordon-Reed's assertion was subsequently corroborated by Eugene A. Foster's research using mitochondrial DNA testing of Y chromosomes, which offers strong evidence that Jefferson fathered Hemings's last child, Eston Hemings Jefferson.[76]

The controversy surrounding the possible exhumation of Lewis's remains has developed into a potentially explosive challenge, revolving around the debate as to whether exhumation is an acceptable method of historiographic inquiry. James E. Starrs, a Georgetown University law professor with a special interest in forensics and who has directed the exhumation of such historical figures as Jesse James, argues that only through exhumation can the controversy about Lewis's death be resolved. He claims that, by tracing the trajectories of the bullets that entered Lewis's body in 1809, he will be able to determine whether Lewis died by his own hand or someone else's. Starrs's efforts have resulted in direct confrontation with such Lewis and Clark popularizers as Ambrose and the award-winning documentary film-maker Ken Burns. In a newspaper interview, Starr criticized Ambrose's methods for relying "on secondary sources. You've got to use the original sources. That kind of scholarship to me is not worth a passing grade."[77] Burns, whose PBS documentary, *Lewis & Clark: An Illustrated History* (1997), featured extensive interviews with Ambrose, responded: "Meriwether Lewis committed suicide. It is a tragedy to his name and to his honor to exhume his body to satisfy the curiosity and the conspiracy theories of some latter-day historian."[78]

Starrs's real battle, of course, is with the National Park Service, to which he first proposed the possibility of exhumation in 1992. The National Park Service, which maintains the Meriwether Lewis burial site at Meriwether Lewis Park, near Hohenwald, Tennessee, is generally unsympathetic to requests for historical exhumations on Park Service land. Although a coroner's jury agreed in June 1996 that Starrs's case was worth considering, and the living descendants of Lewis (through his siblings) support exhumation, the National Park Service denied Starrs's request in September 1997. His appeal to the Park Service's southeast regional director was denied in December 1997 and again in January 1998. Starrs has since resorted to legal action and has brought a suit against the Park Service before a Tennessee judicial court.[79] Jerry Belson, regional director for the Park Service, argues, "The proposed excavation and exhumation is still inconsistent with National Park Service management policies."[80]

Although likely to be delayed for several years, exhumation and testing of Lewis's remains for the purpose of determining the cause and manner of his death might be a means by which the claims of descent from Meriwether Lewis made by Joseph DeSomet in the Yankton Mission registers and by Michael DeSomet in Warren's and Hutton's journals, the circumstantial evidence provided by the journals, and the tradition of a South Dakota family could be addressed. It might also be possible, as in the case of testing for Thomas Jefferson's paternity, that DNA comparison of the male-line descendants of Joseph DeSomet with male-line descendants of Meriwether Lewis's brother might also answer questions about a biological relationship. DNA testing might establish the paternity DeSomet claimed, or it may simply confirm the possibility that his father was indeed a member of the Corps of Discovery, but not specifically Meriwether Lewis. Perhaps we should understand Michael DeSomet's assertion, as recorded by Hutton, in this way: that his father was "Lewis &Clarke," referring not so much to a single individual but to that particular expeditionary group.

One other point of uncertainty that exhumation and DNA testing may be able to resolve is the question of whether the remains in Lewis's tomb, which have been moved once already, are indeed those of Meriwether Lewis. As James Wilkinson reminds us, "Not everything in the past has left traces, and not all traces have survived. In the absence of remains, there can be no evidence, and in the absence of evidence, there can be no history."[81]

Why Not Homicide?: Historians and Their Case for Suicide

John D. W. Guice

Late in the afternoon on October 10, 1809, one of the nation's greatest heroes reined his horse off the Natchez Trace and dismounted in front of a crude log cabin. What occupied Meriwether Lewis's mind we will never know, but many historians insist he was contemplating suicide. Shortly after sun-up the next morning he died. Who held the weapon or weapons that fired the two fatal shots during the night? Probably one of the outlaws who preyed on travelers along the dangerous road that connected Natchez on the Mississippi River with Nashville on the Cumberland.

"Suicide or murder? What difference does it make?" one of my friends asked. A lot of difference, I replied, to an historian concerned with the integrity of the profession, for the accuracy of our nation's history, and for the descendants of the Lewis family. In addition, this debate offers a fascinating study in historiography. How can such an acclaimed writer as Stephen Ambrose declare that Lewis, *without a doubt*, killed himself, when Vardis Fisher, who dedicated over two and one-half years of intensive research for his 1962 book *Suicide or Murder?*, believed it was murder. Other Lewis and Clark scholars before and after Fisher have questioned the evidence offered by proponents of suicide. They include Richard Dillon, author of the most authoritative Lewis biography available, a work praised highly by none other than Stephen Ambrose.[1]

On their return from the Pacific Coast, Lewis and William Clark arrived on the Atlantic seaboard in December, 1806. The next year President Jefferson appointed Lewis as governor of Upper Louisiana, Clark as Brigadier General of the militia and Agent of Indian Affairs, and Frederick Bates as territorial secretary. Though Clark and Bates assumed their posts without delay, Lewis did not arrive in the territorial capital of St. Louis until a year after Jefferson signed his commission. During the interim he was in Philadelphia, the District of Columbia, and Virginia. One task occupying his time was attendance at the Aaron Burr trial in Richmond as an observer for President Jefferson. In Philadelphia Lewis contracted for the publication of his journals, recruited illustrators, attended meetings of the American Philosophical Society, and sat for portraits, to list a few of his many activities.[2]

On his arrival in St. Louis, Governor Lewis found an administration racked with contention caused by the machinations of territorial secretary Bates, a treacherous and implacable enemy. Resolving serious Indian problems consumed much of the governor's energy, though he found time to engage in land speculation. Meanwhile, James Madison replaced Jefferson in the White House and William Eustis became secretary of war. Lewis gave little thought to the new presidential administration until the war department refused to honor a $500 expenditure. This financially strained the outraged Lewis, who boarded a boat for New Orleans on September 4, 1809, the first stage of a planned sea voyage to Washington to resolve his battle with the bureaucracy. When the boat called at New Madrid, Lewis wrote a will, naming his mother his sole beneficiary. After eleven days on the Mississippi, a sick, exhausted Lewis disembarked at what is now Memphis, then known as Chickasaw Bluffs, the site of Fort Pickering, commanded by Captain Gilbert C. Russell. The surgeon's mate prescribed abstention from grain spirits but allowed Lewis some wine.

After six days Lewis gained strength. Meanwhile he decided to continue his journey overland, and after two weeks departed for the Natchez Trace along with three men: his free mulatto servant John Pernier, Chickasaw Indian agent and former militia major James Neelly, and Neelly's slave. Lewis was armed with a rifle, two pistols, a dirk, and a tomahawk. His pack horse carried two trunks and a portfolio containing sixteen leather-bound journals from the Pacific expedition as well as the disputed bills. At the Chickasaw agency the exhausted Lewis rested two days before the party headed up the hilly Trace toward the Tennessee River. The night of October 9 they camped a day's ride beyond the river. While they slept two of the horses escaped. So Lewis rode on with both servants toward a crude inn known as Grinder's Stand, about seventy-three miles southwest of Nashville, while Neelly remained behind to recover the horses. Hence Neelly was not with Lewis the morning of his death.

Collectively, proponents of suicide offer a multitude of arguments including the following[3]:

- The delay in reporting to St. Louis indicates that Lewis was despondent over his failure to find a wife.
- Consequently, he became an alcoholic.
- His inability to cope with administrative affairs—combined with his financial difficulties in St. Louis—led to further despondence.
- The writing of a will at New Madrid indicates he was contemplating suicide.
- According to the CO at Fort Pickering, the boat crew reported that Lewis had tried twice to kill himself and Lewis had arrived in a state of "indisposition" due to over consumption of alcohol. Two years later, Russell described his condition as one of "mental derangement."
- The corrections and uncertain hand in a letter that Lewis wrote from Fort Pickering to President Madison indicate emotional instability.
- Neelly wrote Jefferson that Lewis had killed himself. Pernier delivered this letter.
- Neelly also informed Jefferson that at the Chickasaw Agency, Lewis "appeared at times deranged in mind."

- Mrs. Grinder, over a year later, told famous ornithologist Alexander Wilson that Lewis had behaved strangely the evening before he shot himself.[4]
- Thomas Jefferson accepted the initial report of suicide, and in 1814 he also wrote that "Governor Lewis had been from early lifetime subject to hypochondriac affections," which Jefferson attributed to "a constitutional disposition in all branches of the family."[5]
- William Clark, co-captain on the expedition, allegedly accepted the report of suicide.[6]
- Howard I. Kushner, in a 1981 psychoanalytic inquiry, attributes the assumed suicide to childhood mental trauma.[7]
- Park historian Dawson Phelps contends that the Natchez Trace "was not, in 1809, a dangerous place."[8]
- Lewis made no progress on the editing of his journals while in St. Louis and seldom wrote Jefferson while he was there.
- Lewis killed himself while suffering from the agonizing tertiary effects of syphilis.[9]

Alexander Wilson wrote the most often quoted account of events based on notes taken during an 1811 visit with Mrs. Grinder, the inn-keeper's wife:

> Governor Lewis, she said, came there about sunset, alone, and inquired if he could stay for the night; and alighting, brought his saddle into the house.... On being asked if he came alone, he replied that there were two servants behind, who would soon come up. He called for some spirits, and drank a very little. When the servants arrived...he inquired for his powder, saying he was sure he had some powder in a cannister.... Lewis, in the meanwhile, walked backwards and forwards before the door, talking to himself. Sometimes, she said, he would seem as if he were walking up to her and would suddenly wheel around and walk back as fast as he could. Supper being ready he sat down, but had eaten only a few mouthfuls, when he started up, speaking to himself in a violent manner. At these times, she says, she observed his face to flush as if it had come on him in a fit. He lighted his pipe, and drawing a chair to the door, sat down saying to Mrs. Grinder, in a kind tone of voice, "Madam this is a very pleasant evening." He smoked for some time, but quitted his seat and traversed the yard as before, he again sat down to his pipe, seemed again composed, and casting his eyes wistfully toward the west, observed what a sweet evening it was. Mrs. Grinder was preparing a bed for him but he said he would sleep on the floor and desired the servant to bring his bear skins and buffaloe robes, which was immediately spread out for him; and it being now dusk the woman went off to the kitchen and the two men to the barn, which stands about 200 yards off. The kitchen is only a few paces from the room where Lewis was, and the woman being considerably alarmed by the behavior of her guest could not sleep; but listened to his walking backwards and forwards, she thinks, for several hours, and talking aloud..."like a lawyer" [10] ...she then heard the report of a pistol, and something fell heavily to the floor, and the words "Oh Lord!" Immediately afterwards she heard another pistol [shot], and in a few minutes she heard him calling out: "O madam! give me some water, and heal my wounds." The logs being open, and unplastered, she saw him stagger back

> and fall against a stump that stands between the kitchen and the room. He crawled for some distance, raised himself by the side of a tree, where he sat [for] about a minute. He once more got to the room; afterwards he came to the kitchen door, but did not speak; she then heard him scraping the bucket with a gourd for water; but it appears that this cooling element was denied the dying man. As soon as day broke and not before, the terror of the woman having permitted him to remain two hours in the most deplorable situation, she sent two of her children to the barn, her husband not being home, to bring the servants; and on going in they found him lying on the bed; he uncovered his side and showed them where the bullet had entered; a piece of his forehead was blown off, and had exposed his brains, without having bled much. He begged they would take his rifle and blow out his brains, and he would give them all the money he had in his trunk. He often said, "I am no coward, but I am so strong, so hard to die." He begg'd the servant not to be afraid of him, for he would not hurt them. He expired in about two hours, or just as the sun rose above the trees. [11]

I am a student of territorial history and of the southern frontier. My interest in this subject arose when I wrote a chapter on the Natchez Trace in a recent book on the Old Southwest from which developed my present project—a history of the Natchez Trace. I was astounded that so many historians accepted the verdict of suicide on such flimsy circumstantial evidence—all of it ultimately based on hearsay. Besides, the behavior of Mrs. Grinder was out of character for a woman who lived in Tennessee, one of the most violent American frontiers.

Dawson Phelps clearly approached his frequently quoted 1956 article in *The William and Mary Quarterly* with an axe to grind. That axe was his overstatement of the safety of the Natchez Trace, a position encouraged from his close association with Duke University Professor William B. Hamilton. He and Phelps attempted to counterbalance the fictionalized account of violence on the Natchez Trace by Robert Coates in his 1930 bestseller, *The Outlaw Years*.[12] Yes, by 1809 the Trace was not as dangerous as it was earlier, but it was still so dangerous that the rough, tough boatmen always rode or walked up it in convoy, as Phelps points out in one of his earlier articles. Lewis had reason to arm himself so heavily. Furthermore, if the Trace was so safe, why was Mrs. Grinder so fearful?

The arguments for suicide are readily countered:

- Lewis conducted important business in Philadelphia and attended the Burr trial. Yes, he actively, but unsuccessfully, sought a wife. So have countless other men. His east coast interlude was a dalliance, not a delay. Perhaps, after three years in the wilderness, Lewis was indulging himself.
- Yes, he at times did drink. It is safe to say that at times he got drunk. But drinking in the young republic, and especially on the frontier, was par at a time when par was pretty high. The amount of whiskey drunk on the southern frontier seems astronomical by modern standards. One of the primary products shipped

down the Mississippi in flatboats was whiskey; it was the drink of choice among travelers on the Natchez Trace.

- Lewis handled administrative affairs quite well, especially relating to the Indians and in light of the interference of Frederick Bates. With its French, Spanish, and American heritages, and with its large American Indian population, Upper Louisiana was far more complex than most territories.
- Yes, Lewis had a momentary cash flow problem, but he stood to make a lot of money, and he surely recognized that fact. Territorial officials all over the trans-Mississippi West dealt in the widest range of speculation; they sought those low-paying jobs because of the investment opportunities. Most territorial officials throughout the trans-Mississippi West constantly battled uninformed, parsimonious bureaucrats. Lewis had plenty of company.
- On May 28, 1999, at the Center for Western Studies' Dakota Conference, in Sioux Falls, South Dakota (just months before her untimely death), the late Ruth Colter-Frick read an excellent paper entitled "The Myth of Insolvency: The Financial Affairs of Governor Meriwether Lewis at the Time of His Death." She based her research on the Grace Lewis Miller Collection at the Jefferson National Expansion Memorial Archives in St. Louis, Missouri, as well as on documents from eight other repositories spread cross the nation. Colter-Frick proved that, while Lewis clearly had a temporary cash flow problem, he was far from bankrupt. He had invested carefully in valuable land holdings in St. Louis with an eye toward moving his mother there. He also had assets in other parts of the country.[13]
- Only a terribly imprudent man, facing a sea voyage at any time, but especially just before the War of 1812, would not write a will. He knew he had considerable assets that he wished to bequeath to his mother.
- It is curious that Capt. Russell offered no details of the reported suicide attempts en route to Memphis. Because Lewis was truly a national hero, it is odd that the boatmen did not give the particulars. Had they done so, it is likely that Russell would have mentioned what Lewis is supposed to have done.
- Not only does the text of the letter written by Lewis to President James Madison at Fort Pickering clearly indicate that he was rational, but parts of it were up-beat.[14]
- At this point it is important to refer to the 1996 coroner's inquest in Hohenwald, Tennessee, county seat of Lewis County where Lewis is buried. For most of two days fourteen witnesses, mainly forensic scientists, testified under oath. The transcript contains 364 pages. One can summarize their testimony as follows: It is likely that sufficient skeletal remains exist to permit a forensic examination. Such an examination is practical without disturbing the monument, and it could rule out suicide.
- Documents experts at the coroner's inquest testified that the oft-cited letter to Madison is merely a rough draft, bearing no signs of mental deterioration. A highly qualified certified forensic document examiner studied nine samples of known writings of Meriwether Lewis, five of Gilbert Russell, and one of Jonathan Williams in whose papers one of Russell's most often cited documents was found. The attorney who questioned Gerald B.

Richards focused on the letter which Lewis wrote to President Madison from Fort Pickering.

Q. "Now, do you find anything unusual about the writing in this 1809 letter compared to the 1807 document and the other 1809 letter to his friend Amos?" (Amos Stoddard).

A. "As far as the writing goes, the style of writing, the relative size, the speed, the quality of what we call the rhythm of the writing, it's all totally consistent with the other two examples. The only difference, and it's a very noticeable difference, is there are numerous—and this is what the historians mostly dwelled on—there are numerous corrections, cross outs, additions, deletions throughout the entire document; however, the handwriting itself is stable, it is as solid as he has ever written it before."[15]

Furthermore, from Fort Pickering, Lewis wrote his former Army comrade Amos Stoddard at Fort Adams, just south of Natchez, to let him know of his change of plans. Lewis asked Stoddard to send $200 of Lewis's money on to Washington so it would arrive while he was there. Lewis expressed confidence that he would "put matters right" in Washington.[16] That does not sound like a man contemplating suicide. He tended to other business at Fort Pickering.

- Another fascinating part of the testimony dealt with Gilbert Russell's statement of November 26, 1811, the one in which he describes Lewis as mentally deranged on arrival at the fort and in which he mentions the alleged suicide attempts by Lewis on the boat. This statement was found in the papers of Jonathan Williams, who purportedly wrote on the bottom that Russell sent it to him, i.e. Williams.[17] This Russell statement is another cornerstone of the argument for suicide. However, the expert testified: "Based on these characteristics and numerous other ones I found throughout the writing, it became very obvious that Russell did not write the Russell statement that's purported to describe what happened to Meriwether Lewis." He continued, "...Williams did not write the Russell signature.... Neither he (Williams) nor the purported writer of it who signed at the bottom wrote those particular documents."[18] Perhaps Russell did dictate such a statement, but this conclusion by a highly reputable expert casts great doubt on the authenticity of one of the key documents cited by proponents of the suicide theory.
- The second document examiner was Dr. Duayne Dillon, an expert witness in hundreds of cases. Neither expert knew the other was examining the same set of documents—actually photographic copies of documents. Dillon confirmed that the 1811 statement attributed to Gilbert Russell was not written by either Russell or Jonathan Williams. Nor were their signatures authentic. According to Dillon, the signatures of Lewis at Fort Pickering were "actually superior to many of the other signatures." Likewise, the writing in the text of the letters just before Lewis's death showed no deterioration—"no change at all." Furthermore, Dillon, who has done experimental work on the effect of alcohol consumption on writing,

found no such effects in the writing of Lewis at Fort Pickering.[19] How dare some of our colleagues proclaim that no questions remain regarding the circumstances surrounding the death of Lewis!

It is possible that this testimony vindicates Vardis Fisher. When Fisher read a transcription of the Russell statement provided by Donald Jackson in 1960, Fisher wrote back that it fell upon him like a "bombshell." Fisher, however, doubted its authenticity. "I read half the first page and was so astonished that I went back and reread, knowing that if this is authentic it overthrows my thesis that Lewis did not kill himself. Somewhere early in the second page I was strongly feeling that Gilbert Russell never wrote this, and by the time I reached the end of it, I was convinced that he did not. It is so unlike what he wrote in two letters to Jefferson in its spirit, in its use of the language, and in its statements of what happened. So the question in my mind is, Who wrote it and why? For if Russell wrote it, he had in two years completely changed his attitude toward Lewis and his view of what happened."[20]

Our test of the arguments for suicide continues:

- Neelly wrote to Jefferson that Lewis "appeared at times deranged in Mind" when they stopped at the Chickasaw agency, but while there Lewis wrote a totally rational letter to Russell regarding his excess baggage.[21]
- Because no record exists of Jefferson's meeting with Pernier, we do not know his initial reactions. Jefferson's decisions to hire Lewis as his secretary, to assign him leader of the Pacific Expedition, and to send him to the Burr trial belie his 1814 statement regarding Lewis's "hypochondriac affections" and his tendency to abuse alcohol. Ambrose raises this question with these comments in his introduction to the 1988 reprint of Dillon's book, which he describes as a "model biography": "But the fact that Jefferson selected Lewis as his private secretary and dinner companion, and then to lead the expedition to explore the Louisiana Purchase, tells more about Lewis than anything I could write."
- Virtually all historians agree that the Lewis and Clark expedition was the culmination of Jefferson's life-long curiosity about and fascination with the West. Surely he would not choose a person with a history of mental problems—a manic-depressive alcoholic, as some have painted Lewis—to lead such an expedition and to govern such a critically important territory. Jefferson was aging; acceptance of suicide was a "clean" way to handle the situation. Every hour of every day an official somewhere in the United States is labeling a homicide a suicide because it is the cleanest, easiest decision. So might have Jefferson. Pulitzer prize-winning historian Joseph Ellis in his 1997 *American Sphinx: The Character of Thomas Jefferson* not only emphasizes Jefferson's pragmatism but also suggests that Jefferson had a talent for self-deception. While it is not unusual today for historians to attack Jefferson, Vardis Fisher was raising similar questions over four decades ago. Jefferson's memory may well have been deceiving him.[22]
- Retired physician Dr. William Anderson of Williamsburg, Virginia, whom I first met at the 1996 Coroner's Inquest, is the great, great, great nephew of Lewis. I asked him to explain Jefferson's remark about his family disposi-

tion to mental problems. After reciting a family medical history, which did not include insanity, Dr. Anderson wrote: "I believe that Thomas Jefferson's assertion regarding the family was made in an effort to comfort himself by finding a scientific explanation for the news he had received from others and which he had assumed to be fact. Jefferson was human, like all of us, and he needed to explain things, and, of course, he had known the Lewis family and he was bound to have seen some of them when they were "blue," down, or discouraged. What better conclusion to satisfy his own mind, than to say Lewis could not help himself because he had bad genes for which he was not responsible." Dr. Anderson's opinion fits perfectly into recent research on memory, reported in the July 16, 2001, issue of *Newsweek*, that indicates that memories are often illusions and that we tend to remember things as we want them to be.

- Though William Clark eventually may have believed that Lewis did kill himself, one of Clark's letters from St. Louis before Lewis's death indicates that Clark expected him to resolve matters in Washington and "return with flying Colours to this Country."[23] And Clark equivocates in his initial reaction to a suicide report in a Kentucky newspaper. One wonders how Clark would have reacted had the report referred to a murder instead of a suicide.
- According to many medical experts, the theory that Lewis in 1809 suffered from the final effects of syphilis is highly speculative, at best.
- Could Lewis, if wounded as Mrs. Grinder reported, physically have perambulated around her premises? The late Dr. E. G. Chuinard, a professor of orthopedic surgery at the University of Oregon Medical School, answered this question with a resounding no. Chuinard, past president of the Lewis and Clark Trail Heritage Foundation and founder of its journal, contended that Lewis suffered from malaria, and painted a scenario for murder at the hands of Neelly.[24] Many others question the ability of anyone to shoot himself twice with the long horse pistol that Lewis carried, probably .69 caliber.
- Even if Lewis could have wandered around, a faculty colleague recently proposed that Mrs. Grinder could not have seen him if there had been a new moon on the fateful night of October 10-11, 1809. And there was a new moon at 1:30 a.m. on October 9, 1809. On Tuesday, October 10, the moon was "a waxing crescent with 3% of the Moon's visible disk illuminated." Moonset was 6:21 p.m.[25] In other words, on the heavily forested, highly humid Natchez Trace it was pitch black the night that Lewis died. Mrs. Grinder could not have seen Lewis walk around her yard as she claimed she did. This opens up a whole new set of questions regarding the credibility of Mrs. Grinder as well as Neelly, questions that add a whole new dimension to the debate.
- Finally, we remind you that the 1848 Monument Committee in its report to the legislature concluded—after examining the remains of Lewis—and we quote: "The impression has long prevailed that under the influence of disease of body and mind Governor Lewis perished by his own hands. It seems to be more probable that he died by the hands of an assassin."[26]

- This topic provides a fascinating study in historiography precisely because those entering the fray seem to bring with them pre-conceived notions, often instilled by their mentors. This is particularly true in reactions to Fisher's 1962 book, *Suicide or Murder?*, but these predispositions persist. Despite the depth of Fisher's research and the intriguing nature of the book, many historians continue to view Dawson Phelps's article as the authoritative statement.. His concluding sentence reads: "In the absence of direct and pertinent contemporary evidence to the contrary, of which not a scintilla exists, the verdict of suicide must stand." [27] *The William and Mary Quarterly* refused to print Grace Lewis Miller's well-written thirty-six page typescript rebuttal despite the fact that it was researched equally well, if not better, and contained more primary sources than the Phelps article.[28] Miller was a subject of the correspondence of Phelps, Fisher, and Jackson. An enigma to Fisher, Phelps considered her a joke, and Jackson felt she was incapable of objectivity, writing: "She uses facts like chunks of marble to build the man a shrine, rejecting or ignoring anything that won't do for the purpose."[29] Miller, on the other hand, accused Phelps of "studied selectivity" and of citing "only such details as bear favorably on the suicide theory."[30]

One wonders why *Suicide or Murder?* was not taken more seriously by historians of the American West. Anyone who studies the book carefully and who delves into the Vardis Fisher Papers at Yale University must admit that he was a meticulous, diligent researcher—a man of great integrity and insatiable curiosity. Though he admits that he could not prove murder, Fisher casts considerable doubt on evidence for suicide and presents a long list of possible suspects. So why is his stock no higher? First of all, he made his mark as a prolific Western novelist; his doctorate from the University of Chicago was in literature. Perhaps a better explanation relates to his alienation from Julian Boyd and Donald Jackson—giants in the historical profession. It is easier to understand how he offended Boyd than Jackson.

Boyd, a Princeton historian who for years edited the Papers of Thomas Jefferson, took offense at the manner in which Fisher quoted him. While he did not state so in his correspondence, Boyd probably was antagonized by Fisher's criticism of Jefferson. Even before publication of the book, their exchange of correspondence pertaining to Fisher's efforts to uncover Jefferson memoranda regarding Pernier was not exactly cordial. It became quite heated after Boyd fired off a blistering letter on April 26, 1963, in which he questioned Fisher's integrity and honor.

Fisher immediately requested that James T. Babb, Yale Librarian, return to Fisher the correspondence with Boyd. After satisfying himself that he had not misrepresented Boyd, Fisher defended his statements. Then he unloaded. "What I suspect, my dear Sir, is that you have an idolatrous attitude toward Jefferson, that my book disturbed; *or* that you liked to feel that Jefferson had settled the matter and that nobody less than a Jefferson scholar had a right to raise it; *or* that you feel you have right of preemption in the Jefferson domain and resent intrusions."[31]

More difficult to understand are the comments of Donald D. Jackson, published long after Fisher's 1968 death. Their exchange of numerous letters regarding research for *Suicide or Murder?* and the original manuscript had a warm, friendly—even chummy—tone. On August 3, 1960, after reading his manuscript twice, Jackson wrote Fisher a friendly critique of over seven single-spaced pages. "First," Jackson assured Fisher," I am fascinated by the thoroughness of your research and the expertness with which you have ferreted out material where I have supposed none existed." Toward the end he wrote: "You have convinced me that Neelly probably was a dishonest man and that Mrs. Grinder was a real nut." Then he added that "I am positive that you've got a good book here." His last sentence read: "But I think you owe it to our mutual friend, Meriwether Lewis, to see this thing through."[32]

To be sure, Jackson had a host of criticisms and suggestions, which stand as a tribute to his perception and insightfulness. At the top of his list was a lecture on mental illness and suicide. He wrote in part, "Certainly nobody condones suicide, but it is possible to believe that an admirable, courageous man can commit it under certain conditions....For if Lewis *did* kill himself, how are you and your readers going to salvage any respect for the man?" But Jackson's later published criticism was harsh.

Jackson, in his 1978 edition of *The Letters of the Lewis and Clark Expedition*, describes Fisher's book as "verbose and inexact" and accused him of approaching "the subject not in the manner of a historian but like a detective following a very cold trail."[33] Again in his 1987 anthology, *Among the Sleeping Giants*, Jackson takes Fisher to task for writing as a "storyteller" rather than as an historian. His lists of criticism include Fisher's "manipulation of evidence," "reliance on oral tradition," and "emphasis on negative evidence." Jackson repeats his "detective" imagery.[34]

Because no historian of his generation even approached his prominence in the eyes of scholars of Lewis and Clark, Jackson's denigration of Fisher's work and praise of the Phelps article probably explain why so many historians of the American West place little credibility in Fisher's book.[35] Indeed, a surprising number of historians will not even consider the possibility of homicide. Murder was not only a possibility, but a probability. Lewis's most notable biographer, Richard Dillon, agrees.[36]

Only a forensic examination of the remains can prove homicide. Meanwhile, this historian of the Natchez Trace finds it incredible and inconceivable that any scholar dare state *unequivocally* that Meriwether Lewis contemplated suicide as he rode into Grinder's Stand that pleasant fall evening in 1809. A perfect target for outlaws, Lewis was probably their victim.

The Sacajawea of Eva Emery Dye

Ronald Laycock

Eva Emery Dye* is credited with creating the myth of Sacajawea. Her book *The Conquest: the True Story of Lewis and Clark*[1] is not a true story but rather a historical novel. Actual references to Sacajawea in her novel are few, and, unfortunately, these few references are historically very inaccurate. They portray a Sacajawea that is far different from the Sacajawea we find in the journals of Lewis and Clark.

Eva Emery Dye's reputation as a factual historical novelist has perhaps lent credibility to *The Conquest*. After all, it was supposed to be the "true story of Lewis and Clark," and the American public was about to celebrate the first centennial of the Lewis and Clark Expedition. Not many books had been written about the Lewis and Clark Expedition in 1902, and only condensed, edited versions of the original journals were available at that time. Her book not only met the need for a factual book about the Lewis and Clark Expedition; it gave the American people a heroine, Sacajawea.

Let us look at a few of the references to Sacajawea that are found in *The Conquest*:

> Out of Ross' Hole Sacajawea pointed the way by Clark's Pass, over the Continental Divide, to the Big Hole River where the trail disappeared or scattered. But Sacajawea knew the spot.... "Yonder, see, a door in the mountains."[2]
>
> "Onward" still urged Sacajawea, "the gap there leads to your canoes."[3]
>
> Before them arose, bewildering, peak on peak, but again the Bird Woman, Sacajawea, pointed out the Yellowstone Gap. The Bozeman Pass of today, on the great Shoshone Highway.[4]
>
> Sacajawea, modest princess of the Shoshones, heroine of the great Expedition, stood with her babe in her arms and smiled upon them from the shore. So had she stood in the Rocky Mountains pointing out the gates. So had she followed the great rivers, navigating the continent.
>
> Sacajawea's hair was neatly braided, her nose was fine and straight, and her skin was pure copper like the statue in some old Florentine gallery. Madonna of her race, she had led the way to a new time. To the hands of this girl, not yet eighteen, had been entrusted the key that unlocked the road to Asia.

---

* Dye's spelling of the name, Sacajawea, is retained throughout the paper in place of the more common spelling, Sacagawea.

> Some day upon the Bozeman Pass, Sacajawea's statue will stand beside that of Clark. Some day, where the rivers part, her laurels will vie with those of Lewis. Across North America a Shoshone Indian Princess touched hands with Jefferson, opening a country.[5]

This was the Sacajawea Eva Emery Dye gave to the public in her book *The Conquest*. But her contribution to the myth of Sacajawea went far beyond the pages of her book. To understand the Sacajawea of Eva Emery Dye we must first understand Eva Emery Dye herself. And we must look at a social and political movement that divided and polarized America for over sixty years. We have to look at the woman's suffrage movement, a movement in which Eva Emery Dye was a tireless, dedicated worker, and we must also look at the Equal Rights Amendment to the Constitution of the United States.

The first woman's rights convention was held in Seneca Falls, New York, in 1848, over one hundred and fifty years ago. The woman's rights movement got off to a slow start, but by 1869 two separate woman's suffrage movements had developed. In 1890 the two groups, the American Woman's Suffrage Association and the National Women's Suffrage Association, had merged into the National American Woman's Suffrage Association. Leaders of the movement included Elizabeth Cady Stanton and Susan B. Anthony.

Not surprisingly, not all men—or women—were in favor of granting women the right to vote. In fact, there were many strongly opposed to it. So strong was the anti-suffrage feeling that a National Association Opposed to Woman's Suffrage emerged. It developed into a movement with associations in more than twenty states by the early twentieth century.

Woman's suffrage became a popular subject for the press, with magazine articles, newspaper editorials, and cartoons appearing frequently in the publications of the time. Passionate feelings developed both for and against woman's suffrage. Refined easterners viewed the West as wild and uncivilized. Its inhabitants, both men and women, were considered crude and uncultured; only such people would want women to vote. No woman of culture and class would want to be involved in politics; their place was in the home, not the voting booth. Spokesmen in favor of woman's suffrage asked why only criminals, lunatics and women were denied the right to vote.

One of the ironies of the woman's suffrage movement is the location of its stronghold. It gained momentum not in the so-called liberal and progressive East, but in the new West. The first state to give women the right to vote wasn't yet a state. It was the Territory of Wyoming in the year 1869. Utah followed in 1870, but by 1910 only four states—Wyoming, Utah, Colorado, and Idaho—had granted women the right to vote.

Since men far outnumbered women in the new West, some have suggested that the men of those states had ulterior motives. Perhaps by giving women the right to vote, women would move into their states. Not only could the women vote; they would be available for courting and marriage as well.

Oregon had had an Oregon Equal Suffrage Association since 1873, and Eva Emery Dye was the Clackamus County chairman for the Association. In 1898, at the 25th annual convention of the Association, Abigail Scott Duniway spoke, demanding in an open letter that the state of Oregon ratify the Equal Rights Amendment. The measure was turned down by the voters—men—of Oregon.

Undaunted, the Oregon Equal Suffrage Association regrouped, looking for a personage, a woman, who could exemplify the ideals of womanhood they needed. Eva Emery Dye, in describing her search for such a person, wrote:

> I struggled along as best I could with the information I could get, trying to find a heroine.... Finally I came upon the name of Sacajawea and I screamed, "I have found my heroine!"
>
> I then hunted up every fact I could find about Sacajawea. Out of a few dry bones I found in the old tales of the trip I created Sacajawea and made her a real living entity. For months I dug and scraped for accurate information about the wonderful Indian maid.
>
> The world snatched at my heroine, Sacajawea.... The beauty of that faithful Indian woman with her baby on her back, leading those stalwart mountaineers and explorers through the strange land appealed to the world.[6]

Eva Emery Dye had found her heroine, and so had the woman's suffrage movement.

Following the publication of her book *The Conquest* in 1902, the Woman's Club of Portland formed a Sacajawea Statue Association with Eva Emery Dye as chairman. Their goal was to place a statue of Sacajawea in a city park in Portland, not only to recognize Sacajawea's efforts as a guide and interpreter but also to honor her as the pioneer mother of the state of Oregon. Women from Oregon and across the country sold Sacajawea spoons, mugs, and other souvenirs to raise money for the statue. They were successful in their efforts; a beautiful statue of Sacajawea was erected in Washington Park in Portland, where it stands today.

In 1905 two things happened simultaneously in Portland: both the 1905 Lewis and Clark Exposition and the National American Woman's Suffrage Association met there. Apparently the Lewis and Clark followers bought into the myth of Sacajawea, including noted author and historian Elliott Coues. The Sacajawea Statue Association also joined forces with the National American Woman's Suffrage Association (NAWSA) at this time.

The NAWSA convention opened June 28, 1905, and Sacajawea immediately figured prominently in the proceedings. Dr. Anna Howard Shaw, president of NAWSA, had this to say when she addressed the convention:

> At a time in the weary march when the hearts of the leaders had well nigh fainted within them, when success or failure hung a mere chance in the balance, this woman (Sacajawea) came to their deliverance and pointed out to the Captains the great Pass which led from the forks of the Three Rivers over the mountains.[7]

Dr. Shaw went on to link Sacajawea of the Lewis and Clark Expedition with the woman's suffrage movement when she said:

> Forerunner of Civilization, great leader of men, patient and motherly woman, we bow our hearts to do you honor! May we... learn the lessons of calm endurance, of patient persistence and unfaltering courage exemplified in your life, in our efforts to lead men through the Pass of justice, which goes over the mountains of prejudice...to the land of perfect freedom, one in which men and women together shall in perfect equality solve the problems of the nation.8

On July 6th, 1905, the statue of Sacajawea was unveiled. Susan B. Anthony gave the address, saying:

> The recognition of the assistance rendered by a woman in the discovery of this great section of the country is but the beginning of what is due. Next year the men of this proud state, made possible by a woman, will decide whether women should at last have the rights in it which have been denied them so many years. Let men remember that part that women have played in its settlement and progress and vote to give them these rights which belong to every citizen.[9]

Oregon did not ratify the Equal Rights Amendment in 1906. It was defeated in 1906 and again in 1908 and 1910. Finally, in 1912 Oregon narrowly passed the measure. Eva Emery Dye and others now devoted themselves to helping get the measure passed in other states.

Unfortunately, the woman's suffrage movement leaders, including Eve Emery Dye, were never aware of one important incident in the life of Sacajawea. They did not know of the potential importance of a historic drama that unfolded on November 24, 1805, when the expedition was camped on the north side of the Columbia River near the Pacific Ocean. The party was cold, wet, hungry, and exhausted. They had conquered a continent, yet here they could not find enough food to sustain them or a suitable place for winter quarters. Their equipment was in need of repair. Their clothes were in tatters. A decision must be made: where should they establish winter quarters? Should they stay in their present location or should they move across the river where friendly natives told them more elk were available and suitable sites for winter quarters could be found?

Crossing the Columbia River at its mouth in their clumsy dugout canoes would be dangerous, and they were not sure what the other side would be like. Were there really more elk over there? Would they find suitable winter quarters on the south side? Lewis and Clark were good leaders and they were also good listeners. This was a decision that would affect them all. After talking over their situation with the men and the options they had, Lewis and Clark put the decision to a vote.

On November 24th, 1805, the men of the expedition voted on whether to stay where they were or cross over to the other side. Even York, Clark's slave, voted. And Sacajawea also voted along with the men, and her vote counted along with the votes of the men. One hundred and fifteen years before women were given the right to vote in America and one hundred and forty-three years before Native Americans were given the right to vote, Sacajawea, an Indian woman still in her teens, voted on American soil along with the men of the Corps of Discovery.

Unfortunately, the promoters of woman's suffrage were not aware of this historic moment or they could have used it to further their cause. The image of Sacajawea casting her vote, along with the men, would have made her a true heroine for the woman's suffrage movement.

Imagine, if you will, a painting of this scene, a painting that has never been executed. And let us permit the artist to take some liberties with historical accuracy as they often do. Without a ballot box the members of the Corps of Discovery, one by one, drop their ballots—their votes—into the upturned tricorn hat of Meriwether Lewis. The painter of the scene captures forever on canvas the exact moment when Sacajawea drops her ballot into the hat. Sacajawea voting, casting a ballot, along with the men, on American soil!

What an opportunity this could have been for Eva Emery Dye and the woman's suffrage movement. Think of how they could have used this scene. Sacajawea voting! But Eva Emery Dye was not aware of this event because Sacajawea's participation in the voting was not included in the condensed journals of Lewis and Clark that were at that time the only record of the expedition. Even Patrick Gass, in his journal, does not mention Sacajawea's voting. Eva Emery Dye and the other leaders of the woman's suffrage movement were not aware that Sacajawea could indeed have been a true heroine for the movement.

Because she did not know the real Sacajawea, Eva Emery Dye created a Sacajawea to meet her needs. To further the cause of woman's suffrage a myth was created, a myth that is still being perpetuated to this day. It is the myth of a young girl leading and guiding the men, encouraging the men and urging them on, saving the men from mistakes and misfortune, a myth that never happened but yet is believed by many. It is a myth that masks the real Sacajawea.

The Lewis and Clark Story in the 20th Century: The Emergence of the Outsiders

David Kvernes

The subject of Lewis and Clark in the twentieth century is far more daunting than I had expected since the amount of published material that has appeared in the past 100 years is staggering, to put it mildly. What we know for certain about the expedition is contained in the journals and field notes of Lewis, Clark, and a few of the enlisted men. A great deal of factual material has also been uncovered about the planning of the trip, the places visited along the route, and the lives of the participants both before and after their journey. On this foundation has been built a vast edifice of historical narratives, novels, school textbook accounts, biographies, art objects, films, TV documentaries, and a host of other memorabilia and legend related to the expedition. What I will attempt to show is that most of this great outpouring of words and objects has come since the end of the nineteenth century, and that whereas the focus of the limited amount that appeared before 1900 was on Lewis and Clark themselves, since that date we have seen a growing fascination with the other members of the expedition.

First, a few definitions. The outsiders in my title are all those who made the journey to the Pacific and back except Lewis and Clark, who thus become the insiders. They both had connections with people in power, relatively good educations, commissions as officers in the U.S. Army, and a modicum of wealth, which in Clark's case included slaves. The outsiders, by contrast, lacked all of these advantages, and in the cases of Sacagawea and the black man York, they had the additional disadvantage of being slaves. The others in the crew were mostly white men recruited from the enlisted ranks of the military to serve on this expedition, which was itself a military operation. A few, like Drouillard and Charbonneau, were civilians hired to do special tasks such as hunting or translating from Indian languages to English.

All of these outsiders were relatively unknown to the American public throughout the nineteenth century with the exception of Sergeant Patrick Gass, whose journals had been published and reprinted several times over that century, and John Colter, who was noted for his exploits after the expedition returned. It is doubtful, however, that even theirs were familiar names to the public, as Lewis's and Clark's certainly were. I was therefore surprised to learn how far the captains' fame had diminished as the nineteenth century went on. The first official edition of the journals, prepared in selected paraphrase by Nicholas Biddle, did not appear until 1814, eight years after the explorers returned. It did indeed appear in reprints throughout the century, but by 1890 access to the journals was restricted, mainly because the number in circulation was relatively small. The 1842 edition of Biddle, a truncated version of the 1814 edition, was reprinted about 20 times, but these reprints averaged only 250 copies, making a total of only 5,000, a small number even in nineteenth-century terms (Coues, I, cxxx). Patrick Gass's journal was also reprinted, but usually much condensed (Coues, I, cxvii).

To fill the gap left by Lewis and Clark's failure to publish their journals, apocryphal editions claiming to be genuine appeared in the years immediately after the return of the expedition. They were based mainly on Jefferson's message to Congress in 1806, which in turn was based on material sent down from the Mandan villages by expedition members in the spring of 1805. Thus Jefferson's message covered only the first part of the expedition. The apocryphal editions filled out the rest with spurious matter from Jonathan Carver's *Travels* and a variety of sources, including the writers' imaginations. According to Coues, these editions ceased appearing once the Biddle edition was published in 1814 (Coues, I, cviii-cxvii), but Paul Cutright, in his history of the journals, points out that an apocryphal edition appeared in 1840 and another may have been published by B. F. Ells in 1851 (38). Still, these were of little consequence, and Coues' conclusion is, for all practical purposes, accurate.

The periodical literature on Lewis and Clark that appeared in the nineteenth century is even scantier, only eleven items having turned up in my computer search up to 1893, when the Elliott Coues edition first appeared. About half of these were reviews of the editions of the journals mentioned earlier. Hence it is not surprising that Lewis and Clark's fame receded as the nineteenth century went on or that the other members of the expedition were almost totally ignored.

Stephen Ambrose goes so far as to say that "through most of the nineteenth century [Lewis] was relatively ignored and in some danger of being forgotten." He also maintains that Clark's reputation in the nineteenth century "rested far more on his accomplishments in St. Louis as superintendent of Indian affairs than on the expedition" (Ambrose, 474). These are, in my opinion, exaggerations of their relative obscurity, but it is clear that they were not as well remembered as we are apt to think. Yet their place in the public imagination was far greater than that of the other members of the expedition.

The answers are not far to seek. Lewis and Clark alone were the chief objects of public adulation upon their return, and newspaper accounts and local celebrations in honor of their accomplishments almost invariably included only the two leaders. Sacagawea and her husband and baby left the expedition at the Hidatsa villages, where they had been recruited, while York, Clark's slave, stayed with him but remained a slave rather than a free man, in spite of York's repeated petitions for freedom. Colter and several others left the expedition to join fur-trapping parties before the expedition got to St. Louis. The enlisted men who did return mostly scattered to their homes after a few days or weeks of celebration in St. Louis, where they were lionized.

All this changed with the publication in 1893 of a new edition of the Biddle version of the journals, edited and profusely annotated by Elliott Coues. His notes re-opened the subject for historians and popularizers, and they also gave a sense of how little was known about the outsiders in the nineteenth century. Introducing a list of the expedition members, Coues writes, "Excepting Lewis, Clark, Gass, and Shannon, we know next to nothing more than the names of the men and woman who accomplished an immortal purpose" (253, n8). Coues supplies a paragraph each on Floyd, Colter, Cruzatte, the Field brothers, Labiche, Lepage, Shannon, and Shields. For most of the rest he simply says, "No more known of him." For Sacagawea he says, "...otherwise Bird-woman, with her infant born Feb. 11th, 1804. See note 13, p. 189." That note quotes Lewis's unflattering remark on Charbonneau, "A man of no peculiar merit," and goes on to provide Coues' own comparison of Charbonneau to his wife: "...in the light of the narrative he appears to have been a poor specimen, consisting chiefly, of a tongue to wag in a mouth to fill; and had he possessed the comprehensive saintliness of his baptismal name, he would have been a minus function still in comparison with his wife Sacagawea, the wonderful 'Bird-woman,' who contributed a full man's share to the Expedition, besides taking care of her baby." Here is the earliest source for those legends that were to bloom so luxuriantly throughout the twentieth century.

Coues is also the earliest authority for legendary—and negative—material on York, the slave. His entry in the company list is brief: "York, a negro slave, belonging to Captain Clark. See note 31, p. 159." The note begins: "York was evidently a wag. When he returned to St. Louis and been freed he used to get drunk and tell funny stories...." The note closes with this sentence: "York's stories grew with every glass that went down, till Mr. Biddle might have wondered what his *History of the Expedition* had to do with that multitudinous host who conquered the land, under the leadership of a black drum-major about ten feet tall." Coues provides no authority for these remarks; they seem to come from simple late-nineteenth-century racial prejudice. York, by the way, wasn't freed until later, after he had moved from St. Louis.

The second big boost to Lewis and Clark studies came in 1904 with the appearance of a fairly complete edition of the original journals, in contrast to Biddle's selected paraphrase. Masterfully edited by Reuben Gold Thwaites, it served as the standard edition of the journals until Gary Moulton's definitive edition began appearing in the 1980s. Thwaites' compete original journals supplied much more material on the outsiders than had the Biddle edition, and hence its appearance stimulated great interest in these lesser-known figures.

The Sacagawea revival, however, began even before the appearance of the Thwaites edition; it is clearly based on the stimulus provided by the Coues edition. In 1902 Eva Emery Dye, a worker in the women's sufferage movement, published *The Conquest: The True Story of Lewis and Clark.* As Ronald Laycock tells us in a paper read at this conference in 1999, "Eva Emery Dye is credited with creating the myth of Sacagawea" (429). A fairly competent historian in most respects, she let her enthusiasm for the suffrage movement color her view of Sacagawea's accomplishments. Laycock describes her search for a suitable model of ideal womanhood, quoting from her journals: "I struggled along as best I could with the information I could get, trying to find a heroine....Finally I came upon the name of Sacajawea and I screamed, 'I have found my heroine!" (quoted in Laycock, 432).

The passages devoted to Sacagawea in Dye's book though limited are the most flowery and the best remembered, and they have survived to inspire a number of writings and works of art. One of the earliest was a statue of Sacagawea commissioned for the 1905 Lewis and Clark centennial celebration in Portland, Oregon, a project in which Dye played a key role. Her book also inspired Leonard Crunelle's sculpture entitled *Bird Woman*, which was unveiled in 1910 and still stands on the grounds of the North Dakota state capitol (Kessler, 90, 210).

The most thorough and scholarly treatment of the Sacagawea phenomenon is Donna Kessler's 1996 book, *The Making of Sacagawea: A Euro-American Legend.* She shows how Dye's book not only reflects the author's dedication to the women's suffrage movement but also her perhaps unconscious aim to support the Euro-American myth of manifest destiny (89). Sacagawea is described as the guide to the expedition, making her the key to its success. Also, her "royal birth" (she is the sister of Chief Cameahwait), light skin, slender figure, and fringed buckskin clothing make her a perfect embodiment of white notions of the Indian princess, in sharp contrast to nineteenth-century images of Indian women as squaws and savages. Note, for example, Lewis and Clark's usual references to her as "Charbono's squar" or simply "the Indian woman." They do, however, begin to call her Sacagawea, in various spellings, late in the journals.

Dye's flattering descriptions are carried over into the next important study, Grace Raymond Hebard's *Sacagawea, a Guide and Interpreter of the Lewis and Clark Expedition*, which appeared in 1932. Hebard's main contribution to the legend, however, is to add many years to her life, claiming on the basis of oral testimony that she lived to be nearly 100, ending her days among her own Shoshone people, where she is said to have helped them to assimilate to Euro-American culture. Like Dye's book, this one sold well, and it became the definitive biography of Sacagawea for several decades, providing material for school textbooks and other popular publications (Kessler, 101-02).

Among those popular writings were a number of historical and romantic novels turned out in the 1940s, '50s, and '60s. They are too numerous even to list; suffice it to say that most of them show Sacagawea as an Indian princess, model mother and caregiver, firm supporter of manifest destiny, principal guide to the expedition and, in the romantic novels, the object of white men's romantic attentions. The man she is most often linked with is Captain William Clark, and though he returns her affection, he is barred from a permanent connection by prevailing taboos against miscegenation. Her husband, Charbonneau, who is reported in the journals to have beaten her several times, is cast as the villain. Larry McMurtry, in a recent essay entitled "Sacagawea's Nickname," perpetuates this legend. He doesn't go nearly as far as the romantic novelists, concluding sensibly, "I wouldn't suggest a romance or even a flirtation, but I do think the two had a friendly rapport" (McMurtry, 72). The nickname is "Janey," and it appears once in the journals and again in a letter from Clark to Charbonneau written after the expedition had returned.

Works of art featuring Sacagawea continued to appear throughout the twentieth century, including paintings, statues, a commemorative plate in the Hamilton Collection, and most recently, the Sacagawea gold dollar. All of them more or less reflect the romantic legends that characterize the novels and other popular accounts.

All this is not to deny that Sacagawea was an unusually resourceful, generous, hard-working, and therefore admirable woman. As Lewis and Clark both make clear in the journals, she contributed more than her share to the success of the expedition while at the same time caring for her boy Jean Baptiste, or Pompey, who was only two months old when the expedition set out from the Mandan villages. Sadly, in Lewis's letter to the Secretary of War, listing, with an eye to their compensation, the contributions of each member of the expedition, her name is omitted, and she, along with York, received no compensation whatever (Betts, 149, 192, n4).

Turning now to the enlisted men and civilians who accompanied Lewis and Clark, it is clear that they are a mixed group containing a few who have become well known and a number who received no notice in the nineteenth century and very little in the twentieth. Lewis's letter to the Secretary of War might have made them more familiar to the public, but it was referred to only briefly by Coues and was not published in full until Donald Jackson included it in his *Letters of the Lewis and Clark Expedition* in 1962. In that letter Lewis praises most of the men of the expedition in moving language and singles out a few for special mention.

Exceptions to the general anonymity of the enlisted men in the nineteenth century were Patrick Gass, whose journals were published early in the nineteenth century, and John Colter, whose trials and exploits in the Yellowstone country after 1806 were, according to Coues, "repeatedly told" in the nineteenth century, for example in Bradbury's *Travels* and Washington Irving's *Astoria* (Coues, 254). In addition to Gass's journals, accounts by Ordway, Floyd, and Whitehouse have been published from time to time since 1893, providing material for new publications on them.

The enlisted men's anonymity began to fade with the publication of Coues' edition in 1893, but their rehabilitation was neither so sudden nor so complete as was Sacagawea's. The biggest single addition to the stories of these men came with Charles G. Clarke's *The Men of the Lewis and Clark Expedition: A Biographical Roster of the Fifty-one Members*, which appeared in 1970, although Donald Jackson includes new information on most of the men in his 1962 edition of the letters. Book-length treatments of individuals have appeared, especially after 1950, including three on John Colter in 1926, 1936, and 1952, all of them focusing on his exploits after leaving the expedition, most notably his discovery of the geysers and boiling pots in the Yellowstone area, two on George Drouillard in 1964 and 2000, and one on George Shannon for juveniles in 1941. More than any other historian, James Ronda has done much to direct attention to the outsiders, among other places in his essay, "'A Most Perfect Harmony': The Lewis and Clark Expedition as an Exploration Community" (1988) and in his carefully researched *Lewis and Clark among the Indians* (1984).

The efforts to uncover new material on all the enlisted men have yielded rather satisfying results, enabling writers such as Stephen Ambrose to deal in much greater detail with individual enlisted men than would otherwise be possible. Coming through clearly is his admiration for men such as Drouillard and the Field brothers, who accompanied Lewis on the ill-fated foray up the Marias River. We now see these men as complex human beings much more fully than a reading of the journals alone makes possible.

That applies to York the slave as well as to the white men. His story is the last to emerge in anything like a complete form. Not surprisingly, the journals say little about him, but what they do say makes clear he was as useful a member of the company as the average enlisted man. In addition, his strange appearance in the eyes of the Indians smoothed the way for the party in several difficult situations. A number of articles on York have appeared since 1960, but the most thorough and scholarly work is Robert B. Betts' 1985 book, *In Search of York: The Slave Who Went to the Pacific with Lewis and Clark*. In addition to giving us the facts of his life both before and after the expedition, Betts examines the legends that have grown up around him. Among them are York the buffoon, York the lover of Indian women, and York of the St. Louis taverns. All have some basis in the journals or other reliable sources, but Betts finds many accounts to be exaggerated or unsupported by evidence. He also exposes the untruths and exaggerations in several articles by well meaning writers who have attempted to combat the negative pictures that abound in the literature about York (77-80). He deals at length with one story that may or may not be true, the story put forward by the mountain man Zenus Leonard that York spent his last years among the Crow Indians in Montana, living happily and in high regard among them (135-43). Betts makes a fairly strong case against this having happened. This story oddly parallels the one told about Sacagawea's returning in old age to live among the Shoshones.

In an appendix to the Betts book, James Holmberg explores the question of Clark's ill-treatment of York after their return from the expedition as revealed in newly discovered letters from Clark to his brother Jonathan (151-70). It is a sad story that does no credit to Clark. In May of 1809, Clark writes: "He is here but of very little Service to me. [He is] insolent and Sulky, I gave him a severe trouncing the other Day and he has much mended Sence. Could he be hired for any thing at or near Louisville, I think if he was hired there a while to a Severe Master he would See the difference and do better" (quoted in Betts, 162). He later regretted these actions and eventually freed York, giving him a wagon and six horses, which enabled him to set up in business as a freight hauler in Tennessee and Kentucky. According to Washington Irving's report of a conversation with Clark in 1832, York died of cholera in Tennessee while on his way to rejoin his old master in St. Louis. He had failed in business and was mired in poverty after a few years of freedom (Betts, 119). Studies like this one have brought the outsiders vividly before us, enabling us to appreciate better their contributions to the expedition and their sufferings and worth as human beings.

If we are to gauge public awareness of the outsiders, we cannot fail at least to mention the great impression made by Hollywood films and more recently by TV documentaries such as the 1997 Ken Burns and Dayton Duncan series on Lewis and Clark and the book based on it. There has also been a great surge of publicity in the popular media as local and national organizations prepare for the bicentennial, not least in South Dakota. These recent projects have probably done more to bring members of the expedition to the public's attention than all the books and articles that have preceded them.

A final question might be asked: Why have the outsiders emerged in the twentieth century as important actors in this great undertaking? The appearance of new editions of the journals edited by Coues and Thwaites has already been noted as the first stimulus. Other obvious causes are the women's suffrage movement in the early twentieth century, the feminist movement of the 1960s and after, the Civil Rights Movement, the American Indian Movement, and the recent emphasis in literature and school curricula on multiculturalism. Pervading these movements and going beyond them is what I see as the nearly universal desire to recognize ordinary people. Among other places, we see it in the Vietnam Memorial in Washington, D.C., in the recognition given to police and fire fighters in New York City, and in the series of short articles on individual victims of the 9-11 disaster in *The New York Times*.

We have come to distrust big business, big government, and other institutions controlled by powerful white men, who may no longer be exclusively Anglo-Saxon and Protestant but are nevertheless not admired. We do still admire Lewis and Clark, at least those of us who are white, but I suspect that a survey of opinions among American Indians would yield mixed results at best. Their views are shaped by issues similar to those put forward by revisionists among scholars of western American history such as Patricia Nelson Limerick, whose book *The Legacy of Conquest* has set the tone for many recent discussions of the American West.

A much more extreme statement of this revisionist position can be found in the opening paragraphs of Max Rittgers' paper read at this conference in 1998. Entitled "The Lewis and Clark Expedition Begins with the Amiotte Plate," it sees the Euro-American effort to explore, conquer, and civilize the West as starting, at least in South Dakota, with the Verendrye expedition in 1743 and being carried forward by Lewis and Clark, with much more devastating effects on Native Americans. He would probably agree that Sacajawea, York, and the enlisted men were mostly unwitting accomplices on this adventure and hence worthy, in their struggles and their dedication, of our attention and our praise.

"Over the Hill and Beyond the Sunset": Bernard DeVoto and the Expedition of Lewis and Clark

Robert C. Steensma

As the bicentennial of the epic journey of Lewis and Clark approaches, we can expect the emergence of a cottage industry of scholarly and popular treatments of that great event. Certainly the works of Stephen Ambrose, Dayton Duncan, and Ken Burns, to mention the most prominent, have started our generation's re-evaluation of that expedition, and this is good. Every generation must examine the history and tradition passed down to it, make its own judgments, and then go on from there.

As a Utahn transplanted from South Dakota, I find the great feats of the Lewis and Clark party fascinating. The expedition spent a great deal of time in my home state, and as I have visited Spirit Mound near Vermillion and loafed along the north banks of the Missouri, I have felt the presence of that group. But my first detailed awareness of that expedition came forty years ago through my reading of a volume by a man born in Utah. This writer was Bernard DeVoto, who in his introduction to his abridgement of the Lewis and Clark journals wrote that the expedition provided "the first report on the West, on the United States over the hill and beyond the sunset, on the province of the American future" (*Journals* ix).

The University of Utah, where I have taught, it seems at times, since the days of Meriwether Lewis and William Clark, has little information on a freshman from Ogden in the academic year 1914-1915, but I'm sure that his professors probably didn't realize that the short homely student would transfer to Harvard and from there go on to become one of America's most prominent essayists and historians of the American West.

Bernard Augustine DeVoto (1897-1955) was the son of an apostate Catholic father and an apostate Mormon mother. His paternal grandfather was an Italian cavalry officer who had been trained by the Jesuits and had taught at Notre Dame. His maternal grandfather, Samuel Dye, was a famous Mormon pioneer. Young DeVoto spent his freshman college year at the University of Utah, but received his degree at Harvard in 1919 after a stint in World War I as a lieutenant in the army infantry. He then successively taught at Ogden Junior High School, Northwestern University, and Harvard University before turning to free-lance writing in 1927. During the remaining years of his life he published five novels under his own name and four more under the pen-name "John August." The novels are not the work for which DeVoto is remembered. His real contribution to American intellectual history lies in the "Easy Chair" essays he wrote for *Harper's* magazine after 1935 and four major historical works: *The Year of Decision: 1846* (1943), *Across the Wide Missouri* (1947), which won the Pulitzer Prize for history, *The Course of Empire* (1952), which earned the National Book Award for history, and his one-volume abridgement of the journals of Lewis and Clark (1953). Also of great importance were *Mark Twain's America* (1932) and *Mark Twain at Work* (1942), both of which corrected Van Wyck Brooks' badly astigmatic criticism of Twain.

DeVoto was many things during his career. As Wallace Stegner, his close friend and biographer, has written, he was a "novelist, professor, editor, historian, pamphleteer, critic, and under a half-dozen aliases, hack writer" (*Sound of Mountain Water* 255), a man who "despised literary phonies, narcissistic artists, public confessors, gushers, long-hairs, and writers of deathless prose" (274). He fought at the lectern and in print with liberals and conservatives, Democrats and Republicans, Communists and Fascists, the FBI, and the literary establishment (including Robert Frost and Sinclair Lewis). He won more often than he lost, but he always left his opponents with the knowledge that they had had a lively fight with a first-rate mind. But most of all, he was proud to be an American, as he told Catherine Drinker Bowen in an undated letter. She had been criticized by an academic critic for what he sneeringly called her romantic addiction to American history. DeVoto writes:

> Dear Kitty:
>
> Sure you're romantic about American history. What your professor left out of account was the fact that it is the most romantic of all histories. It began in myth and has developed through three centuries of fairy stories. Whatever the time is in America it is always, at every moment, the mad and wayward hour when the prince is finding the little foot that alone fits into the slipper of glass. It is a little hard to know what romantic means to those who use the word umbrageously. But if the mad, impossible voyage of Columbus or Cartier or La Salle or Coronado or John Ledyard is not romantic, if the stars did not dance in the sky when the Constitutional Convention met, if Atlantis has any landscape stranger or the other side of the moon any lights or colors or shapes more unearthly than the customary homespun of Lincoln and the morning coat of Jackson, well, I don't know what romance is. Ours is a story made with the impossible, it is by chaos out of dream, it began as a dream and it has continued as dream down to the last headline you read in a newspaper, and of our dreams there are two things above all others to be said, that only madmen could have dreamed them or would have dared to—and that we have shown a considerable faculty for making them come true. The simplest truth you can ever write about our history will be charged and surcharged with romanticism, and if you are afraid of the word you had better start practicing seriously on your fiddle (*Letters* 285-286).

One can imagine what DeVoto would have to say about the political correctness of some modern revisionist historians and politicians who surrender to the demands of cultural extremists.

But the one intellectual area that fascinated DeVoto was the history of the American West. Having been born and grown to maturity in Utah, he could never get the West out of his blood, and it continued to engage his mind and his efforts for the rest of his life. He wrote about the history, personalities, problems, and prospects of the West in magazine columns, books, and articles. One of his greatest fascinations, however, was the journey of Lewis and Clark.

As early as 1936, he published an article in *The Saturday Review of Literature* entitled "Passage to India: From Christmas to Christmas with Lewis and Clark." This article deals with the experiences of the party from December 24, 1804, at the Mandan villages, until December 25, 1805, when they moved into Fort Clatsop at the mouth of the Columbia. DeVoto's narrative is enlivened by quotations from the journals of Clark, Sergeant John Ordway, Sergeant Patrick Gass, and Private Joseph Whitehouse, as well as by his own descriptions of Sacajawea, her husband Toussaint Charbonneau, "a bungler, a coward, and a bully" ("Passage" 3), and other members of the party. But DeVoto's novelist's eye is what makes the narrative most engaging. He describes the captains listening to information from the Mandans about the upper Missouri:

> One sees that firelight on intent faces as the Indians draw river courses on the puncheon [rough lumber] floor, scrawling with bits of charcoal the known bends and rapids, and the bearings of distant peaks, shaping a handful of ashes to show how a range loops down from the north, grunting and disputing, sending to the village for a brave whom chance may have led up some unknown creek. The captains listened, trying to check their informants by one another, never sure how much was guessed or rumored or perhaps merely invented about the uncharted waste, so many of whose rivers and summits they were to christen in the months ahead ("Passage" 4).

DeVoto is equally dramatic in describing the toil, the disappointment, the fears, and the perseverance of the party. But his best narrative comes at the end as he describes how Captain Clark perhaps felt as he looked over his Christmas presents at Fort Clatsop:

> A hero's Christmas presents, on the edge of the Pacific, with the now traversed continent behind him and the dream achieved. They attest an immortal deed, the affection of his comrade, the respect of his men. And the warm heart of Sacajawea, whose ailments he had treated with nitre and zinc sulphate and Rush's pills, whom he had delivered from her husband's blows, whose child also he had nursed and doctored, whom he had several times snatched from death, whom he had come to think of not as an Indian squaw but as a woman of extraordinary fineness and staunchness. And whose gratitude and loyalty were his. She has but inadequate words to give him on Christmas, the great medicine day of his race, but, accepting the custom she

> could not comprehend, knowing that he had been kind to her and that this was a day of kindness, she gave him what she had. History will remember William Clark as one of the greatest of its captains, and, remembering him, it will not forget the twenty-four white weasel tails that Janey [Clark's nickname for her] gave him on Christmas Day ("Passage" 28).

This essay was just the beginning of DeVoto's work with Lewis and Clark. In the next decade and a half, he would be doing the research and writing that would eventuate in *The Course of Empire*, with its 120-page narrative of the expedition, and his edition of the journals.

The progress of his work can be traced in Stegner's edition of DeVoto's letters. On April 30, 1944, he writes to Henry Steele Commager, "The job I'm eyeing is Lewis and Clark," and after inventorying his historical knowledge of the period, he confesses, "I'm taking a backward leap into a field where I'm virginal, bucolic, naive, wideeyed [sic], trustful and practically as ignorant as Red [Sinclair] Lewis. So, the idea is, you take me by my little hand and lead me in" (*Letters* 271-2). And he apologizes for asking so much of his historian friend:

> Sure, I know this is unconscionable, and you have more to do than you'll ever get done and who the hell am I to bust in on a busy man, and all that. On the other hand, you've got a stern obligation to your profession, and if amateurs will insist on trying to practice it, you've got to do what you can to keep the resulting damage at a minimum. Right? (*Letters* 272).

About eighteen months later, on December 28, 1945, he writes to another historian friend, Garrett Mattingly, that his book *Across the Wide Missouri* "is in the hand," but that as for the Lewis and Clark book, "I may not live to write it, I may live to learn better than to write it, it may turn out to be about Lewis and Conger" (*Letters* 282).

During the summer of 1946 DeVoto traced by auto the route of the expedition with his 1941 Buick Special and published four "Easy Chair" essays in *Harpers* for August, September, October, and November of 1946. The essays tell us less about Lewis and Clark than about DeVoto's experiences on the road. In an undated letter of December 1946 he tells his historian friend Samuel Eliot Morison,

> The humiliating truth is that I emptied my history tank with the fur trade book [*Across the Wide Missouri*] and am only beginning to refill it with Lewis and Clark. As a historian I have to operate on a small capital with a rapid turnover. Every book I write represents the sum total of my knowledge to the date signed to the preface (*Letters* 284).

By June 5, 1947, he is writing to George Stevens, managing editor of *The Saturday Review of Literature*, that he is planning to write a "book about Lewis and Clark which is supposed to end all books about Lewis and Clark. I have been reading off and on now for it for four years and am slowly swinging into the fundamental research right now" (*Letters* 235).

In May of 1950 DeVoto spent several weeks touring the Missouri River from its headwaters to its mouth with William Lederer, the novelist who wrote *All the Ships at Sea* and *The Ugly American*, and Montana novelist A. B. Guthrie (*The Big Sky*). DeVoto took the trip mainly to get material for an article or series of articles criticizing the Army Corps of Engineers' plan for flood control on the Missouri, but he wrote back to one of his hosts, Brigadier General Samuel Davis Sturgis, Jr., that the trip "was, of course, inestimably valuable to me as a historian. It will directly affect my Lewis and Clark book, making it better than it otherwise would have been" (*Letters* 359-60n. and 360).

But DeVoto never did finish a book devoted exclusively to a historical narrative of the Lewis and Clark adventure. Instead his narrative of the expedition was published as the two final chapters of *The Course of Empire*, which appeared in 1952. Chapter XI, "Westward the Course of Empire" (pages 435-484) covers the expedition from its start on May 14, 1804, to their arrival at the Great Falls of the Missouri on June 13, 1805. Chapter XII, "The Passage to India" (pp. 487-554) deals with the rest of the westbound expedition to Fort Clatsop and ends on December 7, 1805.

DeVoto's narrative of the expedition is a model of good historical writing: clear, lively, forceful, engaging, dramatic. Numerous examples could be cited: the confrontation between the Sioux and the members of the party at the Bad (Teton) River on September 25, 1804 (445-6), and their experiences with the Arikaras and the Mandans (448-70), to name just two. But more engaging and colorful than the customary histories are DeVoto's descriptive accounts of nature along the Missouri. Thus the fall of 1804:

> But the year was drawing in. Ever since they entered South Dakota, the lavender and purple hazes of autumn had softened the bluffs that bordered the river.... The great flights had been going southward, lighting briefly on the river by the hundreds. The sudden rains were bitter cold, the the wind had a honed edge, ice formed in still water at dawn, the clouds were lead-colored in always vaster masses, the gun-metal emptiness of the North made even sunny skies ominous. There had been two short, whirling snow storms. Flannel shirts had long since been issued and lately the skins of deer and elk killed for food had been going to the men, though they must have made uncomfortably stiff robes for there was no time for proper tanning (451).

Or, later, describing their passage through the famous Missouri Breaks:

> The bluffs are innumberably repeated—pyramidal, truncated, domed, writhen with erosion, some steep sides ruffled like the ruffles of a child's dress; white, gray, yellow, red, rust, cobalt, or veined horizontally with gray and black, bare or a little grassed or drab with greasewood or black where the dwarf cedar can grow. The banks crumble with a splash or a groan or a roar...and the olive-drab water boils and a small or a big wave swells toward the other shore. Tree roots snapped by the collapse stick straight out from the new raw bank and trees float off to strand at the next bend, or moor them-

> selves as sawyers, or build new courses on old snags.... Over river, shore, and bluffs is enormousness, the endless sky and the clouds that join and climb. Clouds and a quarter or a half of the sky turn black with inconceivable suddenness. A wind strikes out of them, the water begins to hiss, whitecaps or big waves leap at the boat, and navigation is over till the wind drops half an hour from now, tomorrow noon, day after tomorrow. The wind is as cold as it is violent; snow comes with it, or hail, or a battering and strangling rain. Against the trailing black gauzes of the storm, cottonwood trunks are a pale pure silver and their buds the pale green of the sky at daybreak.... Round such a bend, against such cottonwoods, up the dun-colored water, two pirogues, six dugouts, thirty-one minute figures in drenched and very cold buckskins while the sky flaws with rain (475).

The two chapters on the expedition in *The Course of Empire* clearly show that DeVoto's apprenticeship as a writer of fiction served him well as a historian.

But DeVoto's single volume which is probably read more widely than any of his other works is his abridged edition of the *Journals of Lewis and Clark*, first published in 1953 and reissued in 1997 with a forward by Stephen Ambrose. In the next few years until the bicentennial, DeVoto's single-volume edition will probably be read by far more people than the eight-volume edition of Gary Moulton. As Ambrose has written in his forward, "For the scholar, Moulton's is the definitive edition. For the rest of us, it complements but does not supersede the present volume. DeVoto's condensation is in its own way definitive. It is the ideal selection for the citizen-reader, an American classic in its own right, a book that will be read as long as the Republic lasts" (*Journals* xii).

Time today prevents my discussing little more than DeVoto's method in preparing this work for the press. In his preface he says that "I have omitted no important event and no incident of more than passing interest. I have included as much as seemed possible of the daily routine and the continuous direct observation of the new country the expedition was traveling. I have also included representative descriptions of the flora and fauna and all important descriptions of Indian life, omitting anthropological details" (xiv). DeVoto also omitted navigational and astronomical observations and records of temperature and weather as well as most of the extended discussions of animals and plants (xiv).

DeVoto made use of three earlier editions of the journals: Reuben Gold Thwaites' (seven volumes of text and one of maps, 1904-1905), Nicholas Biddle's (two volumes, 1814), and Elliott Coues' (four volumes, 1893). In addition to abridging the journals, DeVoto also took great pains to try wherever possible to correct factual mistakes made by the earlier editors and to refine their work with information that might bring into question some of their interpretations.

Much of the value of DeVoto's edition lies in the detailed and rich thirty-eight-page introduction in which he sets the expedition in its historical and political contexts. In his magnificent conclusion, he describes the journey of the Lewis and Clark party as the event which precipitated manifest destiny and the fulfillment of the American dream:

> But it gave not only Oregon but the entire American West to the American people as something with which the mind could deal. The westering people had crossed the Mississippi with the Louisiana Purchase and by that act had acquired the manifest destiny of going on to the Pacific. But the entire wilderness expanse, more than twice the size of the United States at the beginning of Jefferson's administration, was a blank, not only on the map but in human thought. It was an area of rumor, guess, and fantasy. Now it had been crossed by a large party who came back and told in assimilable and trustworthy detail what a large part of it was. Henceforth the mind could focus on reality. Here were not only Indians but the land itself and its conditions: river systems, valleys, mountain ranges, climates, flora, and a rich and varied membrane of detail relating them to one another and to familiar experience. It was the first report on the West, on the United States over the hill and beyond the sunset, on the province of the American future. So it was rather as a treasury of knowledge than as a great adventure story that the *History* became a national and international favorite, reprinted, translated, pirated, and counterfeited. It satisfied desire and it created desire: the desire of a westering nation
>
> That, the increase of our cultural heritage, the beginning of knowledge about the American West, must be accounted the most important result of the Lewis and Clark expedition (lx).

Thus Bernard DeVoto, the Utah and western expatriate, went east and then, ironically, became the champion of the region he had deserted in his youth. He died at age 58 of a heart attack at about 6:00 p.m. on November 13, 1955, in his New York hotel room just after an appearance on the CBS radio show "Adventure." In April of 1956, his ashes were scattered, very appropriately, on the Lochsa River in northern Idaho, not far from the Lolo Pass into Montana and not far from where Lewis and Clark made camp on September 9, 1805.

Catherine Drinker Bowen, whose romantic view of American history DeVoto applauded, perhaps best describes both his Utah boyhood and his long fascination with Lewis and Clark: "he knew these journal writers and these journeys as he knew the back of his hand or the Wasatch Mountains and Weber Canyon, where he roamed as a boy" (*Four Portraits* 9). And, as Stegner puts it so rightly, DeVoto's historical works "warrant all the superlatives they have consistently won; they belong on the shelf that contains only Prescott, Bancroft, Motley, Adams; and they are not unworthy of the company they find there" (*Four Portraits* 106).

Lewis and Clark, Harbingers of Colonialism

Rita Easterby Olson

"Behold, the Lord Thy God hath set the land before thee: go up and possess it." These words, which appear on William Clark's tomb, are from the King James version of Deuteronomy 1: 2. Moses is addressing the people of Israel, who are poised on the edge of Canaan. As they invade this unfamiliar territory, the Israelites make decisions regarding the use of the land and the treatment of its indigenous people, and their choices are predicated on their belief that they have a divine right to possess Canaan. These lines from Deuteronomy provide a background for viewing the journey of the Corps of Discovery narrated in *The Journals of Lewis and Clark*. Like the leaders of Israel, Lewis and Clark's choices reflect their status as members of a settler colony moving into unfamiliar territory, and their assessment of the land and treatment of the indigenous people they encounter is predicated upon their belief in their superiority. Using postcolonial methodology to examine the imperialistic attitude seen in President Jefferson's instructions and the explorers' journals leads to the conclusion that these three men regarded both the land west of the Mississippi and all the life dwelling on that land as theirs to possess and exploit.

In 1978 Edward Said published *Orientalism*, which contains his initial discussion of the effects of colonization, a discussion which is the basis for postcolonial theory. Of the three definitions of Orientalism provided by Said, the one pertinent to this discussion, is the "Western style for dominating, restructuring, and having authority over the Orient" (3). According to Said,

> Orientalism is never far from what Denys Hay has called the idea of Europe, a collective noun identifying "us" Europeans as against all "those" non-Europeans…the idea of European identity as a superior one in comparison with all the non-European peoples and cultures.… Orientalism depends for its strategy on this flexible positional superiority, which puts the Westerner in a whole series of possible relationships with the Orient without ever losing him the upper hand. (7)

Said posits that "knowledge of the Orient, because generated out of strength, in a sense *creates* the Orient, the Oriental, and his world" (40). He believes that Europeans were convinced that only they could make the best use of the Oriental artifacts; in return, they would provide their "judgment as to what was best for the modern Orient" (79). As a result, "the Orient of the modern Orientalist is not the Orient as it is, but the Orient as it has been Orientalized" (104).

In *Postcolonial Theory: A Critical Introduction*, critic Leela Gandhi defines postcolonialism as a "disciplinary project devoted to the academic task of revisiting, remembering, and, crucially, interrogating the colonial past" (4). In support of this definition, she uses Asher Nandy's description of two types of conquests: the physical conquest of territories and the "conquest of minds, selves, [and] cultures," which was pioneered by "rationalists, modernists and liberals who argued that imperialism was really the messianic harbinger of civilization to the uncivilized world" (15). One way of "revisiting, remembering, and, crucially, interrogating the colonial past" is to use artifacts produced by the colonizer to examine the strategies used by members of the settler colony as they come into contact with unfamiliar territory and indigenous peoples.

How can one make the leap from the British/French/American response to the Orient and the Euro-American response to its ongoing encounter with Native populations? While I am not naive enough to believe that one may simply insert Native American for Oriental in postcolonial references to the Orient, I do believe that some of the basic tenets of postcolonialism will allow one to use the journals of Lewis and Clark in order to "revisit," "remember," and "interrogate" our colonial past, providing the reader with a new way of viewing the journals arising out of the Voyage of Discovery.

According to Said, "to colonize meant at first the identification—indeed the creation—of interests; these could be commercial, communicational, religious, military, cultural" (100). Thomas Jefferson begins this process of identification by voicing his belief in an "Empire of Liberty," writing that "our confederacy must be viewed as the nest from which all America, North or South, is to be peopled" (qtd. in Ambrose 56). As President, Jefferson clearly articulates his commercial interests in the land west of the Mississippi through the instructions he provides Lewis for the expedition. Written on June 20, 1803, these instructions leave no doubt as to the final outcome of the expedition: the colonization of the area for commercial purposes (Bergon, xxiv). Jefferson states the object of the mission: "to explore the Missouri river & such principal streams of it, as, by its course and communication with the waters of the Pacific ocean…may offer the most direct & practicable water communication across this continent for the purposes of commerce" (qtd. in Bergon xxiv). He instructs Lewis to provide celestial observations for mapping the area and to make observations about "the soil & face of the country, its growth & vegetable productions, the animals of the country…the mineral productions of every kind…and the climate" (Bergon xxv-vi). In addition, Lewis is to compile as much information about the Native populations as possible. Jefferson writes: "It will be useful to acquire what knolege you can of the state of morality, religion, and information among them, as it may better enable those who endeavor to civilize & instruct them, to adopt their measures to the existing notions and practices of those on whom they are to operate" (xxv). Above all, Lewis is to exercise care in the expedition: "We value too much the lives of citizens to offer them to probable destruction....In the loss of yourselves, we should also lose the information you have acquired" (xxvii), for this information is of paramount importance to those settler colonies that will follow this expedition.

The journals that Lewis and Clark kept provide ample evidence of their zeal in carrying out Jefferson's instructions; they can not help but create commercial interest in the land lying west of the Mississippi River. Throughout their journals, the explorers provide descriptions of the land and catalogues of the plant and animal life—descriptions which will encourage the settlement of the area by Euro-American colonizers. In addition, their depiction of the indigenous peoples they encounter provides numerous examples of their belief that these peoples need to be "instructed" by Lewis and Clark, "messianic harbinger[s] of civilization to the uncivilized world" (Gandhi 15).

Both Lewis and Clark consistently describe the land lying between the Mississippi River and the Pacific Ocean in terms of its agricultural value. On July 20, 1804, Clark describes the area near Cass County, Nebraska: "The Praries as far as I was out appear to be well watered, with small Streems of running water" (Moulton 2: 398-99). On May 7, 1805, Lewis describes the land along the Missouri River west of the Poplar River as "the most beautiful plains we have yet seen, it rises gradually from the river bottom to the hight of fifty or sixty feet, then becoming level as a bowling green. Extends back as far as the eye can reach" (Moulton 4: 121). On the return trip Lewis evaluates the land around Camas Prairie, Idaho: his May 9, 1806, journal entry states that he "has no doubt but this tract of country if cultivated would produce in great abundance every article essentially necessary to the comfort and subsistence of civilized man" (Bergon 403).

The catalogues of indigenous plant and animal life would also heighten the nineteenth-century Euro-American reader's commercial interest: these plants and animals are available for immediate use by settlers. As they travel westward, Lewis and Clark are careful to note the edible plants along the trail. Entries record Clark's observation on August 24, 1804, of "great quantities of a kind of current or froot resembling the current in appearance much richer and finer flavd...makes a Delightfull Tart" (Moulton 2: 504), and on September 3rd he reports "great quantities of Plumbs of a most delisious flavour...also Som grapes of a superior quality large & well flavored" (Moulton 3: 44). Lewis's May 6, 1805, entry even provides an enticement for gourmets: it describes the radix as "a tuberous bulb [which] forms a considerable article of food with the Indians of the Missouri....I have no doubt but our epicures would admire this root very much, it would serve them in their ragouts and gravies instead of the truffles Morella" (Moulton 4: 125-6). On

August 1 Lewis writes of meeting "with great quantities of black gooseberries and serviceberries, which I found to be excellent" (Moulton 5: 32).

Not only would the region west of the Mississippi provide tillable acres and ready access to native fruits, but also the vast numbers of buffalo, elk, deer, and other animals catalogued would provide food and clothing for Euro-American colonizers. On April 22, 1805, as he journeys between the White Earth and Yellowstone Rivers, Lewis describes a "delightful view of the country…exposing to the first glance of the spectator immense herds of Buffaloe, Elk, deer & Antelopes feeding in one common and boundless pasture" (Moulton 4: 60). He notes that the "flesh of the beaver is esteemed a delicacy among us; I think the tale a most delicious morsal" (Moulton 4: 100). The July 31 entry testifies to the result of such abundance: Lewis writes, "when we have plenty of fresh meat I find it impossible to make the men take any care of it, or use it at least frugally" (Moulton 5, 18), and there are occasions when buffalo are slaughtered for their humps alone. No thought is given to conserving meat for the indigenous populations or future settlers: like the land, the animal life is theirs to exploit.

Lewis does not simply view the animals as a food supply; he also considers their possible commercial value. He writes of the possible uses of buffalo wool, "which had been bleached by exposure to the weather and became perfectly white…[with] every appearance of the wool of the sheep, tho much finer and more silkey and soft. I am confident that an excellent cloth may be made of the wool" (Moulton 4: 51). His May 25, 1805, description of bighorns refers to their commercial value as well: "I have no doubt but it would [make] eligant and ucefull hair combs, and might probably answer as many valuable purposes to civilized man, as it dose to the savages who form their watercups spoons and platters of it" (Moulton 4: 194).

In addition to cataloging plants and animals having commercial value to any Euro-American settler, Lewis and Clark point out locations for possible forts and settlements, information which will be useful to the military, who will be responsible for ensuring the safety of future settlers. Clark discusses Council Bluffs as "a verry proper place for a Trading establishment & fortification The Soil of the Bluff well adapted for Brick….Great deel of timber abov in the two points….perhaps no other Situation is as well calculated for a Trading establishment" (Moulton 4:41-2). After viewing the three forks area of the Missouri River, Lewis writes, "There is timber enough here to support an establishment, provided it be erected with brick or stone either of which would be much cheaper than wood as all the materials for such a work are immediately at the spot" (Moulton 5: 8).

While the journals provide a description of a land awaiting Euro-American cultivation, they also describe the discovery of the quickest way to get from the Mississippi to the Pacific coast. Even though they did not find the direct passage that Jefferson hoped for, their expedition proved that travel is possible; the land was ripe for colonization by Euro-Americans.

There was, of course, one impediment to the exploitation of these vast natural resources: the Native populations who inhabited the area. Lewis and Clark's treatment of these indigenous populations provides support for Said's belief that the European identity (or in this case the Euro-American identity) was a "superior one in comparison with all the non-European cultures" (7). Lewis and Clark would provide the Native Americans with their "judgment as to what was best" for them (Said 79). The decisions Lewis and Clark make when interacting with indigenous people reveal their strategy for "dominating, restructuring, and having authority" (Said 3) over the Native Americans they meet, a strategy revealed through their references to the Native Americans they encounter, their consistently paternalistic behavior toward the tribes at councils, and their treatment of their guide Sacagawea.

Throughout their journals, Lewis and Clark refer to the Native Americans as "savages" or "thos children of ours," phrasing that places them in the inferior position of those who would need the Euro-Americans to guide them to a civilized state. In addition, the explorers consistently refer to Jefferson as the "Great Father" residing in Washington, a reference intended to reinforce the Native Americans' status as children. It also elevates Jefferson, and the U.S. government, to the paternal position of caretaker for these children. For example, on August 17, 1806, Clark writes that he has told the Mandans that "we Should inform their great father of their conduct towards his faithfull red children and he would take Such Steps as will bring about a lasting peace between them and his faithful red children" (Bergon 473).

Lewis and Clark establish a consistent pattern in their treatment of "thos children" as they journey across the territory. The July 22, 1804, entry describes this pattern: "Send for Some of the Chiefs of [the] nation to let them Know of the Change of Government to Cultivate Friendship with them, the objects of our journey and to present them with a flag and Some Small Presents" (Moulton 2: 408). According to Ambrose, Lewis's speech to the Otos on August 3rd informs them that "the Missouri River country now belonged to the United States, so that all those who lived in that country, whether red or white 'are bound to obey the commands of their great Chief the President who is now your only father....He is the only friend to whom you can now look for protection, or from whom you can ask favours, or receive good councils, and he will take care to serve you, & not deceive you'" (qtd. in Ambrose 156-7). In addition, Clark notes on that date that Lewis also gave "Some advice to them and Directions on how They were to Conduct themselves" (Moulton 2: 440). As obedient children, the Native Americans should not try to stop the expedition; they should, instead, make peace with their neighbors.

At each council Lewis and Clark assert their dominance over the various tribes when they decide who will be the grand chief of each tribe and bestow upon him a medal with Jefferson's face on it—a reminder that the chief's authority now comes from the U.S. government. They also bestow medals of second and third grade to the inferior chiefs. In keeping with their dominant position, Lewis and Clark never write of recognizing leaders from the various tribes; instead, Clark writes on August 3, 1804, of "the names of chiefs made this day" (Bergon 22) and on August 30th he writes of "Preparing Some presents for the chiefs which we intended [to] make by giving Meadels" (Bergon 39). The chiefs have no power in their own right: their power comes from being "made" chiefs by either Lewis or Clark.

In return for their good behavior, the natives will be protected. On August 20, 1805, Lewis answers the Shoshones' request for guns by telling them that "whitemen would come to them with an abundance of guns and every other article necessary to their defence and comfort, and that they would be enabled to supply themselves with these articles on reasonable terms in exchange for the skins of the beaver Otter and Ermin so abundant in their country" (Bergon 251). Both Lewis and Clark believe that status as children dependent upon the benevolence of their "Great Father" in Washington is fair recompense for the Native Americans' giving up their land, their culture, and their way of life.

The first time their authority is called into question, Lewis and Clark act swiftly to put these "children" in their place. On September 28, 1804, several Teton Sioux soldiers take the tow cable used to drag the keel boat up the river. According to Clark, Chief Black Buffalo "told Capt. Lewis who was at the bow the men who Set upon the Roap was Soldiers and wanted Tobacco & then we might proceed. Capt. L. Said [he] would not agree to be forced into any thing, the 2d Chief demanded flag & Tobacco, which we refused" (Bergon 57). If Lewis agrees to pay the toll for passage up the river, he is also agreeing that the Sioux have a right to ask for it: they are equals. He refuses. Clark throws a carrot of tobacco to the Chief and prepares to order Lewis to fire the cannon. The chief pulls the rope away from the soldiers on the shore, and the party moves on, barely averting an armed conflict. When the corps comes in contact with these same Sioux on the return trip, Clark tells a representative to inform the tribe that "we viewed them as bad people and no more traders would be Suffered to come to them, and whenever the white people wished to visit the nations above [them on the Missouri] they would come sufficiently Strong to whip any vilenous party who dare to oppose them" (Bergon 477). As a result of their "bad" behavior (erroneously assuming themselves to be equals of Lewis and Clark), the U.S. government will not only take away their means of trade, but the new settlers will come with enough strength to punish them for any inappropriate behavior.

In addition to portraying the relationships established with the various tribes encountered, the journals also provide an in-depth portrait of Lewis and Clark's relationship with Sacagawea, Charbonneau's Shoshone wife. She, too, is placed in a subaltern position: throughout the journals she is referred to as either "the Indian woman," "squar," or "Charbonneau's squar." She is familiar with Shoshone territory and she comes to the aid of the corps throughout the journals, providing edible plants along the way and saving articles each time the pirogue she is riding in overturns. Lewis, however, cannot quite bring himself to trust her: On July 24, 1805, he writes, "I fear every day that we shall meet with some considerable falls or obstruction in the river notwithstanding the information of the Indian woman to the contrary who assures us that the river continues much as we see it" (Moulton 4: 422).

Lewis decides to leave her behind when he sets out to search for the Shoshone, taking Drewyer instead. Sacagawea would be the obvious choice: she knows the Shoshone language and the land. Choosing Drewyer to accompany him means Lewis must rely on sign language. Why settle for an inferior mode of communication at such an important event? Lewis instead places his trust in an expedition member who is at least half Euro-American. When she recounts the story of her capture by the Minnetares, Lewis misreads her reticence, noting that he "cannot discover that she shews any immotion of sorrow in recollecting this event, or of joy in being again restored to her native country; if she has enough to eat and a few trinkets to wear I believe she would be perfectly content anywhere" (Moulton 5: 9). She is further objectified when Clark writes of his desire for a robe made of two sea otter skins. The robe is procured "for a belt of blue beeds which the Squar-wife of our interpreter Sharbono wore around her waste" (Bergon 324). No mention is made of the men asking Sacagawea for the beads; they simply take them from her. Even when Clark praises her efforts, he refers to her as "The Indian woman who has been of great service to me as a pilot through this country" (Bergon 341), asserting his dominance through his refusal to name her. At the journey's end, Charboneau receives the equivalent of "500$ 33 1/3 cents for his services as an enterpreter" (Bergon 472). There is no mention made of either Sacagawea's contribution to the successful conclusion of the expedition or any payment to her. Perhaps responding to Jefferson's belief that others should "endeavor to civilize and instruct" the indegenous people (Bergon xcxv), Clark offers to raise Pompey, Sacagawea's son, "in such a manner as [he] thought proper" (Bergon 472). Not only is Sacagawea denied presence as a named individual throughout the journals, but also Clark assumes that he himself will do a better job of raising Pompey.

The expedition of Lewis and Clark created interest among the Euro-Americans who had settled east of the Mississippi. Fur trappers and traders were followed by farmers, soldiers, and gold seekers. As Euro-American settlers encroached upon the land granted to the various tribes by treaties, the Native Americans learned that the "Great Father" was *not* "the only friend to whom [they could] now look for protection;" nor was he the one "from whom [they could] ask favors or receive good councils" (qtd. in Ambrose, 156-7). The government of the "Great Father" in Washington broke treaty after treaty, coercing the Native populations into giving up their land, their way of life, and their culture. Forced to subject themselves to the will of the U.S. government, tribes were relocated to reservations where they had to rely on the benevolence of their "Great Father" for subsistence, and any attempt by the tribal leaders to assert their equality was met by a military force willing to use annihilation to assure the right of the Euro-American settlers to possess the land.

There is no doubt that the journey of Lewis and Clark was an historic one. Meriwether Lewis and William Clark took a group of civilians and soldiers and turned them into a well-disciplined, tightly organized corps who made the journey across the Rocky Mountains and back with the loss of only one life. Bergon describes the journey as "the largest and longest of United States expeditions into *terra incognita*. It was also the first,...the most skillfully managed expedition in the history of North American exploration, the one against which all others are measured" (viii). While some may find the makings of an epic in their story, one must balance this accomplishment against the profound effects of the subsequent colonization of Native populations. Instead of functioning as "harbinger[s] of civilization to the uncivilized world" (Gandhi 15), Lewis and Clark were, in fact, harbingers of colonization.

Fort Mandan: Two Hundred Years Later

Elmer S. Odland

The Dream

Dreams have always been a powerful force in the lives and affairs of human beings. It was President Thomas Jefferson's dream to explore the Missouri watershed, to find a portage between the waters of the Missouri and the Columbia, to descend to the Pacific, to take compass, longitude and latitude readings, to make maps of the area, to learn the life, languages, and ways of the Indian people, to make and record observations of the soil, vegetation, animals, minerals, and climate, and to introduce the United States government to the residents of the Louisiana Purchase. Captains Lewis and Clark and the personnel they picked shared this dream and brought it into being as they diligently and faithfully carried out the mandate that President Jefferson had given them. Fort Mandan, which they built to house the expedition for the winter of 1804-05, was part of the plan.

Some 165 years later, a small group of us dreamed of building a replica of Fort Mandan. Further, we were inspired by the words of Professor Donald Jackson, who wrote in the forward to the National Geographic Society's book, *In the Footsteps of Lewis and Clark*:

> When I was a boy growing up near the banks of the Missouri, I thought of Lewis and Clark as western men. Then I moved to Illinois and discovered that the residents of Wood River and St. Louis across the Mississippi felt rather possessive about these two explorers. Now that I live in Virginia, and Merriwether Lewis's birthplace is only a couple hills away, I find that Virginians claim Lewis and Clark as their own.
>
> Why, I have often wondered, does the story of the Lewis and Clark Expedition seem to belong to everyone? Why does each generation discover it over and over again? Probably because it is every man's daydream of ordinary men doing extraordinary, improbable things. No other story in our national history is like this one.

I came to Lignite, North Dakota, in 1962 as a young pastor just graduated from Luther Seminary in St. Paul, Minnesota. An avid interest in history, especially the early history of North Dakota, led me to request books from the state library in Bismarck. They sent me a box of books which included *The Journals of Lewis and Clark*, the Bernard DeVoto edition. I was hooked by the story and used the book to identify sites on modern maps. The book went along with me and my family on two vacations that took us from Sioux City, Iowa, to Fort Clatsop, Oregon. I was fascinated by the Fort Clatsop replica, begun by a county historical society that, in turn, was upgraded by the state historical society and finally completed by the National Park Service. I was disappointed that the only interpretation of Fort Mandan in North Dakota was a marker located in a remote spot telling the story of Fort Mandan but noting that because the Missouri River meanders, the actual site is probably located in the present river channel.

In person, I contacted several government officials and was assured that building a replica was a good idea and that the suggestion would be passed on to appropriate government agencies. The idea was applauded but nothing happened. The dream of building a replica for the people of North Dakota and of the United States seemed very remote. Then I received a pastoral call in 1968 to First Lutheran Church in Washburn, North Dakota, located in the heart of Fort Mandan country.

A Group of Dreamers

In Washburn, one of the first persons I met was a young business man by the name of Ted Walker, who had moved to Washburn a couple of years before my arrival. He had grown up near the Missouri River in Selfridge, North Dakota, and had dreamed of the river exploits of the Lewis and Clark Expedition as well as the river as a highway for the fur trade and the military. Also, he had followed parts of the trail on family vacations. In 1966, he had pitched the idea of building a replica of Fort Mandan to the Washburn Civic Club. He thought they might welcome such a project as a means of stimulating business in the community. The Civic Club deemed it too big a project for them to undertake.

Ted and I shared our dreams and decided to take the idea to the McLean County Historical Society, which had been organized in 1968. At a meeting of the Society in the spring of 1969 we found another person who shared the dream in the person of the first president, Sheila Robinson, of Coleharbor, North Dakota. Sheila had grown up on a ranch in Mercer County and had studied the Lewis and Clark Expedition in school. When she was a Girl Scout leader in the 1950s, she had taught the girls about Lewis and Clark and had written a pageant about the expedition for the girls to present to the public. The McLean County Historical Society had been organized to create a museum where the pioneer history of the county could be preserved and displayed. Our presentation pointed out that this was a noble purpose and should be pursued, as so many counties in North Dakota were doing. In addition, it was stressed that McLean County had a unique history that should be shared with the entire United States, namely that Lewis and Clark had built Fort Mandan a few miles west of Washburn and spent the winter of 1804-05 there.

Although building a replica of Fort Mandan diverged from the organizing principle of the McLean County Historical Society, there was interest in pursuing this aim along with the pioneer museum. We were put in touch with another key figure, Joe Thompson, a Lewis and Clark dreamer who farmed along the Missouri River west of Washburn. Joe also operated a sawmill and was familiar with cottonwood logs and how to work with them. In 1964, Joe had built a mock-up of Fort Mandan as a set for NBC, which was taping a program on Lewis and Clark.

Finding Land for the Dream

At the fall meeting of the McLean County Historical Society in 1969, Ted Walker and I were appointed the co-chairmen of the project, and Joe Thompson was appointed to be the hands-on architect and builder. Our first assignment was to find land on which the replica could be built. Since it is supposed that the actual site was obliterated by the meandering Missouri River, we were charged with finding an alternative site. The guidelines were that it was to be near the original site, to front the river, to be situated on land with "tall and heavy cottonwoods," to be as nearly as possible similar to the original wilderness, and to be accessible to the public.

This was no small task, and that fall and the following spring we tramped the river bottom for a twelve-mile stretch from Washburn to a spot across from the junction of the Knife River and the Missouri. Problems included bottom land that often flooded, visual obstructions such as the power plants across the river, and finding a willing seller. In the summer of 1970, we found a choice piece of bottom land, and the owner, Louie Lorentzen was willing to sell ten acres to the McLean County Historical Society at a cost of $200 per acre. Since the Society didn't have $2,000 dollars, Mr. Lorentzen was willing to grant an option to buy. We felt certain that we could raise that sum.

In August, John Elliott, city editor of the *Minot Daily News*, in a lengthy front page article, wrote:

> There is a spot, not far—but far enough—from the drone of a constantly traveled federal highway. Not far—but far enough—from the sight and sound of power plants converting stacks of lignite to electrical energy.
>
> The spot, an answer to dreams of modern men who thought often of the past, is itself like a dream—still, unsullied, serene. Lush vegetation, shadowed and protected by ancient cottonwoods, lies atop the land, which is a stone's throw from the waters that form the Missouri River.
>
> The highway distance reckoning of our day puts the tree-ringed meadow a few miles west of Washburn. In fact, it could well be the distance between then and now, past and present.
>
> For it is on this land, untouched by the pace of the modern world around it, that a replica memorializing an event unique in the annals of our history will be placed, the wintering site in 1804-05 of the Lewis and Clark Expedition where the party was encamped for five and one-half months.

Sharing the Dream: Finances and Telling the Story

At the September 7, 1970, meeting of the McLean County Historical Society, Ted Walker presented a three-stage fund raising plan. First, there would be a "Captains Club" made up of at least twenty donors who would give 100 dollars. This would enable the society to purchase the land. Second, further funding for the building costs would be sought by enlisting "Trail Blazers" for the sum of a 25 dollar gift. Third, fund-raising events would be conducted as an ongoing effort to generate funds. Immediately, the first fund raiser got underway by selling tickets on three items: a Winchester 94 Centennial Rifle, a dish washer, and an original painting of historic Fort Mandan from the palette of Henry Lorentzen.

The dream of the Society was to build a full-size replica of Fort Mandan, using cottonwood logs and following the general description from the journals. The journal entry for November 20, 1804, reads:

> We this day moved into our huts which are now completed. This place which we call Fort Mandan is situated in a point of low ground, on the north side of the Missouri, covered with tall and heavy cottonwood. The works consist of two rows of huts or sheds, forming an angle where they joined each other; each row containing four rooms of 14 feet square and seven feet high, with plank ceiling, and the roof slanting so as to form a loft above the rooms, the highest part of which is eighteen feet from the ground: The backs of the huts formed a wall of that height, and opposite the angle the place of the wall was supplied by picketing. In the area were two rooms for stores and provisions. The latitude by observation is 47 degrees 21' 47", and the computed distance from the mouth of the Missouri is sixteen hundred miles.

We needed to share the story of the effort to build a replica. I became the "mouth" of the Society, talking to school groups, study clubs, service clubs, civic clubs, Masonic lodges, travel groups, church groups, the newly organized Lewis and Clark Trail Heritage Foundation meeting in Bismarck, North Dakota, the North Dakota Travel Bureau, and other groups. I gave interviews with the *Bismarck Tribune*, the *Minot Daily News*, the *Washburn Leader*, and the *McLean County Independent*, and did a television story with the KX network. I talked to anyone who would invite me and who would listen. The press was very generous with pictures and stories, which brought the story to a large audience.

Along with speaking about Fort Mandan, I wrote a weekly newspaper column beginning in October of 1971 for the *Washburn Leader*. It was titled "Lewis and Clark: 167 Years Ago." From the journals, I summarized what the expedition had done in that particular week 167 years ago, from their arrival in what is now North Dakota in October 1804 to their leaving the state in April 1805. These columns kept the project before the readers on a weekly basis.

The Dream Begins to Take Shape

Even before all the publicity, Joe Thompson began working on the construction shortly after the September 7, 1970, meeting of the McLean County Historical Society. First, concrete footings were to be poured so that the logs would not rot by standing on the ground. The standard joke was that Lewis and Clark built for one season, the Society was going to build for infinite seasons. Eighteen tons of gravel and eighty bags of cement were used to pour 474 feet of footings. The footings for the circumference measured 250 feet. Sixty used grader blades donated by the McLean County Highway department were set vertically in the concrete about four feet apart. Four-foot sections of logs would be bolted to the steel grader blades. The section would be notched to conceal the grader blades.

The cottonwood logs, some 800 of them, were donated by McLean County rancher, Carl Kuehn. Over the winter, Joe was busy felling trees and hauling the logs to his sawmill. Each one was run through the rip saw to make a flat surface on each side so that the logs would fit together squarely when placed vertically. The flattened portion was slathered with linseed oil to prevent rotting.

In the spring and summer of 1971, work was slowed because Joe was a farmer and had to tend to his seeding, haying, and harvesting. Some work was done but it had to be fitted in with the rhythm of farming. Over the fall and winter, Fort Mandan began to take shape. Instead of human muscles, Joe used the hydraulic muscles of his tractors. He manufactured his own tools to handle the demands of this unique construction project. Each of the biggest logs weighed a ton or more. Often he worked alone or with just a couple of men on his payroll. At other times volunteers helped out. There were six men from Washburn and six men from Turtle Lake who could be called out as needed.

When the finished logs were at the site, each one was drilled with three holes using a jig that Joe had made. He calculated that he had drilled 2,400 feet of holes, making him the most "boring" person on the project. The construction was done by hoisting one log at a time into position. The first log was bolted to a grader blade protruding from the concrete. Three steel reinforcing rods were threaded through the holes and then the next log was hoisted and threaded with the rods. When four feet had been completed, that log was bolted to the next grader blade. Additional lengths of rod were welded as each four-foot section was completed. That process was continued until the circumference was in place. In all, 2,400 feet of reinforcing rod was used.

The cabins had plank ceilings and there was a loft above. The roof that sloped from the outer wall to the center was fashioned of planks as well. From the *McLean County Independent* newspaper, 560 used aluminum offset mats were nailed over the planks to make the lofts waterproof, and then cottonwood slabs were laid over the mats and nailed. Joe designed and welded all the hinges and hardware for the doors and gates. Joe estimated that the logs, if sawed into boards, would have amounted to 65,000 board feet. To put that into perspective, he said, "A pretty nice home could be built with 4,000 board feet of wood." In addition to the materials already mentioned, the project required 250 pounds of nails and 200 pounds of bolts.

In addition to the trees donated by Carl Kuehn and the used aluminum offset mats given by the *McLean County Independent*, sixty used grader blades were given by the McLean County Highway Department, which also leveled the site with their highway equipment. The survey work was contributed by the South McLean Soil Conservation District, brushing and tree trimming was done by the Boy Scouts, and peeling the logs and cleaning up the construction site was done by Green Thumb workers.

The Dream Is Dedicated

Throughout the spring of 1972 and right up to the day of dedication, work continued on the replica. There was other work going on as well, which saw the McLean County Historical Society planning for the day of dedication, set for June 23, 1972. It had been decided to present a pageant of life at Fort Mandan. Writing the pageant was assigned to me, which I worked at during the spring. Jim Vranna from the English department at Washburn High School accepted the task of finding actors and staging the pageant.

A pit-beef barbecue was planned by another crew, who had to dig the pit, plan the menu, purchase the food, arrange for the serving, and cook the food. A program committee was appointed to plan the dedication. It was decided to contact Mr. Gus Budde from St. Louis, Missouri, to be the dedication speaker. Mr. Budde had traveled the trail 16 times and had followed the building of the Fort Mandan replica with great interest.

Finally, the day arrived with high anticipation. The skies did not look friendly and the forecasts spoke of rain. However, everything was in motion and it was decided to risk the planned outdoor dedication. Mr. Budde shared his experiences, gained by following the trail sixteen times, and pointed out the developments that had taken place over that time. He praised the McLean County Historical Society and especially the work of Joe Thompson in building an authentic looking replica equally as fine as Oregon's Fort Clatsop.

Sheila Robinson said in her remarks, "Lewis and Clark built for one winter; the McLean County Historical Society is building for the future." I gave a brief history of the project that included the purchase of the land, the finances at present, and the need for additional funding, and how Joe had worked with the cottonwood logs. I expressed the feeling of the dreamers that building the replica of Fort Mandan was an idea whose time had come.

It still looked like rain but the dedication was followed by a delicious barbecue. The cost of the meal was $3.00 and included beef, bread, beans, pickles, and beverage. Much of the food had been donated, so most of the money from the 900 tickets went to help pay some of the bills incurred.

The rain held off for the evening and the pageant followed the meal. Jim Vranna had gathered a cast of over 100 costumed people that included Indian dancers from the Three Affiliated Tribes along with tribal chairman, Nathan Little Soldier, people from in and around Washburn, the I Company of the 7th Calvary, and the Garrison Wagon train. The pageant swept through 168 years of history from the building of Fort Mandan to the present day. The drama portrayed the presentation of the Jefferson Peace Medal to Mandan Chief Sheheke. The pageant concluded with a surprise when Joe Thompson, playing the part of Captain Lewis, presented a facsimile of the Peace Medal to Tribal Chairman Nathan Little Soldier. In remarks of acceptance, Little Soldier noted the good relations between Mandan and Hidatsa tribes and the Lewis and Clark party, who wintered nearby. The rain had held off and it had been a grand day.

The Dream Receives Financing

As soon as the euphoria of the dedication day was over, the Society faced the fact that there was a debt of nearly $4,000, most of it owed to Joe Thompson. There had not been enough $25.00 Trailblazer memberships sold nor had the various fundraisers brought in the amounts hoped for. There was a long shot in terms of the "Better Way of Life Contest" sponsored by Gate City Savings and Loan, which was offering a $10,000 prize. Their slogan was that at Gate City you're saving for a better way of life. Sheila Robinson wrote an application which was similar to writing a grant proposal.

Over the course of the summer and into the fall, we heard that there were 121 applications from throughout North Dakota. Winning the grant seemed a very remote possibility. The society continued with fund-raising efforts and also explored the possibility of borrowing or turning to state and county sources of revenue. State and county revenues were a last resort because it would have meant turning over the land and the replica to an elected state board or to an elected county board. Since there were many things yet to be done, the McLean County Historical Society did not want to give up control at this point.

Just after the dedication, visitors were already beginning to stop to see the reconstructed Fort Mandan, even though it was only a shell. At the December 7, 1972, meeting of the McLean County Historical Society, the guest book revealed visitors from twenty-five states and five foreign countries. Already there were 2,100 names in the book. Before the movie *Field of Dreams* appeared, the Society was experiencing the premise of the movie, "If you build it, they will come." A traveler sent a letter to the McLean County Historical Society writing, "Fort Mandan was the most outstanding achievement along the Lewis and Clark Trail considering how local effort had been responsible."

President Sheila Robinson announced that the Fort Mandan Project was doing well in the Better Way of Life Contest. She said, "Fort Mandan is in the final six out of 121 entries and we have a real good chance of winning." Her words proved to be prophetic, for on January 13, 1973, Fort Mandan was declared the winner of the $10,000 prize. Mr. John Whittlesley, representing Gate City Savings and Loan, presented the check, which was accepted by Sheila Robinson in the presence of a large gathering of the members of the Society.

Mr. Whittlesley read the text of the letter he had sent to the Society, which stated:

> Certainly there were many things about the Fort Mandan Project that appealed to the judges. The judges were particularly impressed with the amount of work that has already been accomplished on the project with so little help other than the determination and generosity of local people.... The Fort Mandan Project will go far in highlighting our state's history and heritage and will enrich the lives of those who visit.
>
> The money would be used as follows:

• Parking lot leveled and paved.	$2,000
• Payment to Joe Thompson—labor and material.	3,900
• Fencing	500
• Sodding around the footings	500
• Summer caretaker	1,200
• Fireplaces, pads, sunken garbage cans	300
• Furnishings for cabins, dugout replica	1,000
• Pamphlets and advertising	300
• Nature trail and tree planting	300
	$10,000

Most of these improvements were made but some were not, such as paving the parking lot, furnishing the cabins, and making a dugout canoe. Instead, some of the money was used to build a log comfort station with flush toilets and to build a gift shop. The attraction of funding from outside McLean County vindicated the Society's efforts and was a sign of things to come. Now that the big effort to put up the replica had been completed, the Society was content to make small improvements and to make the site available to visitors. One highlight was the ceremony at Fort Mandan sending the North Dakota Bicentennial Covered Wagon to Washington, DC, in 1976 for the National Reverse Wagon Train.

Expanding the Dream

At the dedication on June 23, 1972, Tribal Chairman Nathan Little Soldier had noted the good relations that winter among Mandan and Hidatsa people and the members of the expedition. Echoing that point, James Ronda in 1984 wrote in his book *Lewis and Clark among the Indians*:

> Personal relations between explorers and villagers were marked by genuine good feeling with only a few misunderstandings [p.112]. Visiting, hunting, trading, and sexual adventures were all common ground where people from different cultures could talk, joke, haggle, and compete in the shared struggle of life on the northern plains [p. 98].

On December 5, 1970, the *Bismarck Tribune* noted the possibility of establishing a national park on the site of the earth lodge villages on the Knife River, the villages that were there in 1804-1806. Subsequently, that park was established to tell the story of the earth lodge dwellers, the Mandan and Hidatsa people. Another significant event took place with the completion of the Missouri River Bridge at Washburn in December of 1971. The bridge was an ideal link between Fort Mandan and the Knife River earth lodges, symbolizing the cultural exchange that took place when American explorers spent a winter in the neighborhood.

Enhancing the Dream

After 1980, the McLean County Historical Society turned its attention to another aim, a heritage center collecting and displaying items from pioneer times to the present. Fort Mandan was held in a maintenance mode. Small improvements and upkeep were continued, but there was neither the energy nor the funding to fully develop the dream. It had been hoped from its inception that at some point state resources would enter the picture as in the case of Fort Clatsop in Oregon.

The hope was answered in the spring of 1997 when the responsibility for maintaining and programming the Fort Mandan replica site was turned over to the North Dakota Lewis and Clark Bicentennial Foundation, which had been formed to operate the new Lewis and Clark Interpretive Center at Washburn, two miles east of Fort Mandan.

The Foundation, with its staff and resources, introduced a seasonal interpretive program at the Fort, offering presentations every day from 9:00 a.m. to 5:00 p.m. from Memorial Day to Labor Day. In addition, interpreters were made available to school and other groups in the spring and fall. A series of major improvements to the grounds included:

- Paving the driveway and parking lot leading into the Fort area. Numerous contributions were received for this project, including fly ash from the nearby Great River Energy Coal Creek Power Station, which was used in the concrete.
- Extensive cutting and clearing of shrubbery and non-native trees was completed.
- Three picnic shelters were built to accommodate the large number of tour groups and others.
- An extensive trail system is in the process of development which connects the Fort Mandan replica area with the adjacent Fahlgren Memorial Park, a wilderness area which was deeded to the Foundation by the McLean County Historical Society as well.

A number of enhancements are in process with the goal of making the Fort replica more historically accurate. To date the following improvements have been made:

- Wooden floors have been installed in the cabins.

- A working blacksmith shop occupies one of the cabins.
- Stone fireplaces and chimneys have been built.
- Cottonwood slabs for the roof have replaced the cedar shakes which, in turn, had replaced the original slabs.
- A catwalk was added where sentries had been posted.
- Wooden bunks and desks were added, including items that may have been part of the expedition, such as uniforms, clothing, guns, knives, instruments, buffalo robes and trade blankets for the bunks, candle holders, and much more. The rooms are now furnished as if the expedition were still present.

On June 29, 2002, the Foundation dedicated a new Fort Mandan Visitor Services Center at the Fort Site. This 5,400 square foot facility provides a wonderful environment for visitors to experience Fort Mandan year round. A great fireplace, a classroom with an orientation film, and a large gift shop will greet visitors. The entire building is constructed of coal combustion products in a unique partnership with members of the coal and energy industry. The Lignite Energy Council and other trade organizations are providing financial support for the one million dollar facility as well as in-kind donations of construction materials. The National Park Service, The Department of Energy, and The Institute of Museum and Library Services have all provided various forms of funding for the project.

Continued Commitment to the Dream

Elliott Coues wrote in the foreword to his edition of *The Journals of Lewis and Clark*:

> To the people of the great west: Jefferson gave you the country. Lewis and Clark showed you the way. The rest is your own course of empire. Honor the statesmen who foresaw your west. Honor the brave men who first saw your west. May the memory of their glorious achievement be your precious heritage.

In June of 2002, Fort Mandan marked its 30th anniversary of construction by the McLean County Historical Society. This event marks not only the dedication of a new Fort Mandan Visitor Services Center but also a new commitment to have the site open to the public all year long. It thus honors the statesmen and the brave men of the expedition and encourages us to ponder the meeting of two cultures on the banks of the Missouri in the winter of 1804-05.

Spirit Mound, the Natives, and Lewis and Clark

Norma Clark Wilson

It is June 26, 2003, almost 199 years since the Corps of Discovery ventured eight miles from the Missouri River to see the legendary Spirit Mound they had heard about from the Missouri and Oto nations downriver. I have driven five miles from my home in Spirit Mound Township to visit the Mound again. As I approach, I notice she looks like a woman in repose, and I know I have learned to see her shape from Linda Hogan, a Chickasaw poet.

The human experience of this place is bound up with the literary tradition surrounding it. Even the historical marker that has identified Spirit Mound for decades includes a passage from William Clark's journal in which he refers to stories from the indigenous oral traditon. To the Mandans, the Yanktons, and other Native peoples, Spirit Mound has been and continues to be invested with spiritual meaning that reaches back centuries earlier than the arrival of Lewis and Clark in 1804.

Although the literary tradition that spawned the Corps of Discovery's journey westward and which they developed and changed was different in being written, their Euro-American world view shared a common element with that of Native Americans—the acknowledgement of awe in the face of overwhelming natural beauty. Having been educated in the classics, Thomas Jefferson, Meriwether Lewis, and William Clark were no doubt influenced by the Greek philosopher Longinus who wrote in his essay *On the Sublime*: "As if instinctively, our soul is uplifted by the true sublime; it takes a proud flight, and is filled with joy and vaunting as though it had itself produced what it has heard" (63). He noted that in his time, probably the first century A.D., sublimity of literary expression was being eroded by writers' pursuit of wealth and popularity.

In *Notes on the State of Virginia* (1787) Jefferson wrote about the Appalachian Natural Bridge, "It is impossible for the emotions arising from the sublime, to be felt beyond what they are here: so beautiful an arch, so elevated, so light, and springing as it were up to heaven, the rapture of the spectator is really indescribable!" (148). The Bridge provided one of thousands of grand vistas in this world so new to the Euro-Americans. It was at the same time a world ancient and revered by the Native peoples whose stories and songs expressed in far greater detail and eloquence their awe and wonder.

The Yankton name for Spirit Mound is *Caotina Wiconi Paha*, translated as the eternal mountain of little people. The Mandans also have ancient ties to this place they call "Spirit Hill." Formed by a Wisconsin glacier, the mound or hill rises to a height of 1,300 feet above sea level, 100 feet above the surrounding plain and almost 200 feet above the Missouri River. Its central core is of Niobrara chalk, composed of fossil shells deposited in an ancient sea, perhaps 80 million years ago. Spirit Mound was preserved and perhaps partially shaped by the last Pleistocene glacier, which may have covered the area as recently as 10,000 years ago.

To one who has lived among hills, Spirit Mound may at first seem unremarkable. But from its summit, the view spans ten to fifteen miles to the south and east. Regarded as a place of origin by the Mandan, Spirit Mound is also of ceremonial significance to the Lakota and Ponca nations. Contemporary poets of other Native cultures recognize both its significance as a place of birth and regeneration and as a home of spirits and their gifts of vision.

Lewis and Clark's visit to the Mound took them farther from the banks of the Missouri than they had ventured since their departure from St. Louis on May 14th. When I first read references to Spirit Mound in William Clark's journal and climbed to its summit to look at the surrounding landscape in August 1978, I was awed by both the stories and the view. Realizing that I understood very little of the significance of the place, I could only begin to appreciate the spiritual and historical importance of this Mound to indigenous peoples especially and by extension to all of us. I was then and am still troubled by Clark's reference to the *caotila* as devils. Despite the fact that the Corps' interpreter, Pierre Dorion, had lived among the Yanktons for twenty years, he could probably not have understood or explained to Clark the Yankton perspective on the spirit people, and Dorion was not among the party that visited the Mound. This is Clark's journal entry of August 24 describing the location and shape of Spirit Mound and summarizing the stories about the *caotila*:

> In a northerly direction from the Mouth of this Creek in an emence Plain a high Hill is Situated, and appears of a Conic form, and by the different nations of Indians in this quarter is Suppose to be the residence of Deavels. that they are in human form with remarkable large heads, and about 18 inches high, that they are very watchfull and are arm'd with Sharp arrows with which they Can Kill at a great distance; they are Said to kill all persons who are So hardy as to attempt to approach the hill; they State that tradition informs them that many Indians have Suffered by these little people, and among others three Mahar Men fell a sacrefise to their murceless fury not many Years Sence. So Much do the Maha, Soues, Ottoes and other neighbouring nations believe this fable, that no Consideration is Sufficient to induce them to approach the hill. (DeVoto 22)

The first Indians Lewis and Clark met were the Missouris and Otos who lived near present day Council Bluffs. Lewis addressed the Otos on August 3rd. His reference to them as "red children" accentuates the fact that he did not view them as equals (qtd. in Ronda 19). So it is not surprising that Clark interpreted the story of the little people as the superstitious "fable" of a savage people.

Eleven members of the Corps of Discovery crossed the Whitestone Creek, now named the Vermillion River, and climbed to the Mound on the cloudy morning of August 25th. It was such a hot day that they sent their dog back to the river. The party of eleven reached Spirit Mound at noon. Lewis was feeling fatigued and ill, both from the heat and as a result of the Rush's pills he had taken to alleviate the effects of cobalt he had ingested just south of the current site of Sioux City. Clark wrote the account of their visit:

> One evidence which the Inds give for believing this place to be the residence of Some unusial Sperits is that they frequently discover a large assemblage of Birds about this Mound is in my opinion a Sufficient proof to produce in the Savage Mind a Confident belief of all the properties which they ascribe it.
>
> from the top of this Mound we beheld a most butifull landscape; Numerous herds of buffalow were Seen feeding in various directions; the Plain to North N. W. & N. E. extends without interruption as far as Can be seen. (DeVoto 24)

Again, in this passage Clark made a disparaging reference to the Natives, referring to the "Savage Mind;" yet he appreciated the beauty of the landscape and the abundance of buffalo feeding below.

Standing on Spirit Mound for the first time, I felt disheartened. Unlike the view of "Numerous herds of buffalow" and a seemingly endless prairie, the landscape surrounding Spirit Mound in the summer of 1978 featured farm houses, barns, plowed fields, a highway, and a feedlot on the northeast slope. Looking down into the faces of the Hereford cattle that were looking up at me, I was visually shocked by the change in the view. Beside me stood a stone marker erected in 1921 by the Paha Wakan chapter of the Daughters of the American Revolution. Though the D.A.R. members had appropriated their chapter's name from the Indians, their marker mentioned only that Lewis and Clark visited the spot in 1804, saying nothing about the Indians who were there first.

But a visit to Spirit Mound in October of 1978 with Cheyenne poet Lance Henson and Oklahoma poet Frank Parman helped me to appreciate the continuing wonder of the place.[1] As we approached, crows flew low over the Mound. "Did you see the crows?" Lance asked. Crows have spiritual significance to the Cheyenne culture as they are pervasive survivors. Later that year, once winter had arrived, my husband Jerry and I received a handwritten poem by Henson about Spirit Mound:

> at spirit mountain
> one takes small steps that
> lead to the top
> and beyond

the fields plowed
deep furrows that ask you
to see yourself
in the wind's open sound

wind risen in an ocean
of cloud
that in the distance
to the south
falls to rain

wakan land
we lift our eyes to your
mirror
and see the smallness
of ourselves.

Henson's poem expresses the awe and humility that sacred places like Spirit Mound make us humans feel, a sense of the sublime. Henson's poem articulates the spirit of the place as it must have been felt two hundred years ago and can be felt today, and notes also the changes in the landscape non-Indians made during the twentieth century. For indigenous peoples who, like the Cheyenne, have lived on the Great Plains, hills or mounds are places for seeking vision, and this is the aspect of Spirit Mound accentuated in Henson's poem. In the literary tradition, written and oral, that surrounds Spirit Mound, the contemporary Native poetry and the stories from the oral tradition are far more helpful than the *Journals* of Lewis and Clark in relating the spiritual significance of this place.

On the last day of winter in 1980, I climbed Spirit Mound again, this time with Linda Hogan.[2] Earlier Hogan had read Clark's account of it. A few days after Hogan returned to her home in the Colorado Rockies, I received a poem from her, "Day Before Spring," dedicated to me. The poem begins,

In my hand,
bones of the little people
who threw arrows and crows
from Spirit Mound
that grew like a woman
curving this flat body of land.

It's not our words
that absorb us,
not our stories of the little people.
It's the woman's body
preparing for birth,
the small heart growing

to beat inside skin
the world comes through. (55)

I remember Hogan fingering those little fossilized shells that looked like bones as we sat on top of the mound. Hers is a woman's sense of the land, continuously preparing itself for regeneration. It is a celebration of new life, of spring, and of the woman's shape of Spirit Mound. I treasure Hogan's poem because she expressed so well the meaning of our experience on the land when I was pregnant with my first child. The ancient Mandan stories of Spirit Mound refer to it as a place where Lone Man, the first Mandan, acquired a vision of the ceremonial turtle drums (Deaver 6.19). Hogan's Chickasaw culture, which also reveres the turtle, must have provided her with an intuitive understanding of this part of Spirit Mound's meaning and significance.

I learned more of its significance in September of 1980 when Joseph Rockboy, a Yankton Sioux elder born in 1903 and brought up at Greenwood on the Yankton Reservation, spoke to my students about the little spirit people.[3] The Yankton band of the Sioux occupied the lower James and Vermillion River valleys during the early nineteenth century, hunting and trading in the area. Their main village was located on the site of present-day Yankton, which is thirty miles southwest of Spirit Mound. "The old tales about the people we call the tree dwellers, or the *caotila*, began about 12,000 years ago," Rockboy said. "Our people hesitated about coming to this area because of them," he continued, saying that the *caotila* were "traditional enemies of the Sioux" and "omens of death…created out of warfare, made that way through witchcraft when one tribe put a curse on the other." Rockboy said he learned the stories of the little people from his grandfather, who had learned them from his grandparents. He said, "The tree-dwellers made their home around Spirit Mound in this area; and to this day our people stay away from that place."

Rockboy said that ten years earlier a boyhood friend had gone one morning into the nearby feedlot and saw one of the little people standing there. His people took the man to relatives in Wagner, South Dakota, for three months to help him escape the bad luck of the *caotila*. He returned home, only to die suddenly. Rockboy said that his people don't talk much about the *caotila* in modern times. "If we tell this and it gets out and the sanity board gets ahold of it, we'll be off to the state hospital," he said laughing. He said he had never seen a *caotila* himself. "I have never looked for one either," he added. Rockboy's account fixed in my mind the power, continuity, creativity, and humor of the Native oral literary tradition. Never set in stone like writing, the stories carried upon indigenous voices continue to connect the people with the wakan aspect of the place.

Yet Rockboy's account also included the feedlot that altered the view. In her poem "Journey," published in 1983, Dakota poet Elizabeth Cook-Lynn comments on the impact of immigrants on Spirit Mound, questioning whether the *caotila* were in fact eternal:

> Wet, sickly
> smells of cattle yard silage fill the prairie air
> far beyond the timber; the nightmare only just
> begun, a blackened cloud moves past the sun
> to dim the river's glare, a malady of modern times.
> We prayed
> to the giver of prayers and traveled to the spirit
> mounds we thought were forever; awake we feared that
> hollow trees no longer hid the venerable ones we were
> taught to believe in. (n.p.)

Cook-Lynn's poem expresses the desecration of both the land and her people's spiritual life in the two hundred years since the Corps of Discovery climbed Spirit Mound. Clark made no mention of the smell of the air from the top, but it was probably sweet. Cook-Lynn makes us understand that a disrespect and misuse of the land and animals not only pollutes the environment, but also produces a spiritual vacuum.

In August 1998, Lakota scholars Jerome Kills Small and Wayne Evans spoke about Spirit Mound at an Institute for the Spirit program at the W.H. Over Museum in Vermillion. Kills Small said that Spirit Mound is one of several sacred sites in the Missouri Valley. He explained that to the Lakota *wakan* means powerful, neither good nor bad. He said that *caotila* means "They live in the woods," and that the diminutive ending, *la*, means you love them so much for their sacred and mysterious qualities that you use the *la* for "dear little men."[5]

Evans said that as a child he was told not to make himself vulnerable to the *caotila* because if you see one of those *caotila*, they put a spell on you. If you encounter one of them, you won't necessarily die right then, but it will affect your spirit, your logic. "I'm not going up there," Evans said. "I'll go to the base. If you encounter a *caotila*, you need to go to a spiritual person for a ceremony. For me, it's real." Evans said that Americans "don't want to leave anything sacred. If we say that's just a superstition, I think we're short changing our spirit."

On August 25, 2000, at another program at the W.H. Over Museum, the Director of the University of South Dakota's Institute of American Indian Studies, Leonard Bruguier, said that his own Yankton ancestors were probably in the plum bushes on that date, 196 years earlier, gathering food for the winter. Still today, there is no better taste in winter than that of the wild plum that grows on Bruguier's ancestral Yankton land. Both Clark's and Sergeant

Ordway's journals mention finding and gathering plums and other delicious fruit on their way back to camp from Spirit Mound.

Ronald Little Owl of the Mandan nation spoke about Spirit Mound's significance to his people on September 18, 2002, at the W.H. Over Museum in Vermillion. Little Owl said that during a great flood, the Mandans under the leadership of Lone Man built a structure on top of Spirit Mound. He told his people to remain in the circular structure made of cottonwood trees, saying, "As long as you stay in the structure, you'll live because that's as high as the water will come." Little Owl's people built a replica of the structure, which exists in their community today near Lake Sakakawea in North Dakota.[6]

At the same event in 2002, ethnoscientist Sherri Deaver pointed out that Lewis and Clark were reflecting their Judeo-Christian heritage in referring to the *caotila* as devils. She noted that for most Yanktons they are considered dangerous, not evil, but said one should take them seriously: "They are known to appear on Spirit Mound and one should not go up there without respect." Referring to a story edited by Bronco LeBeau which tells the origin of the *caotila*, included in the *Spirit Mound Culture History* which she compiled, Deaver said they are associated with certain plants.

In this story, according to the Lakota, Iktomi the trickster approached the raccoon nation because he was lonely. There were no creatures that would welcome him into their homes. He prepared food for the Raccoon People and invited them to a feast. The leader of the raccoons warned his people that Iktomi might be up to one of his tricks, but Iktomi promised he wouldn't play any tricks on them, and many raccoons accepted his offer. At the end of the feast, Iktomi stood up and told the raccoons about the two-legged people who lived in regions under the earth. He told them the *Pte Oyate* (Buffalo People, or Lakota) were very powerful and said if the four-leggeds could walk like them, they'd be very powerful too. As they left, the raccoons began trying to walk on two legs. Iktomi observed that they were able to pick up foods with their front paws as they ate. After a time the leader of the raccoons and many of the elders came back to talk with Iktomi, and Iktomi told them he was very lonely and wanted someone to be his friend and relative. Iktomi said that if an animal nation would agree to give him one of their own, he could "make that one a Pte and they would be my friend and relative and I would never play a trick on them" (6.33). After some discussion, the raccoons decided that two baby raccoons, a male and a female, would be given to Iktomi if he would promise to never play a trick on these two raccoons or any of the raccoon people. Iktomi agreed. They watched as Iktomi transformed the baby raccoons into small Pte babies. Though he promised to take care of the babies, before the racoons left, Iktomi realized he didn't know how and sought help, first from Double Face Woman, who refused to help, but next from Wakanka the grandmother, who agreed to take care of them. But she told him, "because they are raccoons they will only grow as large as a raccoon." "You have done a very bad thing," she said. Because he had changed them into something different from their own nature, they would "be cunning and play tricks" like Iktomi, "and their happiness will be to trick others into the woods and make them foolish" (6.35).

The *caotila* lived in the woods until a great flood when they came to Spirit Mound for safety. After that time, one of them prayed to the Spirits to help him change his relatives "into a good people who help others and give them good things instead of playing tricks on them." Many of them vowed to never again play tricks or cause harm (6.37). A spirit being then gave them a medicine bundle to use for this purpose. The Santee men would then make these bundles and use the *caotila* spirit medicine to help their people. The spirit Wakinyan said the *caotila* would live until the true children of Iktomi came into the world and drove them out. The children of Iktomi are understood to be the Euro-Americans.

Deaver also said the Mandan turtle drums integral to the historic *Okipa* ceremony and the contemporary sun dance came from the Spirit Mound area. She said that Native Lakota and Mandan people still make offerings and give prayers there because "it's a sacred place to Native people. It's still part of a living spiritual tradition." Deaver explained that the cultural geography of the plains is tied up with people recognizing high points as spiritually significant. Spirit Mound is part of a cultural geography of the Great Plains that also includes other high points such as Bear Butte, the Medicine Wheel, and other sacred sites.

On May 3, 2003, Tsalagi/Huron poet Allison Hedge Coke participated in a community project to plant native grasses and forbs on Spirit Mound. Hedge Coke is writing a book of poems about mounds in the state of South Dakota. As we walked along the east side of the mound on that cloudy day, fitting the roots of violets, spiderworts, and goldenrod into the soil, I anticipated reading her perspective on Spirit Mound. Having come from an agricultural background that reveres the ancient burial mounds, Hedge Coke can be expected to broaden still further our understanding of the eternal meaning of this sacred place even in the face of unprecedented violence and commercialism in American culture. She and the other Native poets and storytellers remind us of our continuing need to nurture the spirit.

During the past quarter century I have visited Spirit Mound in all seasons—I have stood on top looking at the surrounding countryside with my husband, my children, with Oklahomans, with Germans, with a Southern Cheyenne, a Chickasaw, several Yanktons, Lakota, a U.S. senator, a mayor, students, and townspeople. One winter afternoon Cecilia Ragaini, an Italian student, and I climbed to the top through a foot of snow. It was the ancient stories that brought us there. We looked out at the white lands surrounding us, and as we stood there we felt a sense of adventure, but also of awe that we were standing in the company of so many spirits past. Two hundred years after Lewis and Clark visited Spirit Mound, the place and the experience of the sublime still inspire us, for Spirit Mound is home to thousands of years of human history that we can never fully understand.

Each time I visit I see her from a new perspective. Today she is peaceful, at rest, with breezes all around her. She is surrounded by the plants that have grown here for centuries—echinacea, vervain, and meadow rose, as well as newer arrivals like clover, hemp, and brome. The cattle, the feedlot fences, all the farm buildings and even the trees have been removed from the land surrounding her to return Spirit Mound to her approximate condition when Lewis and Clark were here. A sign in the parking lot announces, as if she's a movie, "Coming Soon: A New Look for Spirit Mound." I walk along the new asphalt path but soon must turn and walk through stubble. Spirit Mound Creek has escaped its banks, and the southern base of Spirit Mound is now a wetland. Red-winged blackbirds are singing, grasses are rustling. All is alive and in motion. I won't go up today. I am content to stand and look up at the Mound where thousands of years ago Lone Man stood. I imagine he is holding up the sky. Today it is blue and scattered with cumulous clouds. This newly formed wetland reminds me that Nature has her own ways, whatever our plans. She is always remaking herself, according to her own designs. As I leave, I look back at the shape of Spirit Mound. From the southwest she looks like a turtle whose head is raised to the north. Remembering the turtle drum, I am thankful to Spirit Mound for her strong, enduring heart.

Spirit Mound After Lewis and Clark

Kent Scribner

Two hundred years ago, on August 25, 1804, Meriwether Lewis and William Clark, along with Lewis's dog and eleven other members of their Corps of Discovery, spent the day on a detour from the tedium of the Missouri River. They were determined to investigate a legendary natural landmark in what is now Clay County, South Dakota. Hiking seven miles north and generally following the Vermillion River, then known as the White Stone, the party in due time reached their goal, the prominence we know today as Spirit Mound.

Up to this point in their journey Lewis and Clark had not ventured very far from their river highway, but they chose this place out of curiosity from what Indians and perhaps fur traders had apparently told them as they were coming upriver. Clark wrote on August 24, "...this hill...by all the different Nations in this quater is Supposed to be a place of Deavels or that they are in human form with remarkable large heads and about 18 inches high; that they are watchfull and ar armed with Sharp arrows with which they can kill at great distance; they are said to kill all persons who are so hardy as to attempt to approach the hill."

August 25 was a very hot summer day, and the dog, Seaman, suffering from the heat, had to be sent back to the Vermillion River for water. Despite rumors of danger, the men approached the hill and climbed to the summit, which they estimated to be about seventy feet above the surrounding plain and of natural origin, not man-made. They also noted the abundance of insects near the top, which attracted great flocks of swallows, and the captains speculated that it was the birds that gave the mound its air of mystery.

Lewis and Clark did not see any devils in human form, but they were deeply impressed with the view from Spirit Mound. Clark wrote, "From the top of this Mound we beheld a most butifull landscape; Numerous herds of buffalo were Seen feeding in various directions, the Plain to North N. W & NE extends without interruption as far as Can be seen." He also described the birds and other life they saw and the variety of wild fruit. Uncomfortable from heat and thirst, the Corps members made a beeline east to the Vermillion River, rested, and returned to their pirogue on the Missouri River to rejoin their colleagues and prepare for the next day's journey. Before his day ended, however, Clark drew a map labeling the place they had visited the "Hill of Little Devils."

The above can serve as a backdrop, but it is not my intent here to add to the Lewis and Clark literature of August 1804. It is my intent to survey the subject, "Spirit Mound after Lewis and Clark." "After" begins in September 1806 as they passed the Sioux River on their return trip downriver to St. Louis.

The 1806-to-2004 span can be roughly divided into fifty-year segments. The first of these is the *Era of Indians and Fur Traders*. Native Americans, of course, had lived within sight of Spirit Mound for decades, even centuries. During and after the Lewis and Clark years, these lands were controlled by the Yankton Sioux, whose main village was near the mouth of the James River at present-day Yankton. A smaller community, comprising about 100 lodges, was located near the mouth of the Vermillion River at present-day Vermillion. This latter village, in particular, would have hunted in the Spirit Mound area, but, we are to understand, avoided the mound itself.

Fur traders, however, were relative newcomers to the Upper Missouri. Only two days south of the Sioux River en route home, Lewis and Clark met a trading boat belonging to Auguste Chouteau, who, with several men, was on his way north to trade with the Yanktons. As the Corps neared St. Louis they met other parties of traders preparing to engage the Omahas, Pawnees, and Yanktons in trading beaver furs for all manner of goods prized by the tribes.

It is estimated that during this era up to one hundred fur-trading posts were operating at one time or another in present-day South Dakota. Three of them were at or near the mouth of the Vermillion River, the most substantial of which was the American Fur Company's Fort Vermillion slightly downriver near where Burbank is now. It is easy to envision Yankton Sioux plying the lower Vermillion River and a tributary such as Clay Creek, both within three miles of Spirit Mound, in search of beavers to supply the nearby posts.

Fur traders were not the only newcomers to visit the Lower Vermillion Valley during these times. Father Pierre DeSmet visited the mouth of the river in May of 1839 to secure a pledge from the Yanktons to desist from attacks on Pottawatami bands downriver. John James Audubon reported in his journal a stop at Fort Vermillion in 1843, including some hunting in the area, on his way upriver to Fort Union in present-day North Dakota to complete scientific studies for a book on quadrupeds. Fort Vermillion was also the site of a sizeable Mormon camp from the summer of 1845 to the spring of 1846, when the party received instructions to join the main body of Mormons in Omaha for its westward trek to present-day Utah.

By this time fur trading among the Yankton Sioux and elsewhere was on the wane, brought to decline by a fashion change in men's hats among Easterners and Europeans. Fort Vermillion closed in 1850, signaling the end of an era in what is now southeastern South Dakota.

The decade of the 1850s began for the Lower Vermillion Valley what I will call the *Era of Homesteaders and Community Builders.* Considerable settlement had already occurred in northwest Iowa, and nearby Sioux City was bustling. Minnesota became a state in 1858. Opening the land west of the Big Sioux River for settlers was facilitated by a treaty with the Yankton Sioux ratified by Congress in February of 1859. The tribe agreed to withdraw to a reservation in what is now Charles Mix County, ceding the rest of their lands to the whites for $1.6 million. The departure of the Yanktons for their new homes on July 10 of that year marks the official opening of the future Clay County for settlement. We can only wonder what the tribal members who had called the Vermillion valley home for many years must have thought on leaving such a natural wonderland behind, Spirit Mound included.

A small land rush occurred after July 10 as hopefuls who had gathered along the Nebraska side of the Missouri moved across the river. Vermillion, Yankton, and other towns were quickly established, and nearby farmland was claimed. A movement began almost immediately to obtain Congressional approval for a territorial government. Success came on March 2, 1861, when President James Buchanan, two days before Abraham Lincoln succeeded him, signed the bill creating Dakota Territory. Clay County was formed the next month, with Vermillion as its county seat.

Early in 1862 the territorial capital was officially located at Yankton, and the territorial university was placed in Vermillion, although no funds were appropriated for the latter. Later that year unrest among the Santee Sioux in Minnesota resulted in an uprising that spilled over into Dakota Territory, causing settlers in and around Sioux Falls and Vermillion to flee to Yankton or Sioux City for strength in numbers.

The Homestead Act passed by Congress in 1862, effective the following January 1, was the catalyst for waves of immigration into what is now southeastern South Dakota over the next two decades. Early on, moderating influences slowed settlement: a Civil War in progress until 1865, bad grasshopper years, and intense competition from other areas for land seekers. Conditions improved markedly by 1868, when the Laramie Treaty stabilized conditions along and west of the Missouri River. That same year the railroad reached Sioux City, and the next five years saw the greatest increase in homesteading in and around Clay County.

In the spring of 1868 Nathan Hixson filed a claim in Spirit Mound Township, including a portion of the Mound itself. Besides breaking the sod and otherwise doing what was necessary to maintain his claim under the Homestead Act, he was hired as the construction supervisor for Clay County's first gristmill. It was located along the Vermillion River at the nearby Bloomingdale settlement.

Jonathan and Hannah Kimball and their five children soon arrived in the township from Illinois. Kimball also secured employment at the Bloomingdale mill. His son Charles related many years later that fish, mostly buffalo and carp caught in the mill's nets, were on the Kimball dinner table every day. He also said the family's substitute for coffee was "scorched barley." Charles often climbed Spirit Mound as a boy and recalled in particular the north view, where only one tree could be seen all the way to the far horizon.

In the fall of 1868 brothers Peter and John Cleland from Wisconsin settled near the Kimballs. Peter was a Civil War veteran who had marched across Georgia with Sherman. On June 20, 1869, he wrote a letter to his sister, Belle, back home, saying in part:

> John has commenced to draw lumber for his house and when we get that built would like to have you come and make us a visit. Would ask you to come now, but haven't but one bed and no room for another one. I beg of you don't come until we get it built. You won't, will you? You can tell Nettie that we would like to have her come then, too, if she thought Joe would not care, but don't want him to come for there is too many men here now. All we want in this county is oxen and women.

By 1872 the railroad reached Vermillion, and the next year two stage lines began service past Spirit Mound up the river valley to points north. The national depression known as the Panic of 1873 and some bad grasshopper years in the mid-'70s quieted homesteading fervor, but by that time most of the government land in Clay County was claimed.

Times were hard, but community building continued apace. Five schools were begun during the 1870s in Spirit Mound Township, one of which, the Spirit Mound School, was across the road from the west slope of the Mound. The Sunday School movement sweeping the country hit Spirit Mound Township in 1869, and church-building soon followed. Four denominations built in Spirit Mound Township—Baptists, Norwegian Lutherans, Methodists, and the United Brethren—while others appeared in nearby townships. The Spirit Mound Baptist Church just northwest of the Mound, when abandoned some years later, became the township hall for many years.

The 1880s and '90s brought more prosperous times, and life styles expanded. Spirit Mound Township was formally organized in 1881. The same year Nathan Hixson proved up on his claim to the land that included Spirit Mound and gained title to the quarter section. Also, after twenty years of being a school on paper only, the territorial university finally began classes in 1882 in the Clay County courthouse. The people of Spirit Mound Township were among the jurisdictions voting favorably on bonds to help build the first building on the new campus, University Hall, now called Old Main, which opened in 1883.

A quick listing of leisure activities which became commonplace in these decades demonstrates that folks then were beginning to mix pleasure with their hard work: fishing, boating, ice skating, gun clubs (including one in Spirit Mound Township), lyceum courses, literary societies, debating societies (one of these in the Township, too), fraternal organizations, temperance societies, community bands, drum and bugle corps, drama groups, circuses, ventriloquists, lecturers, even intercollegiate baseball and football at the University by 1889.

The most important happening in 1889, of course, was the long-awaited statehood for South Dakota on November 2. Now all of the governmental, economic, and social institutions were in place. Thus the turn of the century marks a convenient close to the Era of Homesteaders and Community Builders.

The first half of the 1900s was ushered in by at least fifteen years of what some historians have termed the Golden Age of Agriculture. It is important for an observer of Spirit Mound Township to know that this entity has always been completely rural. No incorporated town was founded within these 36 square miles. Only one mile of railroad penetrated, the Vermillion-Yankton line in the far southwest section, and no U.S. highway and no interstate highway have ever been part of the township.

Thus, manifestations of rural progress have been "big news" in this enclave. While we will call this fifty years the *Era of Economic Extremes and Foreign Wars*, during the first segment prosperity was arguably the norm. Spirit Mound Township is blessed with highly arable land. The map shows us that over one-third of the sections are in the rich Missouri River plain. Farmers in this sector fought for and won a huge 1908-1910 project to reclaim thousands of acres of marginal wetlands along Clay Creek, which was channelized into a sixteen-mile canal. The new century's first decade also brought into Clay County extension of the nation's rural free delivery postal system and its first rural telephone lines. Most important, the country's stable farm economy, shared by South Dakota, prospered as a sharply expanded urban population increased the domestic market for farm products.

Once America entered the Great War, Spirit Mound Township furnished its sons to the armed services abroad and responded well on the "home front." By now the Alexander C. McDonald family had come into ownership of the quarter section of land which includes the peak of Spirit Mound, having purchased it from the Hixson family in 1908. The Mound was now destined to shed almost 120 years of relative obscurity as a historical treasure, thanks to the teamwork of Doane Robinson, noted state historian of the time, and the Vermillion chapter of the Daughters of the American Revolution (D.A.R). In December of 1921, as part of a statewide D.A.R focus on marking significant historic sites, the Vermillion ladies contracted for a huge granite boulder faced with a lettered eleven-by-fourteen inch bronze plate to be placed on top of Spirit Mound. Alexander McDonald's son Vergil, whose family resided in the adjacent home, used his team of horses and his stone boat, fittingly, to haul the unusual load to the top. This monument, despite erosion around it, crowned Spirit Mound until recently.

Vergil's daughter, Laura Lou McDonald Marsh, who now lives with members of her family near Hartington, Nebraska, was born two years later in the north slope house. She has shared with me memories of her childhood in the shadow of this Lewis and Clark landmark. Here are some of her recollections:

- I remember picking wild flowers on the Mound—a cactus-type plant with dull gray leaves and large white or ivory blossoms that opened only at night—sweet aroma—"snow on the mountain" plants.
- Grass flowers with pastel colors were picked on the native west slope, but there was not a lot of vegetation because of the chalk rock formations and the extreme drought during my childhood years in the 1930s.
- I remember the awful winter of 1936-37—continuous storms from November to March. Roads were constantly blocked and temperatures were sub-zero for days. My father walked across fields with my teacher (who lived with us) and me to see that we reached school safely.
- The heat was equally awful in the summer. Huge green and yellow grasshoppers hung solidly on fence posts so thick the posts were half again their usual diameter. They ate our corn to stubs, as if a mower had gone across the fields. Mother would hang clothes on the line and stand there with a dish towel fanning it to keep the hoppers from eating holes in the sheets and clothing.
- Sledding on the Mound during the winter was a favorite pastime of kids in the neighborhood.
- My friends and cousins and I loved to go to the top of the Mound and check on the covered pipe embedded in the ground. Visitors to the Mound put names, dates and addresses in it—yes, there were some tourists even in the "Dirty Thirties."

From this point I will "fast forward" through this era. Farm relief and crop management programs under President Franklin D. Roosevelt's tutelage helped rural America turn the corner. The most important of these may have been the Rural Electrification Administration (R.E.A), whose lines first entered Clay County in 1937. The next year highway crews began a project near and dear to Spirit Mound folks, the grading and first gravel on South Dakota Highway 19 north and south through the township. This brought a modern farm-to-market road for the first time to the very slope of the Mound, while at the same time making the site more accessible to visitors. By the time the Depression had run its course, the United States became involved in World War II. Improved economic conditions during and immediately after the war allowed farmers to reduce their indebtedness and build up financial reserves. Thus, the curtain closes in 1950 on our Era of Economic Extremes and Foreign Wars.

The most recent half century, among all the fifty-year segments since 1806, is obviously the most familiar to area residents in 2004. I call it the *Era of Consolidation and Technology*. Here we will narrow our focus to Spirit Mound Township as an example of changes ringing through rural America.

The population of the township by the 1990 census had fallen to 194, or less than half the 1950 figure. None of the township's four houses of worship even survived into this era, having closed or merged prior to World War II. While four of the five one-room schools survived beyond 1950, none made it to 1970 before consolidating with larger districts nearby. Construction during the 1960s of Interstate Highway 29 just eight miles east and parallel to Highway 19, coupled with the widening of South Dakota Highway 50 to four lanes between I-29 and Yankton, changed traffic and living patterns in nearby rural townships like Spirit Mound. It was now easier to commute to the larger population centers for work, shopping, and entertainment. Some farm families even began to move to the towns and drive back to the home place to work the land or tend the livestock.

What is far and away Spirit Mound Township's largest piece of construction, East River Electric Power Cooperative's Spirit Mound generating plant, went on line on a multi-acre site two miles northwest of the Mound in 1978. This imposing facility now competes with the Mound itself for "skyline" honors in the township. An important construction project of a different nature also occurred during the '70s, when the Clay County Rural Water System spread its lines throughout the area.

This decade was significant to Spirit Mound for yet another reason: fledgling efforts began to preserve the Mound site as a public landmark to honor its significance to Native Americans and its importance in the Lewis and Clark story. Local historians spearheaded a move in 1974 to add Spirit Mound to the National Register of Historic Places. After the mid-1980s, efforts to preserve the Mound were led by the small but devoted Lewis & Clark-Spirit Mound Trust, a non-profit organization that doggedly called attention to the deteriorating hill and its importance as a historic site. The Trust organization has been aided strategically in recent years by both local and national attention building up to the bicentennial of the Lewis and Clark Expedition from 2003 to 2006.

Since the arrival of the first homesteaders, ownership of the Mound and its slopes has been in private hands. All four of the principal landowning families in the late 1990s were proud of the historical significance of their property. Each was, in terms of the realty business, a willing seller. They were also anxious to have Spirit Mound restored as much as possible to its condition at the time the Lewis and Clark party climbed it in 1804. Everyone familiar with the site knew that restoration would not be easy, given the numerous incursions on the site brought about mainly by farming practices over some 130 years. However, fortune smiled: a six-acre tract on the west slope, while having been grazed, has never been plowed. The considerable flora and fauna of this prairie remnant were inventoried, and this information and other research helped facilitate restoration planning.

Fortune also smiled in October of 1998 when United States Senator Tim Johnson, who has roots in rural Clay County and whose official voting residence is Vermillion, was able to obtain authorization in Congress for federal funds to purchase the 320-acre site. By March of 2000 additional legislation had passed both houses of Congress and was signed by the President to transfer the federal land purchase funds to the State of South Dakota once an acceptable plan was drawn up by the state for preservation and management of the site.

At the same time Congress was getting involved, South Dakota Governor Bill Janklow was also seeing the merits of preserving Spirit Mound in a more natural environment. In the summer of 2000 the state approved a grant for the restoration, at the same time as an agreement was being reached among the South Dakota Department of Game, Fish and Parks; the National Park Service, and the Spirit Mound Trust to move forward with the project. Game, Fish and Parks became the principal coordinating agency for the restoration, and the National Park Service, the South Dakota Parks and Wildlife Foundation, and the South Dakota Department of Transportation are principal partners in planning and funding the project.

Agreements were reached with the landowners during the winter of 2000-2001, and restoration work began in the spring of 2001. Buildings, fences, driveways, and trees were removed. Prairie grasses and other native plants were reestablished through a massive seeding and planting project over at least three years. About forty species were reintroduced to the half section by way of 2,500 pounds of native grass seeds and 6,000 plugs on the more difficult east slope. Decent rainfall enhanced the efforts, but the visitor to the Mound needs to be reminded that prairies were created over time and that it will take many years before Spirit Mound begins to replicate what it was in 1804.

Part of a grove of large trees on the southeast corner of the site was retained as a shade anchor for a small parking lot and day-use area adjacent to Highway 19. Visitors find restrooms, a drinking fountain, and picnic tables available for their use. An interpretive kiosk is located at the start of a three-quarter mile, recycled-asphalt trail that leads across Spirit Mound Creek and up to the summit of the Mound. The relatively simple visitor services were intended in part to forestall obtrusive incursions at the small 320-acre site.

Those visitors who want more information are directed to the Lewis and Clark Learning Center at the W.H. Over Museum in Vermillion. Ample food and lodging services are also available in this university town. Major improvements to Highway 19 complemented the overall Spirit Mound plan. From Highway 50 at the northwest corner of Vermillion, "Nineteen" has been widened and otherwise modernized. This project also added a new enhancement: a bicycle trail that will generate non-motorized traffic along the attractive seven miles from town to the Mound.

Thus, the Spirit Mound Historic Prairie, as the restoration has officially been named, is ready for the many thousands of visitors expected annually at sites from St. Louis to the Pacific during the Lewis and Clark Bicentennial years and beyond.

It is important that guests experience three elements of the restored Mound. First, it will represent the vast prairies of mid-America before pioneer settlement. Second, it serves as a reminder of the many years the native peoples called this area home, including the final residents, the Yankton Sioux, many of whom now reside on a reservation eighty-five miles west. Finally, the Mound hosted the small, curious Lewis and Clark party on one hot summer day in 1804. The vagaries of nature along the Expedition's trail have wiped away evidence of most campsites and other places they visited, but we know they stood here, marveling at the birds and the buffalo and the vastness of the land they were about to enter.

And what about Spirit Mound Township, until now among the most typical of American rural township communities? Its role will change during the twenty-first century. A nation is about to rediscover an important place in our Native American tradition as well as a true Lewis and Clark landmark deep in the heart of Clay County, South Dakota. The next fifty years—let's call it the *Era of National Rediscovery*—is now dawning at Spirit Mound, two hundred years after Meriwether Lewis and William Clark left their imprint forever on this simple prairie hill.

Endnotes

Before the Corps: Don Alonso Decalves' 1786-1787 "Exploration" of the West, by Rex C. Myers (pp. 1-17)

[1] Stephen D. Watrous, ed., *John Ledyard's Journey Through Russia and Siberia, 1787/1788* (Madison: University of Wisconsin Press, 1966), 259.

[2] Don Alonso Decalves, *New Travels to the Westward, or, Unknown parts of America...* (Norwich: John Trumbull, 1788), iv-v. Hereafter, citations to Decalves are to the 1788 Trumbull edition, through page 32, then from the 1790 Trumbull edition, pages 33-34, unless otherwise noted.

[3] Cyclone Covey, trans., *Cabeza de Vaca's Adventures in the Unknown Interior of America* (Albuquerque: University of New Mexico Press, 1961), 133. All foreign language works cited in this paper are in English translation. For additional translation, I want to acknowledge the assistance of Lawrence University foreign language faculty: Gustavo Fares in Spanish; Patricia Vilches in Spanish and Italian; Judith Sarnecki and Eilene Hoft-March in French; and Randall McNeill in Latin.

[4] Percy M. Baldwin, ed., trans., *Discovery of the Seven Cities of Cibola by the Father Fray Marcos de Niza* (Albuquerque: El Palacio Press, 1926), 15, 19, 23, 30.

[5] Baldwin, 20.

[6] Richard Flint and Shirley Cushing Flint, eds., *The Coronado Expedition to Tierra Nueva: the 1540-1542 route across the Southwest* (Boulder: University Press of Colorado, 1997).

[7] Jerold C. Rodesch, "Jean Nicolet," *Voyageur* (Spring 1984), 4-8.

[8] A. P. Nasatir, ed., *Before Lewis and Clark: Documents Illustrating the History of the Missouri, 1785-1804* (St. Louis: St. Louis Historical Documents Foundation, 1952), Vol. I, 3.

[9] John Gilmary Shea, trans., Louis Hennepin, *A Description of Louisiana* (New York: John G. Shea, 1880; reprinted, Ann Arbor: University Microfilms, 1966), 339, 344.

[10] Reuben Gold Thwaites, ed., Baron De Lahontan, *New Voyages to North-America*, (reprinted, New York: Burt Franklin, 1970), xxii.

[11] Thwaites, Lahontan, 192.

[12] Thwaites, Lahontan, 193-194. A league during the 1700s varied in length from 2.6 to 3.1 miles.

[13] Thwaites, Lahontan, 179.

[14] Thwaites, Lahontan, 214.

[15] Lawrence J. Burpee, *The Search for the Western Sea* (Toronto: The Macmillan Company, 1935), 106.

[16] Burpee, 199, 201.

[17] Burpee, 203-208.

[18] Frank Norall, *Bourgmont: Explorer of the Missouri, 1698-1725*, (Lincoln: University of Nebraska Press, 1988), 105, 107-109, 111. Allen Johnson, ed., *Dictionary of American Biography*, Vol II (New York: Charles Scribner's Sons, 1929), "Etienne Venyard, Sieur de Bourgmont," 482-83.

[19] Donald A. Barclay and Peter Wild, "Pre-Lewis and Clark Exploration Narratives of Western North America," in The Western Literature Association, *Updating the Literary West* (Fort Worth: Texas Christian University Press, 1997), 156; Nasatir, 33-34; Donald Jackson, *Thomas Jefferson and the Stony Mountains* (Urbana: University of Illinois Press, 1981), 4.

[20] Joseph G. Tregle, Jr., ed., M. Le Page du Pratz, *The History of Louisiana* (Baton Rouge: Louisiana State University Press, 1975), xix; Allen Johnson and Dumas Malone, eds.,

Dictionary of American Biography, Vol. V (New York: Charles Scribner's Sons, 1930), "Antoine Simon Le Page Dupratz," 534.

[21] Pierre Laclede Linguest, August Chouteau, and a small group of men founded St. Louis in February 1764 to control trade in the area. Nasatir, 63-64.

[22] Tregle, 299-303.

[23] Jackson, 8.

[24] John Parker, *The Journals of Jonathan Carver and Related Documents, 1766-1770* (St. Paul: Minnesota Historical Society Press, 1976), 193.

[25] Parker, 193-194.

[26] Parker, 133. See also Jonathan Carver's actual journal, *Three Years Travels through the Interior Parts of North America...* (Philadelphia: Joseph Crukshank, 1784).

[27] Parker, 136-139; Carver, xix, 217.

[28] Carver, 53, 59, 61, 180.

[29] Parker, 222-229.

[30] Carver, vi.

[31] H.A. Innis, *Peter Pond: Fur Trader and Adventurer* (Toronto: Irwin and Gordon, 1930), 124.

[32] Jackson, 34-36.

[33] Jackson, 42-43.

[34] Jefferson's letter to Clark appears in Julian P. Boyd, ed., *The Papers of Thomas Jefferson*, Vol. 6 (Princeton: Princeton University Press, 1952), 371. Clark's reply is in Vol, 15 (1958), 609-610.

[35] John Ledyard published *A Journal of Captain Cook's Last Voyage to the Pacific Ocean ...in the Years 1776, 1777, 1778, and 1779* (Hartford: Nathaniel Patten, 1783). Rickman's account of the same trip, first published in London in 1781, appeared in the United States as *An Authentic Narrative of a Voyage to the Pacific Ocean. By an Officer on Board the Discovery* (Philadelphia: Robert Bell, 1783). Donald Jackson, "Ledyard and Laperouse: A Contrast in Northwestern Exploration," *The Historical Quarterly* 9:4 (October, 1978), 496.

[36] Ledyard's quirky efforts and Jefferson's interest in them have attracted scholarly attention in Donald Jackson, *Thomas Jefferson*, cited above, 49-50; also in Jackson's article on Ledyard and Laperouse; and Stephen D. Watrous's *John Ledyard's Journey Through Russia and Siberia*. In his 1821 autobiography, Jefferson took credit for suggesting Ledyard traverse Russia and the Pacific, then walk across North America. Watrous, 259.

[37] Estaban Miro to Antonio Rengel, New Orleans, December 12, 1785. Original in the Bancroft Library. Reprinted in Nasatir, 119-127.

[38] Charles M. Gates, ed., *Five Fur Traders of the Northwest* (St. Paul: Minnesota Historical Society, 1965), 11-15.

[39] Innis, 109-110, 125-26. Alexander Mackenzie arrived in Athabaska in 1787 to replace Pond. There seems little doubt that Pond directed Mackenzie to explore a river that ultimately bore Mackenzie's name, but flowed into the Arctic Ocean rather than the Pacific.

[40] Jefferson's *Notes* is reprinted in Merrill D. Peterson, ed., *Thomas Jefferson: Writings* (New York: Library of America, 1984), 166, 176.

[41] Peterson, 132, 133, 144.

[42] Spanish Ambassador Diego Maria de Gardoqui, in Philadelphia, wrote to his superior Don Jose de Monino y Redondo, Conde de Floridablanca, on June 25, 1789, that he interviewed an Englishman who spent the last five years roaming upper Louisiana and saw his map. The distance to the Pacific "was short." Nasatir, 131.

[43] Carl I. Wheat, *Mapping the Transmississippi West, 1540-1861* (San Francisco: Institute of Historical Cartography, 1957), Vol. I, 143.

[44] Wheat, Vol. I, 143, 148, 213.

[45] Wheat, Vol. I, 237, 142-148, 225, 236; R. V. Tooley, *Maps and Map-Makers* (London: B. T. Batsford, Ltd, 1978), 21; "North America Drawn from the Latest and Best Authority, T. Kitchin del. Engrav'd by G. Terry." Special Collections, Reed College Library [http://www.web.reed.edu/resources/library/maps/] (18 March, 2002).

[46] *The Boston Gazette, and the Country Journal*, May 19, 1788, 4. The same ad also appeared May 26 and June 2. Jim Dowd published a book entitled *The Naratives* [sic] *of Don Alonso Decalves, John Van Delure, and Capt. James Vanleason* (Fairfield, WA: Ye Galleon Press, 1996) in which he reprinted the 1788 John W. Folsom edition of *New Travels*, either the 1812 Wright and Sibley or the 1816 Wright edition of *A History of the Voyages and Adventures of John Van Delure*, and either the 1801 Windsor, NY, or the 1816 Ballston Spa, NY, edition of *A Narrative of a Voyage, taken by Capt. James Vanleason*, — Dowd is not precise with his credits. Dowd provided useful publication information on the related works, but saw the later two as disparate, when content was identical and only title pages differed. Dowd listed twenty different printings as *New Travels* and eight as *Travels*. Charles Evans, *American Bibliography: a chronological dictionary of all books, pamphlets, and periodical publications printed in the United States of America from the genesis of printing in 1639 down to and including the year 1820* (New York: Peter Smith, 1941-1959) lists nineteen editions of Decalves, eight as *New Travels*, ten as *Travels*, and one in German. WorldCat [database online] available from OCLC, Inc., lists nineteen separate editions under both names, corresponding to the Evans listings.

[47] *The Norwich Packet and Country Journal*, March 6, 1789, 1. Identical additional advertisements appeared in the Packet for seven weeks, from March 6, through April 17. Thereafter, Trumbull simply listed the title among others he sold in his bookshop. In Connecticut, *New Travels to the Westward* sold for nine pence.

[48] Decalves, iv. The summary of *New Travels* that follows and all quotes come from this edition. See note #1.

[49] Tomhegan, or Tumtumphegan, was an Abenaki Indian who fought for the British during the American Revolution. On August 3, 1781, Tomhegan and five other Indians raided what is now Bethel, Maine. His name survives in various Maine place names. William B. Lapham, *History of the Town of Bethel, Maine* (Augusta: Press of the Maine Farmer, 1891), reprinted (Sommersworth, NH: New England History Press, 1981), 46-51, 423.

[50] Bernd Knipperdoling or Knipperdolling was a German Anabaptist at Munster, 1534-1536. Catholic forces retook the city and executed him in January of 1536. Sigrun Haude, *In the Shadow of "Savage Wolves": Anabaptist Munster and the German Reformation During the 1530's* (Boston: Humanities Press, Inc., 2000), 12, 16.

[51] Decalves, 12.

[52] Decalves, 8.

[53] Decalves, 12-13.

[54] Decalves, 33.

[55] *Norwich Packet*, March 6, 1789, 1. The site of Athens is the site of St. Louis, then nearly twenty-five years old. A.P. Nasatir's translations of Spanish documents during this period contain no mention of such a town site.

[56] James Gilreath and Douglas L. Wiklson, eds., *Thomas Jefferson's Library* (Washington: Library of Congress, 1986).

[57] Lapham, 60.

[58] See Jackson, "Ledyard and Laperouse," and Watrous. Also useful is Bertha S. Dodge, "John Ledyard: Controversial Corporal," *History Today* 23:0 (September, 1973), 648-655. Ledyard died mysteriously in Cairo, January 10, 1789.

[59] Frank Luther Mott, *Golden Multitudes: The Story of Best Sellers in the United States* (New York: R. R. Bowker Company, 1947), 53; Dowd, 8-9; WorldCat. L. Ray Patterson and Stanley W. Lindberg, *The Nature of Copyright. A Law of Users' Rights* (Athens: University of Georgia Press, 1991), 48, 53-54.

[60] Isaiah Thomas, *The History of Printing in America*, originally published in 1810 with a second edition in 1874. Reprinted by Marcus A. McCorison, ed., (New York: Weathervane Books, 1970), 303, 311. Clarence S. Brigham, *History and Bibliography of American Newspapers, 1690-1820* (Worcester: American Antiquarian Society, 1947), 66. The original source of most biographical information on Trumbull is Frances Manwaring Caulkins, *History of Norwich, Connecticutt: From its Possession by the Indians, to the year 1866* (Hartford: By the Author, 1866), 357-364. John Trumbull began publication of the *Norwich Packet* during 1773 in partnership with Alexander and James Robertson. With the onset of the American Revolution, the Loyalists Robertson brothers left Connecticut for New York City. Trumbull continued as sole editor of the *Packet* until his death in 1802. Connecticut during this period abounded with John Trumbull's as governor, poet, jurist, politician, and painter. Editor Trumbull does not appear to be directly related to any of the more famous personages with whom he shared a name.

[61] Dowd, 8; WorldCat; Evans.

[62] Mott, 53; Patterson and Lindberg.

[63] Caulkins, 364. Almost every issue of the *Packet* during 1787 and 1788 carries notice of a publication for sale. Beginning March 1, 1787, Trumbull issued the Francois-Thomas-Marie, de Bagulard d' Arnaud novel Fanny and advertised it heavily thereafter. At no point does Trumbull credit Arnaud as author.

[64] *Packet*, June 21, 1787, 3; August 9, 1787, 4; and April 3, 1788, 3.

[65] The satire of "The Connecticut Wits" provided inspiration enough. See Leon Howard, *The Connecticut Wits* (Chicago: University of Chicago Press, 1943). The Wits included a different John Trumbull, Timothy Dwight, David Humphreys, Joel Barlow, and incidentally Lemuel Hopkins. A dilemma of possible Trumbull authorship is the fact that the *Packet* did not advertise his 1788 edition, but did his 1789 and 1790 numbers. It seems hard to believe he would have missed this opportunity.

[66] Gilreath.

[67] Dowd, 9; WorldCat. The summary of Vandelure's narrative is taken from the 1801 edition, Evans.

[68] Dowd, 96.

[69] William G. McLoughlin, *Revivals, Awakenings, and Reform: An Essay on Religion and Social Change in America,1607-1977* Chicago: University of Chicago Press, 1978).

[70] Gary I. Ebersole, *Captured by Texts: Puritan to Postmodern Images of Indian Captivity* (Charlottesville: University Press of Virginia, 1995).

[71] Dowd, 8-9; WorldCat; Evans.

[72] Three titles are useful in understanding Spanish administration of Louisiana: Warren L. Cook, *Flood Tide of Empire: Spain in the Pacific Northwest, 1543-1819* (New Haven: Yale University Press, 1973); Abraham P. Nasatir, *Borderland in Retreat: From Spanish Louisiana to the Far Southwest* (Albuquerque: University of New Mexico Press, 1976); and David J. Weber, *The Spanish Frontier in North America* (New Haven: Yale University Press, 1992).

[73] Alexander Mackenzie, *Voyages from Montreal on the River St. Laurence, through the Continent of North America to the Frozen and Pacific Oceans; In the Years 1789 and 1793* (London: T. Cadell and others, 1801) reprinted as March of American Facsimile Series #52 (Ann Arbor: University Microfilms, Inc., 1966); Milo Milton Quaife, ed., *Alexander*

Mackenzie's Voyage to the Pacific Ocean in 1793 (Chicago: R. R. Donnelley & Sons Co., 1931).

[74] Jackson, *Jefferson*.

The Literary Struggle of Lewis and Clark, by Joseph Basile (pp. 23-27)

[1] I am grateful to my brother, Leon E. Basile, to Dayton Duncan, and to my colleagues in the English Department at the University of South Dakota for their helpful suggestions during the preparation of this paper.

[2] Meriwether Lewis and William Clark, *The Journals of Lewis and Clark*, ed. John Bakeless (New York: Menter, 1964), 298. All future quotations from the journals are from this edition and will be cited internally.

[3] I believe that Lewis, in this statement, is alluding to a comparison between the Great Falls of the Missouri and Niagara Falls.

The Rhetoric of Imperialism in the Lewis and Clark Journals: Camp Dubois to the Mandan Villages, by Joan K. Warner Dolence (pp. 28-34)

[1] Mary Louise Pratt, *Imperial Eyes: Travel Writing and Transculturation* (New York: Routledge, 1994), 6.

[2] Ibid.

[3] Meriwether Lewis and William Clark, *The Journals of the Lewis and Clark Expedition, Vol. 3: August 25, 1804-April 6, 1805*, ed. Gary E. Moulton (Lincoln: University of Nebraska Press, 1983-1997), 113.

[4] James P. Ronda, *Lewis and Clark among the Indians* (Lincoln: University of Nebraska Press, 1984), 38-39.

[5] David Spurr, *The Rhetoric of Empire: Colonial Discourse in Journalism, Travel Writing, and Imperial Administration* (Durham: Duke University Press, 1996), 15-16.

[6] Thomas Jefferson, "Expedition to the Pacific: Instructions to Captain Lewis," in *Thomas Jefferson: Writings*, ed. Merrill D. Peterson (New York: Library of America, 1984), 1127.

[7] Ibid.

[8] John Logan Allen, *Passage Through the Garden: Lewis and Clark and the Image of the American Northwest* (Urbana: University of Illinois Press, 1975), xiii.

[9] Ibid., 40-41, 64.

[10] Meriwether Lewis and William Clark, *The Journals of the Lewis and Clark Expedition, Vol. 2: August 30, 1803-August 24, 1804*, ed. Gary E. Moulton (Lincoln: University of Nebraska Press, 1983-1997), 415.

[11] Spurr, 27.

[12] Lewis and Clark, *The Journals of the Lewis and Clark Expedition, Vol. 2: August 30, 1803-August 24, 1804*, 309.

[13] Ibid., 341.

[14] Ibid., 355.

[15] Ibid., 304.

[16] Ibid., 327.

[17] Ibid., 348.

[18] Ibid., 333.

[19] Stephen Ambrose, *Undaunted Courage: Meriwether Lewis, Thomas Jefferson, and the Opening of the American West* (New York: Touchstone, 1997), 57.

[20] Ibid.

[21] Pratt, 204-205.

[22] Meriwether Lewis and William Clark, *The Journals of the Lewis and Clark Expedition, Vol. 2: August 30, 1803-August 24, 1804*, 346-347.

[23] In the case of Lewis and Clark, this proves particularly ironic since they failed to publish an account of their journey until 1814, eight years after the return of the expedition. This first account was, in fact, Nicholas Biddle's paraphrase of parts of the journals and lacked most of Lewis's natural history notes. "As a result," Ambrose notes, "Lewis and Clark got no credit for most of their discoveries." Stephen Ambrose, *Undaunted Courage: Meriwether Lewis, Thomas Jefferson, and the Opening of the American West* (New York: Touchstone, 1997), 480.

[24] Pratt, 202.

[25] Ibid., 205.

[26] Spurr, 32.

[27] Ibid., 31.

[28] Allen, 190.

[29] Ambrose, 105.

[30] Jefferson, 1126-1132.

[31] Spurr, 39.

[32] William H. Goetzmann, *Exploration and Empire: The Explorer and the Scientist in the Winning of the American West* (New York: Knopf, 1966), ix.

[33] Ibid, 3-4.

Sexual Relations of the Lewis and Clark Expedition, by Brad Tennant (pp. 46-53)

[1] Donald Jackson, ed., "Jefferson's Instructions to Lewis," in *Letters of the Lewis and Clark Expedition with Related Documents, 1783-1854*, 2nd ed. (Chicago: University of Illinois Press, 1978), 62-63.

[2] James P. Ronda, *Lewis and Clark among the Indians* (Lincoln: University of Nebraska Press, 1984), 114, 130.

[3] Dayton Duncan, *Lewis & Clark: An Illustrated History* (New York: Alfred A. Knopf, 1997), 60.

[4] Gary E. Moulton, ed., *The Journals of the Lewis and Clark Expedition*, Volume 3 (Lincoln: University of Nebraska Press, 1987), 163.

[5] Eldon G. Chuinard, *Only One Man Died: The Medical Aspects of the Lewis and Clark Expedition* (Fairfield, WA: Ye Galleon Press, reprinted 1999), 332.

[6] Moulton, Volume 3, 161.

[7] Stephen E. Ambrose, *Undaunted Courage: Meriwether Lewis, Thomas Jefferson, and the Opening of the American West* (New York: Simon & Schuster, 1996), 180.

[8] Paul Russell Cutright, *Lewis & Clark: Pioneering Naturalists* (Lincoln: University of Nebraska Press, 1969), 115.

[9] Chuinard, 263.

[10] Duncan, 75.

[11] Moulton, Volume 3, 268.

[12] Ibid., 239; Ronda, 106.

[13] Ronda, 133.

[14] Raymond Darwin Burroughs, ed., *The Natural History of the Lewis and Clark Expedition* (East Lansing: Michigan State University Press, 1995), 24.

[15] Bernard DeVoto, ed., *The Journals of Lewis and Clark* (Boston: Houghton Mifflin Company, 1953), 208.

[16] Ibid., 208-09.

[17] Ambrose, 292.

[18] DeVoto, 289-90.

[19] Ibid., 315

[20] Duncan, 172.

[21] Moulton, Volume 3, 115.

[22] Ronda, 63.

[23] Moulton, Volume, 89.

[24] Chuinard, 340-41.

[25] Cutright, 254.

[26] Ibid., 254-55.

[27] Ibid., 223, 255; Chuinard, 156-59.

[28] Duncan, 60.

[29] Chuinard, 263.

[30] Harry F. Thompson, "Meriwether Lewis and His Son: The Claim of Joseph DeSomet Lewis and the Problem of History," *North Dakota History*, Vol. 67, No. 3 (2000), 25-26.

[31] Chuinard, 263.

[32] ———, "What are the Facts?" *Montana, Magazine of Western History*, Vol. 5, No. 3 (Summer 1955), 36-37.

[33] Chuinard, 259.

Honoring and Gift Giving among the Lakota and Dakota: An Interpretation of Two of Lewis and Clark's Encounters with the Sioux, by Laurinda W. Porter (pp. 54-69)

[1] Various writers divide the Sioux into these three groups. Within the groups are bands, a total of 13, distributed in this way: Lakota (Oglala, Hunkpapa, Miniconjou, Oohenumpa (Two Kettle), Itazipco (Sans Arcs), (Brules) Sicangu, Sihasapa (Blackfoot)), Dakota (Mdewakanton, Sissetowan, Wahpetowan,Wahpekute), and Nakota (Yankton, Yanktonnais). See Severt Young Bear, *Standing in the Light: a Lakota Way of Seeing* (Lincoln: Univ. of Nebraska Press, 1994); Herbert T. Hoover, *The Yankton Sioux* (New York: Chelsea House,1988).

[2] Herbert Eugene Bolton, ed. *Spanish Exploration in the Southwest, 1542-1706*. New York: Barnes & Noble, 1959 (reprint of 1908 edition); "Trade Ventures in the Southwest," in Leroy R. Hafen, *The Mountain Men and the Fur Trade of the Far West, Vol. 1* (Glendale, Calif.: Arthur H. Clark Co., 1965); George P. Hammond, "The Search for the Fabulous in the Settlement of the Southwest," *Utah Historical Quarterly* 24 (1956): 1-19, reprinted in David J. Weber, ed., *New Spain's Far Northern Frontier* (Albuquerque: University of New Mexico Press, 1979).

[3] John Bakeless, ed., *The Journals of Lewis and Clark* (New York: Penguin Books, 1964: 70).

[4] Libby Collection, North Dakota Historical Society, MS A85, Box 28, Folder 15, p.6.

[5] Lawrence J. Burpee, Introduction to J*ournals and Letters of Pierre Gaultier de Varennes de la Verendrye and His Sons* (Toronto: The Champlain Society, 1927). Reprinted by Greenwood Press, 1968.

[6] Grace Lee Nute, *The Voyageur* (St. Paul: Minnesota Historical Society reprint edition, 1955: 7).

[7] *Webster's International Dictionary*, Vol I. Grolier, 1969: 408.

[8] Ibid.

[9] Severt Young Bear, *Standing in the Light—A Lakota Way of Seeing*; Ella Deloria, *Waterlily*; Roger Thundershield, interviews, 1995-97.

[10] Severt Young Bear, *Standing in the Light—A Lakota Way of Seeing*.

[11] Interviews with Roger Thundershield, 4/4 Hunkpapa Lakota, October and November, 1997, at Watkins, Minnesota.

[12] Young Bear, 58-59.

[13] Singing groups, or "drums" as they are referred to, consist of men who devote a substantial portion of their time to learning the songs and the history of songs of the Lakotas. See Severt Young Bear, *Standing in the Light—A Lakota Way of Seeing.*

[14] Ibid.

[15] Young Bear, 57.

[16] Ibid., 57-58.

[17] Ella Deloria, *Waterlily*; Severt Young Bear; Roger Thundershield, op cit.

[18] Young Bear, 58.

[19] Deloria, Young Bear, Thundershield, op cit.

[20] Thundershield, op cit.

[21] Ibid.

[22] Raymond J. DeMallie, "Afterword," in Ella Cara Deloria, *Waterlily* (Lincoln: University of Nebraska Press, 1988) 237.

[23] *Tiyospaye* means "family group" or "extended family"—a group of people related by blood and marriage who lived together, camped together, and followed an agreed-upon leader, within a larger tribal group.

[24] Ella Deloria lived and worked during a time that scholars and book editors called all the "Sioux" Dakotas, even though they knew that there were three distinct groups—Lakota, Nakota, and Dakota. The use of the term "Dakota" is found throughout Ella Deloria's published work.

[25] Manuscript H75.271 Ella Deloria Manuscript, South Dakota Historical Society Archives.

[26] Carolyn Gilman, *The Grand Portage Story* (St Paul: Minnesota Historical Society Press, 1992).

[27] *The Journals of Lewis and Clark*, ed. John Bakeless. New York: Penguin Books, 1964.

[28] Manuscript H75.271 Ella Deloria Manuscript, South Dakota Historical Society Archives, 88.

[29] Ibid.

Fulfillment of Jefferson's Expectations, by Tim S. Beck and Brad Tennant (pp. 87-93)

[1] Stephen E. Ambrose, *Undaunted Courage: Meriwether Lewis, Thomas Jefferson, and the Opening of the American West* (New York: Simon and Schuster, 1996), 68.

[2] Dayton Duncan, *Lewis & Clark: An Illustrated History* (New York: Alfred A. Knopf, Inc., 1997), 7.

[3] Ibid., 8; Ambrose, 71.

[4] Donald Jackson, ed., *Letters of the Lewis and Clark Expedition with Related Documents 1783-1854* (Urbana: University of Illinois Press, 1962), 668.

[5] Ibid., 10-12.

[6] Ibid., 15-16.

[7] Ibid., 16-18.

[8] Ibid., 19.

[9] Ibid., 19-20.

[10] James P. Ronda, ed., *Voyages of Discovery: Essays on the Lewis and Clark Expedition* (Helena: Montana Historical Society Press, 1998), 32.

[11] Duncan, 166.

[12] James P. Ronda, *Lewis and Clark among the Indians* (Lincoln: University of Nebraska Press, 1984), 127.

[13] Ibid.

[14] Paul Russell Cutright, *Lewis and Clark: Pioneering Naturalists* (Chicago: University of Illinois Press, 1969), 394-95.

[15] Arlen J. Large, "All In The Family: The In-House Honorifics of Lewis and Clark," *We Proceeded On*, Vol. 25, No. 4 (November 1999), 12.

[16] Ronda, *Voyages of Discovery*, 33.

[17] Eldon G. Chuinard, *Only One Man Died: The Medical Aspects of the Lewis and Clark Expedition* (Glendale, CA: A.H. Clark Co., 1979), 418-22.

[18] Ronda, *Lewis and Clark among the Indians*, 7.

[19] Ambrose, 206.

[20] Cutright, 393-94.

[21] Ronda, *Lewis and Clark among the Indians*, 129-32.

[22] Duncan, 37.

[23] Ibid., 36, 39.

[24] Ibid., 41.

[25] Ibid., 40.

[26] Ibid., 35.

[27] Ibid., 40.

[28] Ibid., 90; Ambrose, 219.

[29] Sheila C. Robinson, *Along the Lewis and Clark Trail in North Dakota* (Garrison, ND: BHG, Inc., 1993), 93-94.

[30] Duncan, 37, 39.

[31] Cutright, 395-96.

[32] Jackson, 320-23.

Meriwether Lewis and His Son: The Claim of Joseph DeSomet Lewis and the Problem of History, by Harry F. Thompson (pp. 97-115)

[1] Yankton Mission Register, Vol. 1, 10-11, Archives of the Diocese of South Dakota, the Center for Western Studies, Augustana College, Sioux Falls, South Dakota. Other family members listed as being baptized that day are Joseph DeSomet's grandsons, John Paddock Matowakpana and Edwin Kemble Ehakekis. Walter S. Hall, Andrew Jones, and E. Jane Jones are listed as witnesses for all Lewis baptisms, and the Reverend Joseph W Cook is listed as the clergyman. Identical entries are also found in a second Yankton Mission Register, Vol. 2, 48-49. Also found in Vol. 2 is the marriage record of Joseph DeSomet Lewis and Annie Tamakoce Lewis, December 27, 1874, 102-103, where he is again identified as the son of Capt. Meriwether Lewis, of Lewis and Clark's Expedition, and Winona.

[2] Ibid. Roscoe E. Dean, "A Visit with Amy Lewis Carpenter," *The Thirteenth Dakota History Conference Papers* (Madison, S.Dak.: Dakota State College, 1982), gives the name lkpsa pe win to the mother of Joseph DeSomet and indicates that she was a Teton Sioux, 279.

[3] James Wilkinson, "A Choice of Fictions: Historians, Memory, and Evidence," *PMLA* 111 (1996), 81.

[4] Pearl Boe, letter to author, May 14, 1998.

[5] Jeffrey G. Olson, "Family Proud of Ancestor." *Bismarck Tribune* (metro ed; November 26, 1998) June 17, 1999 < http://web.lexisnexis.comuniverse . . . d5 = 8734ee0a2ece246cf8e11 12a26dfacd4 >, 1.

[6] Merrill J. Mattes, "Report on Historic Sites in the Fort Randall Reservoir Area, Missouri River, South Dakota." *South Dakota Historical Collections and Report* (Vol. 24; Pierre: South Dakota State Historical Society, 1949), 555.

[7] Ibid., 556.

[8] Olson, 2.

[9] *Early Settlers in Lyman County* (Presho, S. Dak.: Lyman County Historical Society, 1974), 29.

[10] Mattes, 556.

[11] Louis Pfaller, *Father DeSmet in Dakota* (Richardton, N. Dak.: Assumption Abbey Press, 1962), 29. Professor Hoover notes that Father DeSmet served mass and offered instruction to the Yankton Sioux when he visited in 1839, Herbert T. Hoover, *The Yankton Sioux* (New York: Chelsea House, 1988), 44. See also "Chart of Missouri River from the Mouth of the Platte till Vermillion," attributed to Father DeSmet, IX-DeSmetiana-C8-11, Midwest Jesuit Archives, St. Louis, Missouri.

[12] John L. Allen, "Patterns of Promise: Mapping the Plains and Prairies, 1800-1860," in *Mapping the North American Plains: Essays in the History of Cartography*, eds. Frederick C. Luebke, Frances W. Kaye, and Gary E. Moulton (Norman: University of Oklahoma Press, 1987), 57.

[13] W. H. Hutton, in *Little Chief's Gatherings: The Smithsonian Institution's G. K. Warren 1855-1856 Plains Indian Collection and The New York State Library's 1855-1857 Warren Expeditions Journals*, ed. James A. Hanson (Crawford, Neb.: Fur Press, 1996), 137.

[14] G. K. Warren, in *Little Chief's Gatherings*, 35.

[15] Ibid., 20.

[16] Ibid., 100.

[17] Ibid., 106.

[18] Ibid., 110, 117.

[19] William H. Goetzmann, *Army Exploration in the American West, 1803-1863* (New Haven: Yale University Press, 1959), 410.

[20] Warren, 106.

[21] Ibid.

[22] Ibid.

[23] Hutton, 140-41.

[24] Ibid., 142.

[25] James A. Hanson, in *Little Chief's Gatherings*, 116 n, 14.

[26] Hoover, 42.

[27] James P. Ronda, "'The Writingest Explorers': The Lewis and Clark Expedition in American Historical Literature," in *Voyages of Discovery: Essays on the Lewis and Clark Expedition*, ed. James P. Ronda (Helena: Montana State Historical Society, 1998), 299-303. See also Ronda, *Lewis and Clark among the Indians* (Lincoln: University of Nebraska Press, 1984), 4, 7, 30.

[28] Thomas Jefferson, in *Letters of the Lewis and Clark Expedition with Related Documents, 1783-1854*, ed. Donald Jackson (Urbana: University of Illinois Press, 1962), 64.

[29] Ibid., 166.

[30] Ibid., 61.

[31] Ibid., 165.

[32] Ibid., 65.

[33] Ibid.

[34] Ibid., vii.

[35] Gary E. Moulton, ed., *The Journals of the Lewis and Clark Expedition*, Volume 2 (Lincoln: University of Nebraska Press, 1986), 8.

[36] Ibid., 17.

[37] Ibid.

[38] Moulton, "On Reading Lewis and Clark: The Last Twenty Years," in *Voyages of Discovery*, 284.

[39] Dayton Duncan, *Lewis & Clark: An Illustrated History* (New York: Knopf, 1997), 50.

[40] Ronda, "'The Writingest Explorers,'" 303.

[41] Stephen E. Ambrose, *Undaunted Courage: Meriwether Lewis, Thomas Jefferson, and the Opening of the American West* (New York: Simon & Schuster, 1996), 167.

[42] Moulton, *Journals*, 2:18.

[43] Ronda, "Exploring the Explorers: Great Plains Peoples and the Lewis and Clark Expedition," in *Voyages of Discovery*, 196-97.

[44] Bernard DeVoto, ed., *The Journals of Lewis and Clark* (Boston: Houghton Mifflin, 1953), 25-26.

[45] John C. Ewers, "Plains Indian Reactions to the Lewis and Clark Expedition," in *Voyages of Discovery*, 177.

[46] Moulton, ed., *Journals*, volume 3 (Lincoln: University of Nebraska Press, 1987), 1.

[47] Ibid., 3:24.

[48] Ibid., 3:32.

[49] Ewers, 173-74.

[50] Ronda, "Exploring the Explorers," 184.

[51] Moulton, 3:79.

[52] Ibid., 3:80.

[53] Ibid., 3:82.

[54] Ibid., 3:102, 106.

[55] Ibid, 3:2.

[56] Ibid, 3:117.

[57] Ronda, *Lewis and Clark*, 37.

[58] Moulton, 3:115.

[59] Ibid., 3:116.

[60] Ronda, *Lewis and Clark*, 37.

[61] Moulton, 3:121.

[62] Ibid., 3:126.

[63] Ronda, "'The Writingest Explorers,'" 318.

[64] Moulton, ed., *Journals*, volume 9 (Lincoln: University of Nebraska Press, 1995), 69.

[65] Ibid.

[66] Moulton, ed., *Journals*, volume 10 (Lincoln: University of Nebraska Press, 1996), 33.

[67] Ibid., 10:46.

[68] Moulton, ed., *Journals*, volume 11 (Lincoln: University of Nebraska Press, 1997), 91.

[69] Reimert Thoroff Ravenholt, "Triumph Then Despair: The Tragic Death of Meriwether Lewis," *Epidemiology 5* (May 1994), 372.

[70] Ambrose, 467.

[71] Richard Dillon, *Meriwether Lewis: A Biography* (New York: Coward-McCann, 1965), 285-86.

[72] Ibid., 344-45.

[73] Vardis Fisher, *Suicide or Murder? The Strange Death of Governor Meriwether Lewis* (Denver: Alan Swallow, 1962), 257.

[74] Brenda Smiley, "Fingerprinting the Dead." *Archaeology* 49 (November/December 1996), 66-67.

[75] Annette Gordon-Reed, *Thomas Jefferson and Sally Hemings: An American Controversy* (Charlottesville: University Press of Virginia, 1997).

[76] Eugene A. Foster, et al., "Jefferson fathered slave's last child," *Nature* 396 (November 5, 1998), 27-28. See also Eric S. Lander and Joseph J. Ellis, "Founding father," *Nature* 396 (November 5, 1998), 13-14.

[77] Amanda Ripley, "Bone Hunter," *Washington City Paper* (March 3, 1998), June 17, 1999 <http://www.washingtoncitypaper.com/archives/cover/1998print_cover0313.html.>, 9.

[78] Ibid., 8.

[79] Ripley, 9; David Schwalbe, "The Death of Meriwether Lewis," *American History* (November 22, 1999), November 22, 1999 <http://americanhistory.aboutamericanhistory/library/weekly/ aal21597.htm.>, 7.

[80] Schwalbe, 7.

[81] Wilkinson, 80.

Why Not Homicide?: Historians and Their Case for Suicide, by John D. W. Guice (pp. 116-25)

[1] Vardis Fisher, *Suicide or Murder? The Strange Death of Governor Meriwether Lewis* (1962, reprint, Athens, Ohio University Press, 1993); Richard Dillon, *Meriwether Lewis: A Biography* (New York, 1965).

[2] For an account of Lewis's activities between the end of the expedition in 1806 and his arrival at Grinder's Stand on the Natchez Trace, see John D. W. Guice, "A Fatal Rendezvous: The Mysterious Death of Meriwether Lewis, " *We Proceeded On* 24 (May 1998), 4-12.

[3] For citations to numerous works containing these arguments, see Guice, "A Fatal Rendezvous."

[4] Alexander Wilson, Letter to Alexander Lawson, May 28, 1811, *Port Folio*, 7 (January 1812), 34-47. Numerous articles quote the letter. For instance, see Guice, "A Fatal Rendezvous."

[5] Donald D. Jackson, ed., *Letters of the Lewis and Clark Expedition with Related Documents, 1783-1834*, 2 vols, Second Edition (Urbana: University of Illinois Press, 1978), Vol 2, 591-92.

[6] James J. Holmberg, ed., *Dear Brother: Letters of William Clark to Jonathan Clark* (New Haven: Yale University Press, 2002), 206-228

[7] Harold I. Kushner, "The Suicide of Meriwether Lewis: A Psychoanalytic Inquiry," *The William and Mary Quarterly* 38 (July 1981), 464-81.

[8] Dawson A. Phelps, "The Tragic Death of Meriwether Lewis," *The William and Mary Quarterly* 13 (July 1956), 305-18.

[9] Reinert Thorolf Ravenholt, "Triumph Then Despair: The Tragic Death of Meriwether Lewis," *Epidemiology* 5 (May 1994), 366-79.

[10] It is entirely possible that what Mrs. Grinder heard was a man who was fuming with indignation over the officiousness of federal bureaucrats and who was practicing his lines for a confrontation with them.

[11] Wilson, Letter to Alexander Lawson.

[12] William Baskerville Hamilton, "American Beginnings in the Old Southwest: The Mississippi Phase" Ph.D. diss., Duke University, 1938; Robert M. Coates, *The Outlaw Years: The History of the Land Pirates of the Natchez Trace* (New York: Macauley Co., 1930).

[13] Ruth Colter-Frick, "Meriwether Lewis's Personal Finances," *We Proceeded On* 28 (February 2002), 16-20.

[14] Jackson, *Letters* Vol. 2, 464-65.

[15] Transcript of the Lewis County Coroner's Inquest into the Death of Meriwether Lewis, June 3-4, 1996 at Hohenwald, TN., 216-17.

[16] Jackson, *Letters*, Vol 2, 466-67.

[17] Ibid, 573-75.

[18] *Coroner Inquest*, 223-25. .

[19] Ibid, 274-88

[20] Fisher to Jackson, July 9, 1960, Donald Jackson File, Vardis Fisher Papers, Beinecke Library, Yale University.

[21] Jackson, *Letters, Vol. 2*, 467-68

[22] Fisher, *Suicide or Murder?*, 171-82 In his September 1, 1960, letter to Donald Jackson, Fisher quotes Julian Boyd (*The American Archivist*, 22, 170): "It is also pertinent to observe that Jefferson, whose memory in old age caused him at times to err . . . . "

[23] William Clark to Jonathan Clark, August 26, 1809, in James J. Holmberg, ed., *Dear Brother: Letters of William Clark to Jonathan Clark* (New Haven, 2002), 210.

[24] E. G. Chuinard, "How Did Meriwether Lewis Die," *We Proceeded On* 17 (August 1991), 4-12; 17 (November 1991), 4-10; 18 (January 1992), 4-10.

[25] U. S. Naval Observatory, Astronomical Applications Department, Sun and Moon Data for One Day, Tuesday, October 10, 1809, (http://mach.usno.navy.mil/cgi-hin/aa_pap.pl). For a detailed discussion of this question, see John D. W. Guice, "Moonlight and Meriwether Lewis," *We Proceeded On* 28 (February 2002), 21-25.

[26] James E. Starrs, *Meriwether Lewis: His Death and His Monument* (Washington, DC, 1997), 28-32. In particular, Starrs cites Robert H. White, *Messages of the Governors of Tennessee, 1845-1857*, Vol. 4 (Nashville Tennessee Historical Commission) 385-87 and *Tennessee Journal of the House of Representatives*, 86, 238-40 & appendix.

[27] Phelps, 18.

[28] Grace Lewis Miller, "Letter to the *William and Mary Quarterly*, St.. Louis MO, December 16, 1956," Grace Lewis Miller Papers, Jefferson National Expansion Memorial, National Park Service, St. Louis, MO.

[29] Jackson to Fisher, May 16, 1960, Fisher Papers.

[30] Miller, "Letter to the *William and Mary Quarterly*."

[31] Fisher to Boyd, May 14, 1963, Fisher Papers.

[32] Jackson to Fisher, August 3, 1960, Fisher Papers.

[33] Jackson, *Letters*, vol. 2, 748

[34] Donald D. Jackson, *Among the Sleeping Giants: Occasional Pieces on Lewis and Clark* (Urbana: University of Illinois Press, 1987), 68-70.

[35] See John D. W. Guice, "Fisher and Meriwether Lewis" in *Rediscovering Vardis Fisher: Centennial Essays,* ed. Joseph M. Flora (Moscow: University of Idaho Press, 2000), 147-63.

[36] Dillon, *Meriwether Lewis*, 335-50. In an exchange of phone calls and post cards with the author, Dillon, some 20-25 years after the original publication of his Lewis biography, held fast to his conviction that Lewis was murdered. Furthermore, in rather salty language he insisted that many historians started with the premise of suicide and then sought evidence to support their position. Dillon encouraged me to continue studying the topic.

The Sacajawea of Eva Emery Dye, by Ronald Laycock (pp. 126-30)

[1] Eva Emery Dye, *The Conquest: The True Story of Lewis and Clark* (Chicago: A.C. McClurg & Co., 1902).

[2] Ibid., 283.

[3] Ibid., 284.

[4] Ibid., 285

[5] Ibid., 290.

[6] Ronald W. Taber, "Sacajawea and the Suffragettes—an interpretation of a myth," *Pacific Northwest Quarterly*, Vol 58. Number 1 (January 1967), 8.

[7] Ibid., 9.

[8] Ibid., 9.

[9] Ibid., 10.

See also Billie Barnes Jensen, "In the Weird and Woolly West. Anti-Suffrage Women, Gender Issues, and Woman's Suffrage in the West." *Journal of the West* (July 1993), 41-51.

Spirit Mound, the Natives, and Lewis and Clark, by Norma Clark Wilson (pp. 164-72)

[1] Lance Henson, a Southern Cheyenne poet who grew up on a farm near Calumet, Oklahoma, visited the University of South Dakota, October 12-13, 1978. He read and commented on his poetry for an American Indian Literature class the afternoon of October 12. On the morning of October 13, he worked with creative writing students. That evening at 8 p.m., he presented a reading with me and Oklahoma poet Frank Parman. The handwritten poem on Spirit Mound was written in ink on yellow, lined paper and prefaced by "For Norma and Jerry."

[2] Linda Hogan, a Chickasaw writer, presented two sessions: "Literature by and about Native American Women" in the morning and a reading from her manuscript, "The Diary of Amanda McFadden," at 8:30 p.m., for Women in the Arts day of Women's Week at the University of South Dakota, March 19, 1980.

[3] Joseph Rockboy was employed as a consultant to the W.H. Over Museum in Vermillion from 1972-1981. He spoke to students in my seminar, "Images of American Indians in American Literature," and the general public at the Center for Continuing Education September 9, 1980, at 7 p.m. The University of South Dakota Office of Student Services and Public Information sent out a press release about the session. Articles on the presentation subsequently appeared in the *Vermillion Plain Talk*, November 6, 1980, and in *The Sioux City Journal*, November 13, 1980. Mr. Rockboy died in 1982.

[4] The Institutes for the Spirit are a series of retreat, renewal, and enrichment programs offered by the Vermillion United Church of Christ, Congregational. The "Exploring Spirit Mound" institute was held August 28-30, 1998, in Vermillion.

[5] Dr. Evans teaches in the School of Education; Mr. Kills Small teaches Lakota language at the University of South Dakota.

[6] Ronald Little Owl and Sherri Deaver spoke to an audience at the W.H. Over Museum in Vermillion on September 18, 2002. Their presentations were part of a project to present the cultural history surrounding Spirit Mound to our community.

Bibliographies

Before Lewis and Clark: The Monument of Perrin du Lac, by Tom Kilian (pp. 18-22)

Jennewein, J. Leonard, ed. *Dakota Panorama*. Sioux Falls, SD: Midwest Beach Printing Company, 1961.

Kingsbury, George. W. *The History of the Dakota Territory*, vol. 1. Chicago: S. J. Clarke Publishing Company, 1915.

Karolevitz, Robert F. *Challenge the South Dakota Story*. Sioux Falls, SD: Brevet Press, Inc., 1975.

Robinson, Doane. *A Brief History of South Dakota*. New York: American Book Company, 1905.

———. *Doane Robinson's Encyclopedia of South Dakota*. Pierre: South Dakota State Historical Society, 1925.

Robinson, Will G. Personal Letter. January 31, 1961.

Schell, Herbert S. *History of South Dakota*. Lincoln, NE: University of Nebraska Press, 1968.

South Dakota Historical Collections, vol. 7. Pierre: South Dakota State Historical Society, 1914.

South Dakota Historical Collections, vol. 23. Pierre. South Dakota State Historical Society. 1947.

South Dakota Historical Collections, vol. 24. Pierre. South Dakota State Historical Society. 1949.

South Dakota Historical Collections, vol. 41. Pierre. South Dakota State Historical Society. 1982.

The Literary Struggle of Lewis and Clark, by Joseph Basile (pp. 23-27)

Ambrose, Stephen E. *Undaunted Courage: Meriwether Lewis, Thomas Jefferson, and the Opening of the American West*. New York: Touchstone, 1997.

Duncan, Dayton and Ken Burns. *Lewis & Clark: An Illustrated History*. New York: Knopf, 1997.

The Federalist Literary Mind: Selections from the Monthly Anthology and Boston Review, 1803-1811 Including Documents Relating to the Boston Athanaeum. Ed. Lewis P Simpson. Baton Rouge: Louisiana State University Press, 1962.

Heat-Moon, William Least. *Blue Highways: A Journey into America*. Boston: Houghton, 1982.

Kuralt, Charles. *Charles Kuralt's America*. New York: Putnam's Sons, 1995.

Lewis, Meriwether, and William Clark. *The Journals of Lewis and Clark*. Ed. John Bakeless. New York: Mentor, 1964.

———. *The Journals of Lewis and Clark*. Ed. Bernard de Voto. Boston: Houghton, 1953.

The Rhetoric of Imperialism in the Lewis and Clark Journals: Camp Dubois to the Mandan Villages, by Joan K. Warner Dolence (pp. 28-34)

Allen, John Logan. *Passage Through the Garden: Lewis and Clark and the Image of the American Northwest*. Urbana: University of Illinois Press, 1975.

Ambrose, Stephen. *Undaunted Courage: Meriwether Lewis, Thomas Jefferson, and the Opening of the American West*. New York: Touchstone, 1997.

Goetzmann, William H. *Exploration and Empire: The Explorer and the Scientist in the Winning of the American West*. New York: Knopf, 1966.

Jefferson, Thomas. "Expedition to the Pacific: Instructions to Captain Lewis." *Thomas Jefferson: Writings*. Ed. Merrill D. Peterson. New York: Library of America, 1984.

Lewis, Meriwether, and William Clark. *The Journals of the Lewis and Clark Expedition: Vol. 2. August 30, 1803-August 24, 1804*. Ed. Gary E. Moulton. Lincoln: University of Nebraska Press, 1983-2001.

Pratt, Mary Louise. *Imperial Eyes: Travel Writing and Transculturation*. New York: Routledge, 1994.

Ronda, James P. *Lewis and Clark among the Indians*. Lincoln, University of Nebraska Press, 1984.

Spurr, David. *The Rhetoric of Empire: Colonial Discourse in Journalism, Travel Writing, and Imperial Administration*. Durham: Duke University Press, 1996.

We Proceeded On—Without a Doctor: A Combat Flight Surgeon Comments on the Medical Aspects of the Lewis and Clark Expediton, by Jerry L. Simmons (pp. 35-45)

This bibliography is obviously for the casual reader. All of the cited works are interesting. Several are written by physicians with a passion for Lewis and Clark (Chuinard, Loge, Paton, and Peck). All have extensive references for the more compulsive enthusiast.

Chuinard, Elden G. *Only One Man Died: The Medical Aspects of the Lewis and Clark Expedition*. Fairfield, WA: Ye Galleon Press. 1979

Lentz, Gary. "Meriwether Lewis's Medicine Chests." *We Proceeded On* 26 (2000): 10-17.

Loge, Ronald. "Two Dozes of Barks and Opium." *The Pharos of Alpha Omega Alpha* 59 (1996): 26-31.

Moulton, Gary. *The Journals of the Lewis and Clark Expedition*. Lincoln: University of Nebraska Press, 1983-2001.

Paton, Bruce C. *Lewis and Clark: Doctors in the Wilderness*. Golden, CO: Fulcrum, 2001.

———. "Foreword," in *Wilderness Medicine*, 4th ed. Ed. by Paul S. Auerbach. Mosby, 2001

Peck, David J. *Or Perish in the Attempt: Wilderness Medicine in the Lewis and Clark Expedition*. Helena, MT: Far Country Press, 2002.

Ronda, James P. *Lewis and Clark among the Indians*. Lincoln, NE: Bison Books, 1988.

Snoddy, Donald. "Medical Aspects of the Lewis and Clark Expedition." *Nebraska History* 51 (1970): 115-152.

Native American Trade from the Great Plains to the Interior Plateau Encountered by Lewis and Clark, by Ralph J. Coffman, Jr. (pp. 70-86)

Appleman, Roy E. *Lewis and Clark: Historic Places Associated with Their Transcontinental Exploration (1804-06)*. Washington, D.C.: United States Department of the Interior, National Park Service, 1975.

Blakeslee, Donald. The Plains Interband Trade System. Ph.D. diss., University of Wisconsin-Milwaukee, 1975.

Borden, Charles E. 1961. "Notes and News: Northwest." *American Antiquity* 26:4 (1961): 582-85.

Bowers, Alfred W. *Mandan Social and Ceremonial Organization*. Chicago: University of Chicago Press, 1950.

Brain, Jeffrey P. and Philip Phillips. *Shell Gorgets: Styles of the Late Prehistoric and Protohistoric Southeast*. Cambridge: Peabody Museum Press, 1996.

Brown, Everett. S. *The Constitutional History of the Louisiana Purchase*. Berkeley: University of California, 1920.

Buechel, Rev. Eugene. *A Dictionary-Oie Wowpi Wan of Teton Sioux*. Pine Ridge, South Dakota: Red Cloud Indian School, Inc, Holy Rosary Mission, 1983.

Converse, Robert N. "A highly developed tubular pipe." *Ohio Archaeologist,* 44:3 (1994): 19.

Densmore, Frances. *Indian Use of Wild Plants for Crafts, Food, Medicine and Charms.* Smithsonian Institution, Bureau of American Ethnology, United States Government Printing Office, Washington, D.C., 1928.

Dorsey, George Amos. *The Arapaho Sundance.* Field Museum, Publication 75, Anthropological Series 4. Chicago, 1903.

———. *The Cheyenne.* Chicago: Field Museum of Natural History, 1905.

Ehrensperger, Edward C. *South Dakota Place Names.* Enlarged and revised. Vermillion: University of South Dakota, 1941.

Ekman, Leonard C. *Scenic Geology of the Pacific Northwest.* Portland: Binfords and Mort, 1962.

Ewers, John C. *Indian Life on the Upper Missouri.* Norman: University of Oklahoma Press, 1968.

Fisher, William. *An Interesting Account of the Voyages and Travels of Captains Lewis and Clarke, in the years 1804-5 & 6: giving a faithful description of the River Missouri and its source ... to which is added a complete dictionary of the [Cree] Indian tongue.* Baltimore: P. Mauro, 1813.

Fletcher, Alice C. *The Hako: A Pawnee Ceremony, 22nd Annual Report of the Bureau of American Ethnology,* Part II. Washington, D.C.: Government Printing Office, 1904.

Ford, James A. *A Comparison of Formative Cultures in the Americas: diffusion or the psychic unity of man.* Smithsonian Institution Press: City of Washington, 1969.

Fowke, Girard. *Archeological History of Ohio.* Columbus: Ohio State Archeological and Historical Society, 1902.

Frémont, John C. *Memoirs of my life, including in the narrative five journeys of western exploration, during the years 1842, 1843-4, 1845-6-7, 1848-9, 1853-4.* Chicago: Belford, Clarke, 1887.

———. *The Expeditions of John Charles Fremont,* 3 vols. Ed. by Donald Jackson and Mary Lee Spence. Urbana: University of Illinois Press, 1970-80.

Fuller, George W. *A History of the Pacific Northwest.* New York: A. Knopf, 1931.

Gilmore, Melvin R. "Some Comments on Aboriginal Tobaccos," *American Anthropologist,* n.s., 24 (1992): 480-81.

———. *Uses of Plants by the Indians of the Missouri River Region.* 1919. Reprint. Lincoln: University of Nebraska Press, 1977.

Hall, Robert L. "The Evolution of the Calumet-Pipe." In Guy Gibbon, ed., P*rairie Archeology: Papers in Honor of David A. Barreis.* University of Minnesota Publications in Anthropology, no 3, 37-52, 1983.

Hatch, James W., Joseph W. Michels, Christopher M. Stevenson, Barry E. Scheetz, and Richard A. Geidel. "Hopewell Obsidian Studies: Behavioral Implications of Recent Sourcing and Dating Research." *American Antiquity* 55 (1990): 461-479.

Hodge, Frederick Webb, ed. *Handbook of American Indians North of Mexico.* Washington, D.C.: Government Printing Office. 2 parts, 1912.

Hosmer, James K. *The History of the Louisiana Purchase.* New York: D. Appleton, 1902.

Houck, Louis. *A History of Missouri from the Earliest Settlements until the Admission of the State into the Union,* 3 vols. Chicago: R. R. Donnelly, 1908.

Jackson, Donald. *Letters of the Lewis and Clark Expedition with Related Documents, 1783-1854.* 2nd ed., with Additional Documents and Notes. Urbana: University of Illinois Press, 1978.

Jelks, Edward B. "Notes and News." *Plains Anthropologist,* 7:15 (1962): 70-74.

Johansen, Dorothy O. and Charles M. *Empire of the Columbia: A History of the Pacific Northwest*. 2nd ed. New York: Harper and Row, 1967. (Orig. pub. in 1957.)

Keyser, James D. *Indian Petroglyphs of the Columbia Gorge: The Jeanne Hill Rubbings*. The Dalles, Oregon: J. Y. Hollingsworth Co, 1994.

Kroeber, Alfred L. "Ethnology of the Gros Ventre." American Museum of Natural History, Anthropological Papers, 1 (1908): 141-281.

Lepper, Bradley T., Craig E. Skinner, and Christopher M. Stevenson. "Analysis of an Obsidian Biface Fragment from a Hopewell Occupation Associated with the Fort Hill (33HI1) Hilltop Enclosure in Southern Ohio." *Archaeology in Eastern North America* 26 (1997): 33-39.

Lewis, Meriwether and William Clark. *The Journals of the Lewis and Clark Expedition*, 13 vols. Ed. by Gary E. Moulton. Lincoln: University of Nebraska Press, 1983-2001.

Lowie, Robert H. *Culture and Ethnology*. New York: D. C. McMurtrie, 1917.

Mason, Otis T. "Aboriginal American Indian Basketry: Studies in a Textile Art without Machinery." *Annual Report of the Board of Regents of the Smithsonian Institution ... for the Year Ending June 30, 1902*. Washington: Government Printing Office, pp. 171-548, plus 248 plates, 1904.

Mithun, Marianne. *The Languages of Native North America*. New York: Cambridge University Press, 1999.

Nicollet, Joseph. *Hydrographical Basin of the Upper Mississippi River from astronomical and barometrical observations surveys and information in the years 1836, 37, 38, 39, and 40; assisted in 1838, 39, & 40, by Lieut. J. C. Frémont, of the Corps of Topographical Engineers*. Washington, D.C.: Published by order of the U.S. Senate, 1843.

Perrin du Lac, Francois-Marie. *Voyage dans les deux Louisianes et chez les nations sauvages du Missouri, par les Etates Unis, l'Ohio et les provinces qui le bordent en 1801, 1802, et 1803*. Lyon, 1805.

Prucha, Francis P. *Indian Peace Medals in American History*. Madison: State Historic Society of Wisconsin, 1971.

Prufer, Olaf Herbert. The Hopewell Complex of Ohio. PhD. Diss. Harvard University, 1961.

Ramenofsky, Ann F. *Vectors of Death: The Archaeology of European Contact*. Albuquerque: University of New Mexico Press, 1987.

Ramsey, Alexander. *Report*. [Washington, D.C.], 1849.

Rees, John. "The Shoshoni Contribution to Lewis and Clark," *Idaho Yesterdays*, 2 (1958): 2-13.

Riggs, Stephen R. *A Dakota-English Dictionary*. Edited by James Owen Dorsey. St. Paul: Minnesota Historical Society Press, 1992.

Robinson, Doane. *A History of the Dakota or Sioux Indians*, 1904. Minneapolis: Ross and Haines, 1956.

Ronda, James P. *Lewis and Clark among the Indians*. Lincoln: University of Nebraska Press, 1984.

Robertson, James A. *Louisiana under the Rule of Spain, France, and the United States, 1785-1807*. 2 vols. Cleveland: Arthur H. Clark, 1910-11.

Ross, Alexander. *Adventures of the First Settlers on the Oregon or Columbia River*, ed. Milo M. Quaife. [1849] Chicago:The Lakeside Press, 1923.

Sahlins, Marshall D. "On the Sociology of Primitive Exchange." In *The Relevance of Models for Social Anthropology*, ed. Michael Banton, pp. 139-236. ASA Monographs 1. London: Tavistock, 1965.

Schlick, Mary D. *Columbia River Basketry: Gift of the Ancestors, Gift of the Earth*. Seattle: University of Washington Press, 1994.

Speck, Frank G. *The Tutelo Spirit Adoption Ceremony, reclothing the living in the name of the dead.* Harrisburg: Pennsylvania Historical Commission, 1942.

Struever, Stuart and G. L. Houart. "An Analysis of the Hopewell Interaction Sphere." In *Social Exchange and Interaction*, ed. by E. N. Wilmsen, pp. 47-79. University of Michigan Museum of Anthropology Anthropological Papers No. 46, Ann Arbor, Michigan, 1972.

Strong, William D., W. Egbert Schenck and Julian H. Steward. *Archaeology of the Dalles-Deschutes Region.* University of California Publications in American Archaeology and Ethnology, 29 (1930-32): 1-154.

Tabeau, Pierre-Antoine. *Tabeau's Narrative of Loisel's Expedition to the Upper Missouri*, ed. Annie Heloise Abel. Trans. from the French by Rose Abel Wright. Norman: University of Oklahoma Press, 1939.

Thwaites, Reuben Gold, ed. *The Jesuit Relations and Allied Documents, Travels and Explorations of the Jesuit Missionaries in North America (1610-1791).* New York: A and C. Boni, 1898.

———, ed. *Early Western Travels, 1748-184*, 32 vols. Cleveland: Arthur H. Clark Co, 1904.

Vehik, Susan C. "Late Prehistoric Plains Trade and Economic Specialization." *Plains Anthropologist* 35:128 (1990): 125-145.

Vehik, Susan C. and Timothy G. Baugh. "Prehistoric Plains Trade." In *Prehistoric Exchange Systems in North America*, ed. by Timothy G. Baugh and Jonathon E. Ericson, pp, 249-274. New York: Plenum Press, 1994.

West, George A. "Tobacco, Pipes and smoking customs of the American Indians." *Bulletin of the Public Museum of the City of Milwaukee*, 17 (1934).

Whitaker, Arthur P. *The Mississippi Question, 1795-1803; A Study in Trade, Politics and Diplomacy*. New York: Appleton-Century Co., Inc., 1934.

Wood, W. Raymond. "Plains trade in prehistoric and proto-historic intertribal relations." In W. Raymond Wood and Margot Liberty, eds. *Anthropology on the Great Plains.* Lincoln: University of Nebraska Press, 1980.

The Lewis and Clark Story in the 20th Century: The Emergence of the Outsiders, by David Kvernes (pp. 131-38)

Ambrose, Stephen E. *Undaunted Courage: Meriwether Lewis, Thomas Jefferson and the Opening of the American West.* New York: Simon and Schuster, 1996.

Betts, Robert C. *In Search of York.* Boulder: University of Colorado Press, rev. ed. 2000. (First ed., 1985.)

Coues, Elliott, ed. *History of the Expedition under the command of Lewis and Clark.* 3 vols. New York: Dover Publications, 1965. (Annotated reprint of Nicholas Biddle's 1814 edition of the journals. The Coues edition was first published in 1893.)

Cuttright, Paul Russell. *A History of the Lewis and Clark Journals.* Norman: University of Oklahoma Press, 1976.

Duncan, Dayton. *Lewis and Clark.* New York: Knopf, 1997.

Jackson, Donald, ed. *Letters of the Lewis and Clark Expedition with Related Documents.* 2 vols. 2nd ed. Urbana: University of Illinois Press, 1978. (First ed., 1962.)

Kessler, Donna J. *The Making of the Sacagawea: A Euro-American Legend.* Tuscaloosa: University of Alabama Press, 1996.

Laycock, Ronald. "The Sacagawea of Eva Emery Dye," in *Papers of the Thirty-first Annual Dakota Conference*, compiled by Arthur R. Huseboe and Harry F. Thompson. Sioux Falls, South. Dakota: Center for Western Studies, 1999: 429-37.

McMurtry, Larry. "Sacagawea's Nickname," *New York Review of Books* (20 Sept. 2001): 71-72.

Rittgers, Max. "The Lewis and Clark Expedition Begins with the Amiotte Plate," in *Papers of the Thirtieth Annual Dakota Conference*, compiled by Arthur R. Huseboe and Harry F. Thompson. Sioux Falls, South Dakota: Center for Western Studies, 1998: 523-29.

Thwaites, Reuben Gold, ed. *Original Journals of the Lewis and Clark Expedition*, 1804-1806. 7 vols. and Atlas. New York: Antiquarian Press, 1959. (First published 1904-05.)

"Over the Hill and Beyond the Sunset": Bernard DeVoto and the Expedition of Lewis and Clark, by Robert C. Steensma (pp. 139-45)

Bowen, Catherine Drinker, Edith Mirrielees, Arthur Schlesinger, Jr., and Wallace Stegner. *Four Portraits and One Subject: Bernard DeVoto*. Boston: Houghton Mifflin, 1963. Stegner's essay was later reprinted in his volume of essays, *The Sound of Mountain Water* (see below).

DeVoto, Bernard. *The Course of Empire*. Boston: Houghton Mifflin, 1952.

DeVoto, Bernard (ed.). *The Journals of Lewis and Clark*. Foreword by Steven E. Ambrose. Boston: Houghton Mifflin, 1997.

DeVoto, Bernard. *The Letters of Bernard DeVoto*. Edited by Wallace Stegner. New York: Doubleday, 1975.

DeVoto, Bernard. "Passage to India: From Christmas to Christmas with Lewis and Clark," *The Saturday Review of Literature*,15:6 (December 5, 1936), 3-4, 20, 24, 28.

Stegner, Wallace. *The Uneasy Chair: A Biography of Bernard DeVoto*. Salt Lake City: Peregrine Smith Books, 1988.

Stegner, Wallace. "The West Emphatic: Bernard DeVoto," *The Sound of Mountain Water* (New York: Dutton, 1980), pp. 250-275.

Lewis and Clark, Harbingers of Colonialism, by Rita Easterby Olson (pp. 146-53)

Ambrose, Stephen. *Undaunted Courage: Meriwether Lewis, Thomas Jefferson, and the Opening of the American West.* New York: Simon and Schuster, 1996.

Bergon, Frank, ed. *The Journals of Lewis and Clark.* New York: Penguin Books, 1989.

Gandhi, Leela. *Postcolonial Theory: A Critical Introduction.* New York: Columbia University Press, 1998.

Holy Bible. King James Version. Cleveland OH: The World Publishing Company.

Moulton, Gary, ed. *The Journals of Lewis and Clark Expedition.* 13 vols. Lincoln: U of Nebraska Press, 1983 -2001.

Said, Edward. *Orientalism.* New York: Random House, 1994 (first published in 1978).

Spirit Mound, the Natives, and Lewis and Clark, by Norma Clark Wilson (pp. 164-72)

Ambrose, Stephen. *Undaunted Courage: Meriwether Lewis, Thomas Jefferson, and the Opening of the American West.* New York: Simon and Schuster, 1996.

Cook-Lynn, Elizabeth. *Seek the House of Relatives.* Marvin, SD: Blue Cloud Quarterly Press, 1983.

Deaver, Sherri. *Spirit Mound Culture History.* Pierre: South Dakota Historical Society, 2002.

DeVoto, Bernard. *The Journals of Lewis and Clark.* Boston: Houghton Mifflin Co., 1953.

Hogan, Linda. *Seeing Through the Sun.* Amherst: Univ. of Massachusetts Press, 1985.

Jefferson, Thomas. *Writings.* New York: The Library of America, 1984.

Longinus, "From *On the Sublime.*" In *Criticism: the Major Texts*, Ed. Walter Jackson Bate. New York: Harcourt, Brace & World, Inc., 1952.

Moses, Lloyd R., ed. *Clay County Place Names.* Vermillion, SD: Broadcaster Press, Inc., 1976.

Ronda, James P. *Lewis and Clark among the Indians.* Lincoln: University of Nebraska Press, 1984

Index

D

E

F

G

H

I

J

K

L

M

N

O

T

U

V

W

Y

Z